Reading Du Fu

Reading Du Fu

Nine Views

Edited by Xiaofei Tian

HKU
PRESS
香港大學出版社

Hong Kong University Press
The University of Hong Kong
Pok Fu Lam Road
Hong Kong
https://hkupress.hku.hk

© 2020 Hong Kong University Press

ISBN 978-988-8528-44-8 (*Hardback*)

British Library Cataloguing-in-Publication Data
A catalogue record for this book is available from the British Library.

Digitally printed

Contents

Figures

Acknowledgments

This book originated in an international conference on Du Fu that was held at Harvard University in October 2016, generously sponsored by the Andrew W. Mellon Foundation, the Fairbank Center for Chinese Studies at Harvard University, the Harvard-Yenching Institute, and the Department of East Asian Languages and Civilizations at Harvard University. I am indebted to the staff of the Department of East Asian Languages and Civilizations and the Fairbank Center, as well as to the graduate student coordinators, Lu Kou and Kate Monaghan, for all they did to make the conference a successful event. I am grateful to all the paper presenters and discussants for their participation, and to the two anonymous readers of this volume. I owe thanks to Dominic Toscano for helping me prepare the index, to Eric Mok, former acquisitions editor at Hong Kong University Press, for his warm encouragement of this project even before its genesis, and to Joan Vicens Sard, Clara Ho, and the editorial staff at Hong Kong University Press for their efficiency and professionalism.

Introduction

Xiaofei Tian

The Origin

The An Lushan Rebellion that broke out in 755 set in motion forces that led to the gradual decline of the splendid Tang Empire but helped create a great poet. In 759 Du Fu 杜甫 (712–770) left the capital region and began wanderings through west and southwestern China that would occupy the rest of his life. His post-rebellion poetry chronicled the life of a man and his family in a chaotic age. Arguably the greatest Chinese poet, he was certainly the most influential of all Chinese authors in any genre because of the long-lasting and far-reaching impact of his poetry.

In October 2016, a two-day international conference was held at Harvard University on the Tang poet. The conference celebrated the inauguration of the Library of Chinese Humanities, a bilingual, facing-page translation series featuring important works in the premodern Chinese cultural tradition. The first title of the series, published at the end of 2015, is the first complete translation, with notes, of the poetry of Du Fu. This volume grows out of that conference.

Du Fu is well known and well studied in Chinese, with the reception of Du Fu having itself become a special area of focus in the popular field of reception studies. He is so well studied that, first, it draws attention away from the fact that Du Fu's poetry is *not* so well studied in English-language scholarship, and, second, the study of Du Fu in Chinese scholarship has some notable gaps that largely elude notice precisely because of the great number of books and articles produced since the 1980s. One of the gaps is a theoretically inflected close engagement with Du Fu's poems themselves.[1]

In classical Chinese literature Du Fu's stature is like that of Shakespeare in English literature or Dante in Italian, and Du Fu is also widely known outside his native tradition, just as Shakespeare and Dante are. Prior to the complete English translation in

---

1. As the summary of the 2017 annual conference of the Association of China's Du Fu Studies points out, of more than seventy papers received, fewer than ten are dedicated to "the form, style, and art of Du Fu's poems or Du Fu himself." Poetic form, style, and art, such as the use of quatrain or long regulated poems (*pailü*), are habitual topics of traditional "remarks on poetry" and do not exactly constitute any new conceptual territory. The summary henceforth calls for "treating Du Fu himself and Du Fu's poems as the basis" and as the "core issues." Hu Kexian, "Du Fu yanjiu," 93.

2016, Du Fu has been partially translated many times by different hands. Still, when we turn to criticism and interpretation, the books and articles do not exactly constitute a considerable amount of scholarly output on a major poet, let alone a towering figure like Du Fu.[2]

This lack of attention to Du Fu in English-language scholarship is partially due to the changes in the field of Chinese literary studies, which on the one hand took a cultural-historical and materialist turn in recent decades and, on the other, responded to the general trend of canon revision in Western academia in the second half of the twentieth century: some of the traditional criteria were questioned; once-marginal authors were rediscovered; women writers and minority writers received their deserved attention. With the increasing popularity of the studies of modern and contemporary Chinese literature and culture, film, and media in recent decades, premodern literature, especially the literature of the Middle Period (roughly from the Eastern Han through Song, or the first through thirteenth centuries), became a road less and less traveled by the younger generation. These changes are without a doubt also happening in Chinese academia, but such changes can be obscured by a number of factors, including the sheer size of Chinese departments in terms of both faculty and students in colleges and universities. In contrast, overseas sinology is a much smaller enterprise.

To a large extent, however, the lack of attention to Du Fu can also be attributed to, ironically, his canonical status. Many scholars and students find themselves under the impression that Du Fu "has already been done." In addition, the clichéd image of Du Fu the "poet sage" and "poet historian" has overshadowed, even eclipsed, simply "the poet" Du Fu and, even worse, Du Fu's poetry. From the Song dynasty onward, the reception of Du Fu has veered heavily toward his "Confucian" qualities—loyalty to the ruler and concern about the state, summed up in the saying that Du Fu "did not forget his lord even for the interval of one single meal."[3] Such a grossly simplifying image does not always inspire a modern reader's interest. The light-hearted, quirky, and funny Du Fu known for "playful topics and amusing discussions" during his lifetime has all but disappeared into the halo put around his head in the subsequent ages down to the present day.[4] The unbearable weight of the neo-Confucian sagehood attributed to Du Fu was only intensified when, come the twentieth century, it was seamlessly welded to patriotism and Marxist-inflected "compassion for the sufferings of the laboring mass." It is best illustrated in the contrast of two extremes: at one end, we have a popular imaginary portrait of Du Fu, widely known through its use in Chinese high school textbooks, which shows the poet exactly as how he is perceived to be: looking solemnly, concernedly, into the distance, apparently with the fate of the state and the common folk on his mind; at the other end, the doodling and spoofing versions of this portrait that went

---

2. William Hung's (1893–1980) *Tu Fu: China's Greatest Poet*, published in 1952, is a biographical account of Du Fu's life with translations of more than 300 of Du Fu's poems. Between then and the time of our conference, three English-language monographs on Du Fu had been published: they are respectively by David McCraw (*Du Fu's Laments*, 1992), Eva Shan Chou (*Reconsidering Tu Fu*, 1995), and David Schneider (*Confucian Prophet*, 2012). The latest publication is Ji Hao's study of Du Fu's reception (*The Reception of Du Fu*, 2017). A quick search in JSTOR yields just over a dozen research articles with Du Fu featured in the title, printed in the course of a little more than half a century.

3. Su Shi, *Su Shi wenji*, 318.

4. The comment is attributed to a contemporary Fan Huang 樊晃 (fl. 770s), supposedly made in the decade after Du Fu's death. Xiao Difei, *Du Fu quanji*, vol. 12, 6579. Translation is Owen's, *The Poetry of Du Fu*, vol. 1, lxiv.

viral overnight on the Chinese internet in 2012, which marked the 1,300th anniversary of the poet's birth. High moral seriousness became the target of mockery, and the act of worship could find balance only in ridicule.[5] Neither, however, does justice to Du Fu the poet. Worse, neither side—the worshippers or the ridiculers—spends time reading Du Fu's 1,400 poems, closely or widely.

The chapters in this volume represent an effort to read the poems attentively and, as we will discuss in the following section, to read the poems anew by interrogating and cross-examining the poems from different angles and in different contexts. Before Du Fu was anointed the "poet sage," he had commanded attention with nothing but his poems. It is always worthwhile to revisit the canon, for the writings themselves, for a better understanding of the subsequent works influenced and shaped by those writings, and for the reflection on literary history that must by definition include the ordinary and the extraordinary—it would be a mistake to only embrace one end of the spectrum without seeing how interdependent they really are. In the case of Du Fu, we also want to go beyond the famous pieces, whether it is the sets of "Threes," the "Stirred by Autumn" set, the quatrains on poetry, or the poems included in popular anthologies and school textbooks.

There is a parochial desire on the part of some Chinese scholars to take ownership of classical Chinese literature as "ours" (or at best East Asian) and to downplay the right and authority of "outsiders" to interpret and give meaning. Such a desire, encouraged by the state as part of its nationalistic project, would lead to this great literature being read and appreciated by no one but the Chinese themselves, to a cultural isolationism that benefits neither the culture in question nor human civilization. Yet, though written in (Tang) Chinese, Du Fu's poetry belongs not only to the Chinese but also to the world. A collection of essays on Du Fu in English is long overdue.

The Chapters

This volume is divided into three sections, each focusing on a particular set of inter-related issues that not only underscore a hitherto less explored aspect of Du Fu studies but also pertain to the studies of Chinese literary tradition in general. The first section, "Home, Locale, Empire," consists of four chapters. These chapters explore how the poet, moving from place to place, negotiates his longing for "home" with the building and tending of temporary homes and with the larger concerns of the empire. They also discuss how the poet contemplates the questions of mobility and circulation, the local and the state, in his poetry, and how poetry itself is both the object and the venue of transportation in a world filled with blockages.

Though his family held an estate near Luoyang (in modern He'nan), Du Fu's exact birthplace is unknown. In his younger days Du Fu had spent a decade in the capital, Chang'an, seeking, largely unsuccessfully, fame, recognition, and political advancement. After the rebellion broke out, he was trapped in Chang'an for a while, then escaped and joined Emperor Suzong's (r. 756–761) court, in which he served briefly

---

5. A reviewer of "a century of Du Fu studies" notices the link between the elevation of Du Fu, pursued by scholars and avidly assisted by the Ministry of Culture and various local governments, and the viral meme known as "Du Fu Is Busy" and opines, "The study of the 'poet sage' has too much seriousness and lacks liveliness; suppose we study and advertise Du Fu as a 'mortal,' not as a 'sage,' maybe there will be a different sort of phenomenon with Du Fu's 'busy-ness.'" Peng Yan, "Du Fu yanjiu," 124.

before he managed to offend the emperor and was demoted to a lowly position in Huazhou 華州 (in modern Shaanxi) in 758. He soon decided to quit that job and thus began a life of wandering, living off his friends' and associates' goodwill and patronage. He first went to Qinzhou 秦州 (in modern Gansu) in 759, then to Tonggu 同谷 (in Gansu), and finally on to Chengdu 成都 (in Sichuan) near the end of the same year. Du Fu settled in Chengdu for a few years, where he built his famous Thatched Cottage (*caotang* 草堂), with the support of the military commissioner Yan Wu 嚴武 (726–765). After Yan Wu died, Du Fu took his family down the Yangzi River to Kuizhou 夔州 (modern Fengjie 奉節 County, Chongqing 重慶, Sichuan), at the mouth of the famous Three Gorges. He lived at Kuizhou from 766 to 768 under the protection and employment of local supervisor-in-chief Bai Maolin 柏茂林 (also romanized as Bo Maolin). The Kuizhou period was one of his most prolific, as he composed about 400 poems there, almost one-third of his entire extant oeuvre. But in early 768 he resumed his wandering again and eventually died of illness on Lake Dongting in 770.

In the midst of this turbulent itinerant life, Du Fu writes that, on a desolate autumn river, "the life I used to have at home is the longing in my heart" 故國平居有所思.[6] *Guguo* 故國 is used here in the sense of the former home, not that of the former country or the former dynasty; yet it is not *just* the former home he longs for but rather the kind of life he used to have in that home in a different age. *Ping* 平 is peaceful, uneventful, ordinary, perhaps a tad boring—the exact flavor of "home" after one loses it. As Jack W. Chen observes, Du Fu here is "also speaking of 'dwelling' or 'inhabiting' a space of a lost sense of the ordinary . . . in the aftermath of rebellion" (p. 19). That life is no longer possible because it was bound up with the age of peace and prosperity. Beginning with "No Return," a poem lamenting a cousin who died in war, and ending with "Return in Spring," a poem on returning to the Thatched Cottage after interruption caused by a local rebellion, Chen's chapter discusses how "the idea of home" comes to occupy a place of central importance in Du Fu's works after the rebellion. Chen argues that the longing for home is "at its heart, a wish for the return to the ordinary" (p. 16), a carving out of a non-social and non-political space where he lives his life as a private individual, even though the gesture is possible only in exile, against the backdrop of the dynastic trauma, and from the margins of the empire. While Du Fu is often seen as the poet who bears witness to the grand historical events and the tragedy of the times, Chen calls attention to the other side of the poet, who allies himself not with the body politic but with the individual body, its desires, comforts, and aches and pains.

If Chen explores the poet's vision of home by largely focusing on Du Fu's Chengdu poems, Stephen Owen's chapter turns to a place where the poet tries very hard to make a home and yet can rarely feel "at home" in. This is Kuizhou, the exotic borderland of the empire, where Han and non-Han peoples live in close quarters, and the local customs seem foreign and savage to the poet from the capital. Few other locales in the Tang Empire would, Owen suggests, so readily invite thoughts about the imperial and cultural system of circulation far beyond home. Owen's chapter shows how in Kuizhou Du Fu "think[s] through poetry" about circulation, *tong* 通, from local commerce— a local girl's exchange of fish for coins—to that of the merchants moving around on the Yangzi for profit, and to the imperial courier system bringing tributary gifts to the emperor. The poet also thinks of men who are "blocked," the opposite of *tong*, in

---

6.   The fourth of the "Stirred by Autumn" set. Translation is Owen's, in *The Poetry of Du Fu*, vol. 4, 354–55.

their political advancement, but manage to circulate themselves through their traveling poems, literary reputation, and memory. The innocent taking of sustenance from nature in the first poem of the sequence—the mountain birds feeding their young with red berries—ends with the corruption of imperial power by bringing lychee for the emperor's beloved consort through the empire's courier system; yet the lychee fruit itself becomes corrupted on the way to the capital. The immediacy of local experience can never be captured, except in memory and in poetry. Here we see another form of poetic success as pitched against the failure of empire.

Gregory Patterson's chapter contemplates the same issues of *tong*, circulation, communication, and getting through on the vehicle of poetry, from a different perspective: that of history. He likewise centers on Kuizhou, conceding, as Owen does, that "in Kuizhou thinking about communication was unavoidable" (p. 41). He sees, however, in the physical traces at Kuizhou the creation of a unique communicative form through Du Fu's poetic commemorations of two cultural heroes from the past: one is the mythical King Yu, who is credited with channeling the great flood by opening up the river gorges and saving the people from drowning; the other is Zhuge Liang, the legendary loyal minister who, like Yu, had left an indelible material mark on the local landscape. Patterson's chapter is thus a powerful reminder that Du Fu, the acclaimed chronicler of his life and his times, is every bit as much the "poet historian" as the "poet geographer," who "wrote in such unprecedented detail about the unique landscapes, culture, and histories of these temporary 'perches' that they form distinct identities within his larger corpus, like semi-independent provinces within the empire of the collected works" (p. 41).

This ingenious metaphor takes us to the chapter by Lucas Rambo Bender. Bender returns to the issue of empire, which many commentators and scholars consider to be at the heart of Du Fu's poems. In contradistinction to Chen's chapter, Bender argues that the Kuizhou poems on humble topics are in fact complex creations emerging from the incongruity between imperial and domestic concerns, and that they both speak to a commitment to imperial values and ironize those same values. Bender regards these poems as enunciations of the poet's alienation from the empire precisely in his attachment to it. With an acuity finely tuned in to the poetic texts themselves, he sheds light on a moving emotional complexity in these poems, which are self-consciously comic in their grandiosity and tinged with a dark hue of melancholy—a melancholy that is again always undercut by humor.

However, if as Bender argues these poems on humble topics—vegetables, home improvements, faithful servants carrying out domestic tasks—"fit into a narrative of the poet's evolving thoughts about the empire over the course of his life" (p. 72), then maybe one can indeed make a case that the two visions of Du Fu, one confirmed by Chen's chapter and the other presented by Bender's, "derive from different portions of his very large and diverse poetic corpus" (p. 57), because the poet was going through changes just as the world around him did. One may pause here to think of Du Fu's position in literary and cultural history. He was on the threshold of a profound cultural sea change. Before Du Fu, the court and the capital were still the center of cultural accomplishments and cultural production, and in that world poems complaining about bad vegetables, thanking one's servants for domestic labor, or instructing one's son to build a chicken coop were simply unthinkable; but, after Du Fu, that old order crumbled even as the capital Chang'an still stood. Just as the central government's authority and control were weakened by powerful regional military governors, there was a centrifugal pull in cultural terms when the provinces—especially in the Jiangnan and Shu regions—began to assume much larger importance. The cultural world would be transformed with the emergence of the wild and quirky mid-Tang generation, many members of which were Du Fu's admirers, who picked up something from him and carried it even further. Du Fu was a figure emerging from the watershed transition and impacted the transition with his writings.

It is thus indeed interesting to contemplate these humble topics more deeply, since their sheer novelty tends to be forgotten; Du Fu's immense influence had turned them into normative themes for later poets. But no one else, "setting up a household, has poems begging for fruit trees and crockery. No one else writes irritated poems when promised grain does not arrive on time or the vegetable delivery is substandard. No one else celebrates a bamboo piping system that brings water from a mountain spring into his kitchen or the construction of a chicken coop."[7] And "like no one else in his day, we know his servants by name because he wrote poems for them and named them in his poems."[8] This last point may not seem much—or it may even seem discomfortingly condescending—to a modern reader, but if we judge him by the social norm of his day, Du Fu was a veritable revolutionary, as Tang slaves had very low social and legal status, and many Tang masters and mistresses, including famous writers, were known to have treated their servants ignobly. Wang Bo 王勃 (649–676), one of the "Four Outstanding Men of the Early Tang," once killed a slave; Xiao Yingshi 蕭穎士 (735 jinshi) was known for beating an old servant in his frequent violent outbursts; Yu Xuanji 魚玄機 (ca. 844–ca. 868) flogged her maid to death. Many such abusive incidents are recorded in Tang narratives. It is staggering, when we look around, to see how unusual and "strange" Du Fu was in the Tang world. Unfortunately, later poets after the Tang only inherited the topics and themes but not Du Fu's spirit of difference—which perhaps *is*, after all, a mark of individual genius, having nothing to do with empire, even though it was brought out by the decline of the empire and by his isolation in the strange backwater Kuizhou, where the old capital world of glamor and sophistication fell away.

On one level, we can attribute the newness of Du Fu's poetry to his extraordinary originality as a poet or the fact that he was increasingly writing in isolation, away from the old world of the capital and court elite; on another level, he is both a product of the great changes afoot and a prescient usher of the new world. Seeing larger issues in domestic life is a symptom of the old world where order is immanent in everything, but it is also a perversion of that old world. Right after Du Fu, the mid-Tang was one of the most remarkable eras in Chinese cultural history, and it was this mid-Tang generation that "discovered" Du Fu.

We need a deep dive in time. Radical historicization is required to rediscover Du Fu, whose greatness is not, despite what one may think of the "immortal masters,"

---

7. Owen, *The Poetry of Du Fu*, vol. 1, lx.
8. Owen, *The Poetry of Du Fu*, vol. 1, lv. Only after Du Fu do we see the gesture of naming one's servants and expressing gratitude for them in poetry, most notably in Wei Zhuang 韋莊 (ca. 836–910). *Quan Tang shi*, 700.8044, 700.8047. Wei Zhuang, perhaps not coincidentally, was the compiler of an extant Tang poetic anthology (i.e., *Youxuan ji* 又玄集) in which Du Fu's poems made their first appearance; not only that, but Du Fu appears at the head of this anthology. As Paul W. Kroll reminds us, "This is the only extant Tang anthology to include Du Fu." Kroll, "Anthologies in the Tang," in Denecke, Li, and Tian, *The Oxford Handbook*, 311.

timeless in itself. With that we turn to the next section, "Poetry and Buddhism," a topic that does not receive major attention in Du Fu studies, as another attempt to extricate Du Fu from the clichéd image of the good "Confucian" constructed of him since the eleventh century. This section includes a pair of chapters, each discussing the general question of studying "literature/poetry and religion/Buddhism" with Du Fu's poems as specific examples. Both chapters in this section invite us to take into serious consideration Buddhism's *social* presence and yet to also focus on the ultimate *poetic* success of the poems themselves.

Paul Rouzer outlines some of the major pitfalls in writing about Buddhism and Chinese literature. Observing that Buddhist vocabulary may simply be used for the sake of rhetorical effectiveness, Rouzer stresses the need to carefully examine the social context of a poem and the use of allusions in the poem when examining the impact of Buddhism on a poet. Rather than treating Buddhism as a system of belief influencing the aesthetics of a cultural tradition, or trying to ascertain the extent of the poet's commitment to the faith, Rouzer emphasizes the importance of thinking of Buddhism as a form of living practice and regarding Buddhist activities as being part of the educated elite's daily life. He calls for carefully considering the situational nature and social function of poetry, and suggests viewing Buddhist elements in a poem not as spiritual autobiography but as "part of a poet's toolbox, used to create an effective poem" (p. 80). With perceptive readings of a series of Du Fu's poems to the monk Zan, Rouzer shows how the level of Du Fu's engagement with Buddhism varies widely from poem to poem and in particular demonstrates Du Fu's "ability to adapt or ignore Buddhist materials to suit his occasional expressive needs" (p. 89).

Xiaofei Tian's chapter opens with questioning the usefulness of the vexed category of "religious poetry," proposing instead to draw on the more productive formulation "religion *and* poetry" to open up space for thinking about the dynamic ways in which these two distinct traditions interact with each other. While agreeing with Rouzer that it can be difficult to prove how "a Buddhist worldview is subtly influencing the aesthetics of the poem with no explicit Buddhist content" (p. 76), Tian nevertheless argues that it is important to do so when there are obvious clues in the internal properties of a text and when external historical situations invite such speculation, especially because Buddhism is such a prominent part of society and daily life. Tian's chapter thus takes the topic of Du Fu and Buddhism in a different direction by examining a famous set of travel poems, the Qinzhou-Tonggu series, from a Buddhist perspective. Tian opts out of the fragmentary reading practice predetermined by the explicit Buddhist content of any particular poem; instead, she reads the set of twelve poems as a carefully orchestrated sequence that constitutes "a coherent Buddhist narrative of transformation and enlightenment" (p. 94), informed by the multimedia presence of Buddhism on and off the poet's travel route.

The last section of this volume, "Reception and Re-creation," highlights the creative aspect of the reception of Du Fu's poetry. Christopher M. B. Nugent's chapter provides a unique perspective by asking how contemporary Tang readers may have received Du Fu and, specifically, how difficult—or not—Du Fu's poetry might have been for an average member of the medieval literary elite at an early stage of mastering the cultural competency required of him. For his test cases, Nugent chooses "Stirred by Autumn," the famous poetic series that has accrued a massive amount of commentaries over the centuries, and Du Fu's *fu*, a genre well known for lexical difficulty, examining them against a series of what he refers to as benchmark texts for acquiring basic literacy and literary vocabulary as well as against popular anthologies. Nugent argues that poetic difficulty, on one hand, is often created more by expectations and assumptions than by the poetic works themselves and, on the other hand, can be a product of intricacies in poetic thought and expression other than vocabulary and allusions. He calls attention to conditions of material reality under which Du Fu composed poetry—the poet was not surrounded by a well-stocked library in his largely itinerant later years—and those under which his contemporary readers read them.

Indeed, Du Fu has admitted as much about his own reading practice: "When I read, I pass over the hard words" (讀書難字過).[9] He was certainly not one who generally prized lexical difficulty as an aesthetic value, even though his long, regulated poems (*pailü* 排律) demonstrate an allusive density that in many cases was perhaps designed to impress the poems' direct addressees and recipients. There is, to be sure, lexical and allusive intricacy in Du Fu's poetry, yet such intricacy often lies elsewhere: for instance, in his highly unusual use of words out of their "proper" register or context, such as his application of a commonplace modal expression in the *Analects* to denounce substandard vegetables as if they were defective disciples. On another occasion, he writes to his friends about his humble life in Kuizhou:

敕廚惟一味   Edict to the kitchen: just one dish,
求飽或三鱔   to get to eat my fill, sometimes I eat three eels.[10]

The poet can afford only "one dish" per meal, but he conveys this as an "order," as if he had an option; the verb, *chi*, which is specially used to refer to an imperial instruction after the Southern Dynasties, is chosen with irony. Du Fu may not have intended his poetry to be "an object of scholarly study" (p. 127), but to recover how something sounded requires a certain linguistic competency beyond mere recognition of allusions.

Ronald Egan's chapter shows us that there were many different ways of reading Du Fu in late imperial times. Turning to the visual re-creation of Du Fu, Egan examines a series of "paintings of Du Fu's poetic thoughts" (Du Fu *shiyi tu* 杜甫詩意圖) by Wang Shimin 王時敏 (1592–1680), Shitao 石濤 (1642–1707), and the mid-Ming painter Xie Shichen 謝時臣 (1488–1547). As Egan states at the opening of his chapter, the artists' treatment of Du Fu's poetic lines may be viewed as "a distinctive part of the great poet's reception history, a part that is often overlooked" (p. 129). From their selection of couplets to their individualized visual representation of the words, the literati painters' imaging of Du Fu's poetry tells us much about how Du Fu could be read, and also reveals what they have deliberately, sometimes militantly, omitted. Discussing the artistic appropriations of Du Fu with sensitivity to both images and words, Egan picks up on evocative tensions between the visual and verbal realms of representation and their productive interactions.

---

9. From no. 2 of "Haphazard Compositions" 漫成. Owen, *The Poetry of Du Fu*, vol. 3, 2–3.
10. From "Writing My Feelings in Kui on an Autumn Day, Respectfully Sent to Director Zheng and Li, Advisor to the Heir Apparent: One Hundred Couplets" 秋日夔府詠懷奉寄鄭監李賓客一百韻. Owen, *The Poetry of Du Fu*, vol. 5, 204–5. "Three eels" is an allusion to the story about Yang Zhen, a learned scholar, into whose hall a stork once dropped three eels, taken to mean he would rise to high office, which he did. The allusion is used literally here, creating a comic effect, and despite their plurality the three eels indeed make up only "one dish" (*yiwei*, lit. "one flavor").

What is particularly fascinating about Egan's chapter is that he shows paintings to be a space where Du Fu can be dehistoricized in a way that would have been otherwise unthinkable in the voluminous commentaries since the Song. By dehistoricization I do not mean Xie Shichen's anachronistic rendering of Du Fu's sarcastic poems about a group of boisterous young aristocrats partying with singing girls as an all-male "elegant gathering" of literati members; rather, I am thinking of the much more radical example of Shitao's transformation of a poem about the desolation of war into a leisurely contemplation of a tranquil landscape. Equally telling is the way in which painters, as Egan notices, tend to present a lone male figure, without his wife and children, even while the original poem very much accentuates their presence, real or visualized. Speaking of Shitao's painterly vision of the poet, Egan observes that "Du Fu has become the iconic 'poetry sage' who stands apart, moving serenely through the landscape as he describes it" (p. 139).

There is something both disturbing and exhilarating about such a dehistoricized interpretation of Du Fu. At the very least, we realize that the Taiwan poet Luo Qing's 羅 青 (b. 1948) ironic observation about the anachronistic portrayal of the past in "On How Du Fu Was Influenced by Luo Qing" 論杜甫如何受羅青影響 (1994) had already begun in the fifteenth century, and that the configuration of history through the lens and interests of the present day is perhaps itself timeless. Luo Qing is one of the poets discussed in David Der-wei Wang's chapter, "Six Modernist Poets in Search of Du Fu," which brings the volume to the present day. Wang's tour-de-force chapter constitutes a miniature literary history, as well as a macro poetic map, of modern China and the wider sinophone sphere in changing historical circumstances over a century. In a sweeping spatial and temporal canvas nuanced with close readings of individual poems, Wang demonstrates how, "for all the iconoclastic impulses of modern Chinese literature, Du Fu continued to enjoy being an icon and a ground for cultural and even political contestation throughout the twentieth century, inspiring and challenging poets of various styles, generations, and ideologies" (p. 144). Specifically, through emulating and simulating Du Fu, Wang argues that these poets invoke Du Fu the "poet historian" as a yardstick for measuring poetry's social and moral obligation to record modern experiences, and that Chinese literary modernity of the twentieth century, instead of implying a radical break from the past, thus reaffirms its meaningfulness and its "ethical . . . implications in the present" (p. 163). For these poets, then, evoking the name of Du Fu is very much a political act. Not only Du Fu himself but his poetry is writ large in this newest version of his reception and re-creation.

Afterthoughts

In his chapter Ronald Egan makes a thought-provoking observation on how "feminine presence" and Du Fu's family are erased in Xie Shichen's paintings on Du Fu's poems. Xie Shichen's omission is perhaps more representative, and indicative of larger issues, than just one painter's preferences or his personal interpretation of Du Fu.

From the Song dynasty on, Du Fu has come to be exclusively identified with Confucian patriarchal values: loyalty to the ruler or dynasty, concern for the state, and compassion for the common folk. This image is perpetuated by numerous later poets, especially poets who are caught in a national crisis, of which there was no shortage in the past centuries. In this regard, female poets from late imperial China who were inspired by Du Fu, just like their male counterparts, tended to pay particular attention to Du Fu as a poet of sorrows and cares at a time of national and personal trauma.[11] In modern times, Du Fu is even more avidly placed on a pedestal precisely for those very qualities perceived to be dominant in his person and his poetry. It is notable how, as David Der-wei Wang's chapter shows, so many modern poets regard Du Fu as Social Conscience personified: Feng Zhi 馮至 (1905–1993) sees a halo around Du Fu, whose "tattered robes" emit a light as if in a painting of a Christian apostle, "sage" being easily conflated with "saint" in modern Chinese (both *sheng* 聖); when "paying tribute" to Du Fu, Xiao Kaiyu 蕭開愚 (b. 1960) chose to write a poem of ten sections, each featuring a social problem or a political issue in contemporary China. In such a vision, the History of the "poet historian" has a capital *H*: it is the history of an empire, a dynasty, a nation-state, a society, or a cultural tradition; not that of one individual man or woman or that of one single family, lived out in all its mundane details—kids, bean sauce, chickens, a flood, home improvement, gardening projects, all of which preoccupied Du Fu's mind and appear frequently in his poetry.

It is perhaps not a coincidence that the community of modern poets devoted to the vision of poetry as History is as all male as the "elegant gathering" of literati portrayed in Xie Shichen's paining. We have a gender issue here, embroiled in social and cultural changes since the Tang. Gender segregation is prominent in social and representational realms, but it does not do justice to Du Fu's poetry. In fact, it never fails to strike me, a woman scholar who has worked for many years on early medieval literature and court poetry, what an incredibly domestic man and poet Du Fu is, as represented in his poetry. Such representation is in dramatic contrast with the poets before him. Whether or not he endows the quotidian with any large meaning, the poet's delight in family life and his absorption in an assortment of house-related tasks and activities are nothing short of impressive. It has been observed that Du Fu writes about his wife and his children a great deal; even more remarkably, he writes amorously about his wife, describing her sweet-smelling coiffure and alabaster arms. While a premodern male poet could write romantically and erotically about concubines, female entertainers, courtesans, and cat-amites, he would not and could not do that about his wife—in fact love poems to one's wife are usually only written when she is dead, in the established subgenre of "poems lamenting deceased spouse" (*daowang* 悼亡詩). But Du Fu is exactly the opposite: for a poet acclaimed for stylistic and thematic variety and inclusiveness in his oeuvre, he surprisingly does not have any "romantic poems" (*xiangyan shi* 香豔詩 or *yanqing shi* 豔情詩).[12] A quatrain he wrote in Chengdu is a rare indication of a momentary tempta-

---

11. For instance, the late Ming woman poet Xu Can 徐燦 (ca. 1610s–after 1677) or the late Qing poet Li Changxia 李長霞 (ca. 1830–ca. 1880).

12. When he does, he does with a self-conscious "playfulness." Once he writes to a friend teasingly inviting him to host raucous parties and even prodding him to call a couple of local girls, naming the girls specifi-cally. This is "Written in Sport on a Spring Day: Provoking Prefect Hao" 春日戲題惱郝使君兄. Owen, *The Poetry of Du Fu*, vol. 3, 196–97. Another time he writes two "erotic songs" (*yanqu*) but ends with advising his friend not to fool around. This is "Often Accompanying Li of Zizhou Sailing on the River with Girl Musicians in All the Boats, I Playfully Compose Two Erotic Songs to Give to Li" 數陪李梓州泛江有女樂在諸舫戲為豔曲二首贈李. The last couplet of the second poem reads: "The prefect has his own wife— / don't imitate the wild mandarin ducks" 使君自有婦, 莫學野鴛鴦. Owen, *The Poetry of Du Fu*, vol. 3, 216–17.

tion, about which commentators remain largely silent.[13] Du Fu's domesticity tends to be overlooked in comparison with his concerns about dynastic fate, ruler, and empire.

It is, of course, not the domestic activities Du Fu did or the family man he was that matters but rather the fact that he would write them into poetry, a high cultural form in the Tang. If we accept the concept of history in lowercase, then we say that Du Fu is a faithful historian of his own life. That life itself is not so striking, but the way he writes it certainly is. He notices and speaks of moments and details in life that contemporary poetic discourse and polite society do not notice or speak of, and he thinks about them, provocatively, in well-wrought poetic lines. That is why he endures. Later poets cannot do it because they all try to "do Du Fu" while Du Fu was just being himself, and he was like nobody else.

This volume is thus assembled with the modest hope that, along with the complete English translation of Du Fu's collection, these writings will bring the reader closer to Du Fu's poems.

---

13. This is "What Happened" 即事: "A hundred jewels adorn the sash at her waist, / pearls wrap around her leather armlets. / When she smiles, flowers near the eyes; / when the dance is done, brocade wraps her head" 百寶裝腰帶, 真珠絡臂韝, 笑時花近眼, 舞罷錦纏頭. Owen, *The Poetry of Du* Fu, vol. 3, 98–99. A few moralistic commentators insist that it is a criticism of luxury or a disguised satire of a general whose surname is Hua 花 ("flower"). Xiao Difei, *Du Fu quanji*, vol. 5, 9.2542.

Section I

Home, Locale, Empire

1
Foundings of Home

On Du Fu and Poetic Success

Jack W. Chen

> Thus inevitably does the universe wear our color, and every object fall successively into the subject itself. The subject exists, the subject enlarges; all things sooner or later fall into place.
>
> —Ralph Waldo Emerson, "Experience"[1]

Much has been written on the historical stakes of Du Fu's poetry, on how he writes against the backdrop of war and disaster, bearing witness to the fate of the dynasty. To read Du Fu in terms of history is to argue for a conception of poetry as embodying significance, often understood in the literary tradition as bound up with moral judgment. However, pervading Du Fu's poetry is a broken conviction about the significance of poetry, one that undercuts easy didacticism. On the one hand, Du Fu clearly believes that the composition of poetry is invested with moral, political, and historical significance, seeking in poetry the means to put forward arguments about himself and the circumstances around him. Yet, on the other hand, he constantly expresses worry over the ineffectiveness of his poetic acts and gestures, painfully wondering whether what he does truly means anything, whether anything can be salvaged through poetry.

The hope of poetic success—and its constant shadowings of failure—haunt Du Fu even as they spur him ever onward in the writing of poetry. I take the notion of poetic success from the poet and critic Allen Grossman, who writes, "The function of poetry is to obtain for everybody one kind of success at the limits of the autonomy of the will."[2] What Grossman argues here is that poetry offers redress against a reality that cannot be otherwise changed, which for him is the condition of our mortality. Poetry thus becomes a means of speaking desire, of expressing what one would will, if one only had the power to effect one's will. Stephen Owen identifies this quality in Du Fu when he speaks about the optative in his poetry, noting moments in which Du

---

This is a revision of the first graduate school paper that I wrote for Stephen Owen in the fall of 1997, and as such, I am indebted to him and to my classmates in his seminar on early and High Tang poetry. During this time, I was also taking seminars with the late Stanley Cavell, whose influence can be seen throughout this essay and whose memory I wish to acknowledge.

1. Emerson, "Experience," *The Essays*, 263–64.
2. See Grossman, "Summa Lyrica," in Grossman with Halliday, *The Sighted Singer*, 209.

Fu expresses a hope for things to be other than they are.[3] To be sure, we find optative gestures in poetry that long precede Du Fu, beginning with the earliest examples of classical poetry at the end of the Han dynasty, but, in Du Fu, the voicing of hopeful desire is more acutely felt in his knowledge of its impossibility and, indeed, may be said to go beyond mere literary convention, constituting a recurring and integral theme of his work. Before turning to the main part of my argument, I wish to acknowledge also Paul Rouzer's essay "Du Fu and the Failure of Lyric Poetry," which takes up some of the same concerns, though framed in the broader contexts of contemporary poetic interpretation.[4] My argument runs parallel, in many ways, to Rouzer's, both in terms of the entwined themes of hope and failure and in terms of the stakes of poetry.

In examining the question of poetic success for Du Fu, I focus on the idea of home and the importance of home after the An Lushan Rebellion (755–763). It will be my larger argument that the gestures in Du Fu's poetry to found and locate a sense of home are, in fact, attempts to find significance beyond the context of empire and dynastic trauma, to find it even (or especially) within the ordinary, a concept that I borrow from Stanley Cavell and to which I will return throughout this chapter.[5] For Du Fu, the hope for success is frequently tempered by his awareness of failure, and, even when he claims to win out over his circumstances, he undercuts his victory with ironic realization or returns to a scene of disappointment by thematizing his personal failure itself as the subject of poetry. This is a hope that persists in spite of his failures, uncertainties, and realizations of self-misprision. In this way, Du Fu comes to his poetic powers as essentially an ironic reader, one who may admire the hyperbolic self-imagination of a poet such as Li Bai 李白 (701–762) but cannot himself play the roles that Li Bai plays—at least, not without a sense of distance and self-consciousness.

However, the idea of home represents for Du Fu the hope that there might be a form of poetic success that will persist after one's failures or, perhaps rather, despite them. Home is often considered a fixed place within our memories, a site of nostalgia—or, indeed, the site of nostalgia—around which our past is constructed and our present understood. Yet we have many homes throughout our lives, and the act of finding—and of founding—a home carries us through our lives. Throughout Du Fu's poems, there is a constant longing for home, and this longing becomes ever more pronounced after the near collapse of the Tang Empire, as Du Fu travels from one location to another. It is difficult to think of Du Fu outside of the An Lushan Rebellion and its aftermath, having emerged within literary historical memory as the one poet who bore witness to Tang dynastic crisis. Yet he is also the poet for whom the ordinary could be the stuff of poetry, and the longing for home is, at its heart, a wish for the return to the ordinary, to a sense of life that both precedes and postdates the trauma of momentous events.

I begin with the poem "No Return" ("Bu gui" 不歸), which is set during the rebellion but views the rebellion's tragedy through the poet's memories of his dead cousin:

---

3. Owen, *The Great Age*, 205.
4. The question of failure as a central theme of modern lyric (and how Du Fu embodies a similar consciousness) is examined at length in Rouzer, "Du Fu and the Failure of Lyric," 27–53.
5. Cavell explores the idea of the ordinary throughout his work, but one might begin with the title essay of *Must We Mean What We Say? A Book of Essays*, and with *In Quest of the Ordinary: Lines of Skepticism and Romanticism*. Also, see the excellent overview of Cavell's thought in Charles Petersen, "Must We Mean What We Say? On Stanley Cavell."

不歸　　　　No Return[6]

河間尚征伐　There is still fighting in Hejian,
汝骨在空城　your bones lie in a deserted city.
從弟人皆有　Everyone has cousins,
終身恨不平　but all my life this bitterness will not calm.
數金憐俊邁　I am touched by your superiority when counting coins,
總角愛聰明　I cherish your cleverness when your hair was tied in tufts.
面上三年土　Over your face lie three years of earth,
春風草又生　and once again plants grow in the breeze of spring.

The fighting of the poem's opening line alludes to the retaking of Luoyang by the imperial forces after their loss to An Lushan's armies in the rebellion. However, in the second line Du Fu immediately changes the scale of the stakes from that of the empire's fate to that of his dead cousin's, beginning an apostrophic address that comprises the rest of the poem in which he laments the bones of his cousin in the ruined city. In the third couplet, Du Fu recalls his cousin to him through two precise memories that still haunt him, memories that have no significance to anyone but Du Fu. His cousin's quickness at counting money and cleverness as a young child are moments of the ordinary, moments that might have otherwise been forgotten, that are transformed by tragedy into images of what Du Fu has personally lost because of the war. In the poem's close, he admits the undeniable, that his cousin is buried and gone, and remarks on the remorseless progress of the seasons, how spring has returned, plants growing over the bodies of the dead. The indifference shown by spring's renewal reveals the final irony, that the seasons may return each year but that his cousin never will.

Still, at least for the space of the poem, Du Fu is able to summon his cousin into presence through an apostrophic gesture. Within the forensic contexts of classical rhetoric, Quintilian defines apostrophe as the "turning away from the jury," by which he means the diverting of speech in oratory to address someone other than the judges of the contest (who are the expected addressees).[7] However, this meaning has changed within contemporary criticism, becoming understood instead as a turning away to address some other, who may or may not be present in the scene and indeed may be dead or immaterial.[8] In this more recent context, apostrophe names a class of tropes that privileges poetic speech at a moment when human limits are experienced, for which the most prominent member of would be *deisis*, or the poetic invocation of the divine (for inspiration, among other occasions). Thus, the moment of apostrophic speech is also a moment of poetic society, for apostrophe breaks from the poem's discourse to call to a "you/Thou," naming the absence and seeking to fill it with another kind of presence, one born out of poetry, making the gesture one of turning *toward* in the moment that the speaker turns *away*.

---

6. For the Chinese text, see Qiu Zhaoao, *Du shi xiangzhu*, 511; for the translation, see Owen, *The Poetry of Du Fu*, vol. 2, 70–71.
7. Quintilian, *The Orator's Education*, 4.1.63, 9.1.17.
8. J. Douglas Kneale provides a useful survey of apostrophe in its classical and postclassical contexts while disputing its usage in poststructural criticism. See Kneale, "Romantic Aversions," 91–105. Kneale is responding specifically to Jonathan Culler's chapter on apostrophe in *The Pursuit of Signs: Semiotics, Literature, Deconstruction*. See also Johnson, "Apostrophe, Animation, Abortion," in *A World of Difference*, 184–99; and Alpers, "Apostrophe and the Rhetoric of Renaissance Lyric," 1–22.

Yet apostrophe is limited by the fact that it may succeed in only one way: it is voiced only in absence of the addressee. If one speaks to the absent other only in the full knowledge of the other's absence, apostrophe fails—and cannot but fail—in all the other ways that might be important to the speaker. Du Fu names "your bones" (*ru gu* 汝骨) only when the "you" has become a thing, mere bones, separated by both distance and calamity. Moreover, because Du Fu is addressing a "you" of absent bones, there is another facet to his apostrophe: when we speak of bones either in poetry or in philosophy, we are speaking not only of traces and remainders but of the ineluctable truth that underlies the social world. The bones of Du Fu's young cousin mark the limits of poetic imagination because no matter how the poet gives shape and voice to the dead other, the thingness of the bones, their uncanny otherness, still resists and negates the efforts of human society. There is thus a second degree of distance here. When Du Fu speaks to the bones, he is speaking to traces that are themselves absent and must be first summoned into presence by apostrophic speech, just so they may be acknowledged as mere traces. Yet the poet's address cannot be reciprocated. Like the (absent) "deserted city" (*kongcheng* 空城), the bones are merely the (absent) remaining index of a permanent loss. Even where poetic gesture may succeed—in naming the trace as something present to the poetic self—it still must fail; the bones may not be given life again.

The title of "No Return" names a concern with home through its impossibility, the impossibility of the poet's dead cousin to ever return. Yet home does not name the particular building in which one dwells; rather, it is a particular transformation of social space—a staking of the locus in which the self may turn toward the other and the other may respond in kind. The turn toward cherished memory emphasizes the intimacy of the space, preserving the private significance of the other for the self in the elements of the ordinary that no other person might have noticed. There is a way in which Du Fu sketches a relationship between "returning" as a general movement and "home" as that to which one turns or that one seeks. Within Du Fu's two instanced memories, which capture the intimate ordinary, a vignette of home appears. After all, the notion of home is constructed in part by the sense of the ordinary, a shift from the heightened sensibility of poetic experience to a familiarity so unremarkable that it becomes invisible: let us say, domestication. It is society, an immersion in other lives, but without wonder or shock, merely the comfortable passage through shared space. When Stanley Cavell insists in his essay "Declining Decline" that Wittgenstein's *Philosophical Investigations* emphasizes a returning of language from the abstracted realm of the metaphysical to its ordinary usages, he is equating the ordinary with a notion of home.[9] But, of course, we come to recognize home only when we are in exile; when we are home, we immediately forget and displace our comfort with boredom. It is in this way that Du Fu first experiences home when he is lost to it, able to touch its familiar textures only in poetic appeal.

The question of home comes to occupy a great share of Du Fu's middle-period and later poetic work, constituting a kind of literary topography of exile. His poems on this theme are numerous, and they include more idyllic poems, such as the many poems on the Thatched Cottage (*caotang* 草堂) in Chengdu, and the poetry of loss, such as those that take wandering as their theme. Most famous are the pieces that compose the "Stirred by Autumn" set of eight poems ("Qiuxing bashou" 秋興八首), in which Du Fu's poetic vision flickers back and forth between historical and imaginary landscapes on the

---

9. Cavell, *This New Yet Unapproachable America*, 66.

one hand and the actual sites through which the traveler makes his way on the other.[10] What gives rise (*xing* 興) to the poetic travels, as well as to Du Fu's own experience of exile, is represented as the loss of home. This can be seen in the last line of the fourth poem of this set: "The life I used to have at home is the longing in my heart" 故國平居有所思.[11] Owen translates the phrase *pingju* 平居 as "the life I used to have," though Du Fu is also speaking of "dwelling" or "inhabiting" a space of a lost sense of the ordinary, one that comes to signify his "homeland" (*guguo* 故國) in the aftermath of rebellion. Here, the gesture to his former home takes the form of an apostrophic gesture without address, as a turning toward a space and a life that no longer is possible. Instead of a human other (or the traces of a once-human other), the poet names a specific site in the past for which he longs but knows he can no longer have.

To come to rest at a place (*ju* 居) is to found a home (*jia* 家). The term *guguo* identifies one such home, but it is an imagined space and community, rather than a precise geography. This is not the political space of the modern nation-state (*guojia* 國家) but rather something that seems to fall between a political homeland and a "home-land" (the actual piece of earth upon which one builds one's home), and we may hear both the evocation of a state order and the memory of a domestic space. However, the concept of home is far richer than this. In nineteenth-century America, Ralph Waldo Emerson will write that "I know that the world I converse with in the city and in the farms is not the world I *think*."[12] Emerson does not name the notion of home explicitly, but when Geoffrey H. Hartman writes, "we are born aliens into a world which is at most a foster home, or substitute heaven," Hartman makes explicit the oblique echo.[13] Home is what lies beyond this world of limitations, a realm in which our hopes may become realities. In this sense, Du Fu's gestures toward home become efforts to found a home, optative statements that acknowledge the hard facts of reality and seek to rise above them.

In turning to the question of home in Du Fu, we must also turn to biography and the itinerary of Du Fu's travels. The set of poems that compose "Stirred by Autumn" come near the end of Du Fu's life, when he finds a brief refuge in Kuizhou in the years 766–768.[14] However, there is a period of relative peace and happiness that precedes this: the famous Chengdu years, or the years in the Thatched Cottage. A series of poems from "Siting a Dwelling" ("Bu ju" 卜居) to "My Cottage Is Finished" ("Tang cheng" 堂成), and others, bears witness to the poet in the process of poetically declaring himself to be home.[15] For example, in "As a Farmer" ("Wei nong" 為農), he writes, "I site my dwelling, to grow old from this moment on, / being a farmer, far from the capital" 卜宅從茲老, 為農去國賒.[16] Du Fu here adopts, like the poet Tao Qian 陶潛 (365?–427), the role of the rustic, a persona whose selfhood is evinced by the refusal of political subjecthood. The sense of political loyalty and desire that one hears in "Stirred by Autumn" is presented here as a deflection of subjecthood: the poet allies himself not with the body politic (the state and public society) but rather with the individual body (personal

---

10. Qiu Zhaoao, *Du shi xiangzhu*, 1484–99; Owen, *The Poetry of Du Fu*, vol. 4, 352–61.
11. Qiu Zhaoao, *Du shi xiangzhu*, 1489; Owen, *The Poetry of Du Fu*, vol. 4, 354–55.
12. Emerson, "Experience," 266.
13. Hartman, "Wordsworth Revisited," *The Unremarkable Wordsworth*, 16.
14. On Du Fu's years in Kuizhou, see McCraw, *Du Fu's Laments*, 41–60.
15. For "Siting a Dwelling," see Qiu Zhaoao, *Du shi xiangzhu*, 729–30; Owen, *The Poetry of Du Fu*, vol. 2, 290–91. For "My Cottage Is Finished," see Qiu Zhaoao, *Du shi xiangzhu*, 735–36; Owen, *The Poetry of Du Fu*, vol. 2, 296–97.
16. Qiu Zhaoao, *Du shi xiangzhu*, 739–40; Owen, *The Poetry of Du Fu*, vol. 2, 300–301.

desires). However, we cannot avoid noticing how society circumscribes this individual choice; after all, it is not a private choice that Du Fu makes. He cannot simply declare his private identity but must physically remove himself to the geographical margins of the state. In so doing, the poet does not contest state hegemony but rather affirms it.

On the level of poetic claim, however, Du Fu attempts to refashion within the notion of home an explicitly nonpolitical and nonsocial representation. Gestures may be made from the isolated locus of the poetic enunciation toward society (sometimes depicted as the capital, sometimes as a city or village) in the interests of contrast, but these are negative statements, thoughts of difference. For the most part, the poet confines his statements to the consciousness of isolation and the kinds of pleasures that one might find in this. With this in mind, one cannot argue that the poetry of these years is uncomplicatedly happy, an echo of the fraught nature of Tao Qian's own withdrawal from society. A vision of what home might be is articulated clearly in the set of three poems entitled "Hiding My Traces" ("Bingji sanshou" 屏跡三首):

屏跡三首   "Hiding My Traces: Three Poems"[17]

I.

衰顏甘屏跡	In declining years I gladly hide my traces,
幽事供高臥	seclusion provides for resting above it all.
鳥下竹根行	A bird walks, having descended to roots of bamboo,
龜開萍葉過	a turtle passes, sweeping duckweed leaves open.
年荒酒價乏	The harvest was bad, I lack the price of ale,
日並園蔬課	I make a day's food last two, seeking garden vegetables.
猶酌甘泉歌	But I still sing, pouring a drink from a sweet spring,
歌長擊樽破	as my song lasts long, I tap the cup and break it.

II.

用拙存吾道	By ineptness I preserve my Way,
幽居近物情	I dwell hidden, close to the sense of things.
桑麻深雨露	Mulberry and hemp deepen in rain and dew,
燕雀半生成	swallows and sparrows, half grown to maturity.
村鼓時時急	From time to time the village drums beat urgently,
漁舟個個輕	fishing boats, each of them light.
杖藜從白首	Let my hair turn white as I lean on my cane,
心跡喜雙清	I rejoice that both mind and traces are pure.

III.

晚起家何事	I get up late, nothing to be done at home,
無營地轉幽	without bustle, the place becomes more secluded.
竹光團野色	Light on the bamboo concentrates wilderness colors,
舍影漾江流	the reflection of my cottage ripples in the river's current.
失學從兒懶	I allow my son to be lazy, abandoning study,
長貧任婦愁	and let my wife worry about being always poor.
百年渾得醉	May I attain a hundred years of general drunkenness
一月不梳頭	and not comb my hair for a whole month.

17. Qiu Zhaoao, *Du shi xiangzhu*, 882–83; Owen, *The Poetry of Du Fu*, vol. 3, 94–97.

In each of these three poems, Du Fu combines the notion of home—either house-hold, *jia* 家; or the act of resting, *wo* 臥; the state of dwelling, *ju* 居; and the house structure itself, *she* 舍—with hiddenness, *you* 幽. Du Fu is able to conceive a home only in a space that is not only emptied of other people but also invisible to society in general: it is a home that is defined by its hiddenness. The idea of hiding has a rich and complicated history in Chinese philosophical thought, starting from the general concept in the *Yi jing* 易經 (*Classic of Changes*) and its appended commentary, the "Xici zhuan" 繫辭傳 ("Appended Statements") to its deployments in the *Laozi Dao de jing* 老子道德經 and related recluse lore, to Legalist accounts of the state.[18] For those such as the *Zhuangzi*'s Robber Zhi and Old Fisherman, dwelling in hiddenness may provide a respite from political dangers and social entanglements. In literary writings, the trope of hiddenness is usually equated with this last kind of reclusion (the model presented by Du Fu's "As a Farmer," above), and while Du Fu does not infuse "dwelling in hiddenness" with the political complexities of the philosophical tradition, one does hear a certain attention to the political.

Each of the three poems in "Hiding My Traces" begins with idyllic claims: "In declining years I gladly hide my traces, / seclusion provides for resting above it all"; "By ineptness I preserve my Way, / I dwell hidden, close to the sense of things"; "I get up late, nothing to be done at home, / without bustle, the place becomes more secluded." Hiddenness, broached in the first couplet in each of the poems, is equated with peaceful, rustic life. Du Fu even makes the direct allusion to Tao Qian, by citing his favorite self-description, "ineptness" (*zhuo* 拙). These seem to be poetic lines about leisure and empty days; the poet rises without concern about the hour, and no labor is either visible or audible to the poetic consciousness. In the most idyllic of the three poems, the last one, the peacefulness of the scene becomes a negative synesthesia, turning the silence (absence of sound) into invisibility (impossibility of vision).

The second couplets of the three poems turn from his situation to the scenery around him; here, the poet gives order to the surrounding world and allows a sense of place to emerge: "A bird walks, having descended to roots of bamboo, / a turtle passes, sweeping duckweed leaves open"; "Mulberry and hemp deepen in rain and dew, / swallows and sparrows, half grown to maturity"; "Light on the bamboo concentrates wilderness colors, / the reflection of my cottage ripples in the river's current." The third poem in the set, again, contains the most interesting insight, exploring the way in which light and vision interact in tableau-like scenes. We follow the reflection of light upon the shiny bamboo surface to the reflection of the cottage in the rippling water, as the glow of light (*guang* 光), becomes color (*se* 色), and finally reflected image (*ying* 影).

The poet's home is never directly represented in the scene of the poem, though the turn toward light and the play of light in nature allows the poet a way to glimpse the dwelling place despite its hiddenness, so that we see his cottage through the river's reflection. What is hidden, by necessity, cannot be apprehended directly, and this indirect vision of the cottage is a way in which the poet may affirm the quality of hiddenness without destroying it. We somehow know that the hidden thing is there, but we have to resort to a metonymic logic of cause and effect to prove its presence. Thus, we search not for the thing itself—knowing that it can never be found—but rather for

---

18. For recent studies of hiddenness in Chinese culture, see Varsano, ed., *The Rhetoric of Hiddenness in Traditional Chinese Culture*.

its signs, representations, metaphors, indexes, traces, and tracks. We recall that Du Fu tropes here the Thatched Cottage as "dwelling in hiddenness" (*youju* 幽居), making a particular poetic claim about the nature of the building. Though we do see the building represented in other poems, this set of poems, with their consciousness of the hidden, defer representation and focus attention on the conscious absence, the negated thing. In this sense, dwellings are not unlike bones, hidden from human sight, from society, and called back into presence by poetic figuration.

The other prominent theme that runs through "Hiding My Traces" is that of social and economic poverty. In the third couplet of each of the poems, Du Fu raises this specter: "The harvest was bad, I lack the price of ale, / I make a day's food last two, seeking garden vegetables"; "From time to time the village drums beat urgently, / fishing boats, each of them light"; "I allow my son to be lazy, abandoning study, / and let my wife worry about being always poor." The consciousness of an exterior social realm to his hermetic one cannot be completely blocked or hidden. Du Fu speaks about his own poverty and hardships, as well as rural entertainments (the village drums), his neighbors' poverty (the empty fishing boats), and his family's social displacement (his son's neglect of study). This is the reality that pierces through the poetic construction of home, the poet's admission that imagination cannot entirely succeed in recasting reality.

However, I want to suggest another way of looking at the economic intrusion into poetic idyll. When Gaston Bachelard speaks about the hermit's hut in *The Poetics of Space*, he is depicting a relationship between the human and the divine that is grounded in a particular cultural framework. Nevertheless, he addresses an element common to both Du Fu's conception of eremitism and a Judeo-Christian one:

> The hermit is alone before God. His hut, therefore, is just the opposite of the monastery. And there radiates about this centralized solitude a universe of meditation and prayer, a universe outside the universe. The hut can receive none of the riches "of this world." It possesses the felicity of intense poverty; indeed, it is one of the glories of poverty; as destitution increases it gives us access to absolute refuge.[19]

Du Fu is not typically viewed as a poet of the divine, and even where he turns to the divine (or the mortal and architectural representatives of the divine), there is a steadfast refusal to enter into *ekstasis*. However, we find a concern with the hidden and impoverishment in both Bachelard's account of the hermit's hut and in Du Fu's account. Bachelard states the matter very plainly: it is the very condition of impoverishment that creates the power of refuge for the hermit. That is to say, though the hermit dwells in utter destitution, he nevertheless has access to an absolute refuge because of his destitution. His economic condition—that is, his lack—hides the hermit from this world, preserving his life for another world. What hides Du Fu from the world is also this impoverishment, which takes the form of "hiding traces." The poet empties his world of people and social relationships, and, in so doing, he restricts himself and his family to a diminished existence. Without society, there can be no hope for social advancement, and so his son does not study. Du Fu neglects any form of labor or livelihood, and so his wife alone concerns herself with the family's support. Despite this suffering, poverty is ironically what gives Du Fu and his family refuge from the fighting that is approaching his idyll; in the absence of society, a man such as Du Fu becomes

---

19. Bachelard, *The Poetics of Space*, 32.

insignificant and therefore safe. It is a transformed idyll that Du Fu constructs, one that weaves together both the utopian themes of the poet-recluse topos and the reality of his actual destitution.

In this poem, hiddenness and impoverishment become entwined tropes, neither possible without the other. The notion of home, then, must somehow encompass both the sense of rest that hiddenness contains and the painful condition of destitution. In the last couplets of the three poems, we see how Du Fu resolves his situation, finding a sense of peace, if only for the moment: "But I still sing, pouring a drink from a sweet spring, / as my song lasts long, I tap the cup and break it"; "Let my hair turn white as I lean on my cane, / I rejoice that both mind and traces are pure"; "May I attain a hundred years of general drunkenness / and not comb my hair for a whole month." The resolve found in the first of these endings may last just for the space of a drink and a song (after which the cup is broken and the spell gone), but the second ending points to a longer duration—that of old age—and the poet's contentment with his lot. The last of the closing couplets points to the future, enunciating the wish that he will be able to sustain this joy, be it for a month or for a century.

The Thatched Cottage in Chengdu is a dwelling for Du Fu, and, as a place of safe dwelling, it becomes a home for him, but we should remember that it is a second home, a home marked very strongly by its secondariness. It is not the place of origin, a place in which all wounds are healed and losses are given restitution, but a place haunted by the memory of wounds and loss. And yet we remember home only after we are evicted from it. The Afrikaans poet and former political prisoner Breyten Breytenbach writes:

> In the beginning there is the hearth, the ancestral fire, and you are a native of the flames. You belong there and therefore it belongs to you. Then comes exile, the break, the destitution, the initiation, the maiming which—I think—gives access to a deeper sight, provides a path into consciousness through the imitation of thinking. Now you can never again entirely relax the belly muscles. . . . Henceforth you are at home nowhere, and by that token everywhere.[20]

If we have not home, then we are in the world, and we must find a way to make of the world a home, a place in which we might dwell. Poetry becomes a way in which we attempt to redeem for ourselves—as for society—our lost patrimonies; the poetic gesture opens for us a kind of passage beyond and through our present condition. Yet, when we come to a place that we claim as our home, it is within the shadow of belatedness that we do so. The gesture toward home will never restore us to the original state of undifferentiation or innocence, but it is what we do in the absence of choice. We inhabit our selves and houses poorly, full of the suffering of experience. The second home—the only home we can ever know—is always a home of destitution, as well as of refuge.

Still, there is still a measure of hope that we, as poor beings, cannot afford to let pass. When we construct a house and call it home, we stake for ourselves a place within the world to which we may return. The claiming of home gives to us, allows for us, the possibility of returning. As Breytenbach says, "Henceforth you are at home nowhere, and by that token everywhere." Or, as Du Fu says in the closing couplet of the occasional poem "Accompanied by Attendant Censor Wang I Feast at the Wilderness Pavilion on East Mountain at Tongquan" ("Pei Wang shiyu yan Tongquan Dongshan Yeting" 陪王侍御宴通泉東山野亭): "Singing wildly, just too wonderful, / getting drunk, home is right

---

20. Breytenbach, "The Long March from Hearth to Heart," 74.

here" 狂歌過於勝，得醉即為家.[21] We find this possibility of return in the moment that we name a strange land our home, a poetic gesture that succeeds despite the knowledge that it cannot be sustained beyond the moment.

Here I turn to the last poem I will discuss in this chapter:

春歸	Return in Spring[22]
苔徑臨江竹	Mossy path, bamboo overlooking the river,
茅簷覆地花	thatched eaves, flowers that cover the ground.
別來頻甲子	Many sixty-day cycles since I left,
倏忽又春華	now coming back, suddenly spring is in bloom.
倚杖看孤石	Leaning on a cane, I look at a lone rock,
傾壺就淺沙	I go to sandy shallows to drain my jug.
遠鷗浮水靜	Far off gulls serene, float on the waters,
輕燕受風斜	light swallows slant, catching the wind.
世路雖多梗	Though obstacles are many on the roads of the age,
吾生亦有涯	my life too has its limits.
此身醒複醉	This body sobers and gets drunk again,
乘興即爲家	when I follow my whim, that is home.

There is a sadness in the poem, expressed in the passage of time and the solitary vision of the poet as he gazes upon his home at Chengdu. Qiu Zhaoao 仇兆鰲 (1638–1717) dates this poem to the second year of the Guangde reign (764), when Du Fu returned to Chengdu after going to meet the newly appointed Governor Yan Wu 嚴武 (726–765). He had wanted to take a trip down the Western Han to Lake Dongting but, because of social obligations, could not. As often is the case, the claim to hiddenness, with its attendant social and economic privations, is discarded when a social occasion presents itself. The poetic vision of the hermit's hidden dwelling now gives way to a different, and more complicated, conception of home.

Du Fu begins the poem with parallel couplets, describing the scene upon his return and piecing together the traces of the human that have fallen back into nature, as if reverting back to the wilderness: "Mossy path, bamboo overlooking the river, / thatched eaves, flowers that cover the ground." The path is overgrown with moss and shielded by the river's bamboo; by the thatched eaves of the cottage, the poet sees no one, only fallen flowers. The poet had left in a certain season, at a certain moment in time, and he is surprised to find that time had passed while he was away from his home, that his home had been indifferent to his absence. There is also a marked absence of other human beings here, a sense intensified by the poet's gazing upon the "lone rock" while at the "sandy shallows." Yet where we might expect a different sort of poem to follow from this moment, Du Fu restores a sense of quiet calm by turning to the "distant gulls" and "light swallows," the only other moving creatures here. That is, the view of the rock does not bring the poem into lament; its potential pathos is balanced by the serenity of the flying birds.

The moment of lyric insight turns the poet back from the vista to his own self, and again, where one might expect a modulation into pathos, Du Fu surprises us by transforming the melancholy moment: "Though obstacles are many on the roads of the

---

21. Qiu Zhaoao, *Du shi xiangzhu*, 963; Owen, *The Poetry of Du Fu*, vol. 3, 180–81.
22. Qiu Zhaoao, *Du shi xiangzhu*, 1110; Owen, *The Poetry of Du Fu*, vol. 3, 348–49.

age, / my life too has its limits. / This body sobers and gets drunk again, / when I follow my whim, that is home." The penultimate couplet acknowledges the limitations not only of the age—a time of social chaos and upheavals—but also of the mortal being who inhabits the limited and obstructed age. This is a double limit, a limit within a greater limit, that the poet faces: in his public life, he cannot advance or rise above his poverty; in his private life, he cannot overcome his mortality. The deflection of subjecthood that we have seen in Du Fu's inhabiting of the roles of rustic-recluse ("As a Farmer") and hermit ("Hiding My Traces") now stand revealed as poetic games, as legerdemains. Neither reclusion from society nor from mortality can be won absolutely within poetic gesture. The poet makes his claims and inhabits his roles, but he still has not gained redress. Here is the pinnacle of the poet's lament, the most elegiac moment given to us as the stark admission of failure. Yet, at this same moment, Du Fu turns from his own pain to understated meditation on his life's sobriety and drunkenness, the repetitions of balanced moments throughout his life. Public and private, happiness and sorrow, pleasure and pain—these sets of repeated balances may be heard in the simple movement between sobriety and drunkenness. I do not think Du Fu intends to characterize his life as extreme points between which the poet's life rushes back and forth but, rather, to enunciate the range of his life, which he gives as two simple, domestic everyday conditions.

The last line brings closure with a beautiful gesture that does not equate home with the conditions of happiness or safety or restitution but only with "whim." This phrase *chengxing* 乘興 (translated by Owen as "I follow my whim") refuses seriousness insofar as it embodies an alternative choice to the deliberate, to calculation. Du Fu alludes to Wang Huizhi 王徽之 (338–386), in a famous anecdote from the fifth-century anecdote collection *Shishuo xinyu* 世說新語 (translated by Richard B. Mather as *A New Account of Tales of the World*), who turns back from his nightlong journey to visit his friend once the mood to see him is gone.[23] Like Wang Huizhi, the poet claims to follow his whims and allows himself to be given over to his inclinations, whenever they may arise. Yet recall, again, Breytenbach's words: "Henceforth you are at home nowhere, and by that token everywhere." Home is what has to be claimed by the poet as home after its initial loss; it can be found by him only where he happens to find it. In such an admission of chance and fate, the poet confesses to us that he has failed to impose happiness upon himself through an effort of will. Home is never sustained by "wild song," that mannered appeal to uncaring eccentricity or hyperbolic imagination. Rather, home is what is found as if by chance, not through forceful will but through a settling into place, an allowing of things to be as they are. The forced home, like the forced poem, represents only a tattered kind of success. We see this in the following couplet from the poem "River Pavilion" ("Jiang ting" 江亭), in which Du Fu is unable to return home and so tries to find consolation in poetry: "Not yet able to go back to the groves of home, / I push back gloom and force myself to trim a poem" 故林歸未得, 排悶強裁詩.[24] The poem so constructed must bear the marks of its hard birth, a painful state discernible in the acknowledged impossibility of home and visible in the ragged edges of the cutting. Just as when Du Fu claims to find home with the gesture of wild songs, we do not quite believe his claim to poetic success in the forcing of poetry here. But why should

---

23. For this story, see Liu Yiqing, *Shishuo xinyu*, 23.47; and Mather, *Shih-shuo hsin-yü*, 419.
24. Qiu Zhaoao, *Du shi xiangzhu*, 800–801; Owen, *The Poetry of Du Fu*, vol. 3, 6–7.

his other claim to found home through whim then seem persuasive? And how do we measure poetic success?

I would answer, tentatively, that Du Fu's success in "Return in Spring" is bound to his admission of failure, his acknowledgment of limits that directly precedes his settlement with the world. It is in these last four lines that we bear witness to the capacity of the poet to see what may still be won beyond inevitable failure and so to wrest from the experience a better kind of success than one taken uncontested. Although Allen Grossman will argue that poetic success is, in the end, meant to win for us transcendence from our mortal condition, it seems to me that what is more convincing in Du Fu resides instead in the modesty and ordinariness of his hope, which is to find settlement with the world, and thus a sense of home. For Du Fu, the individual poetic claim or gesture matters, becomes meaningful, insofar as it acknowledges the distance he continually measures between claim and self-awareness, a mediation that allows him to make peace, even if momentarily. What remains to the poet is how he negotiates this ironic knowledge, which is not knowledge of failure in some absolute or final sense but a kind of wisdom that can be salvaged only through the experience of necessity and limits, and the poet's own insistence that he try again.

2
Thinking through Poetry

Du Fu's "Getting Rid of the Blues" (*Jie men*)

Stephen Owen

"Thinking through poetry" might suggest Heidegger's "poetic thinking," which, for a literary scholar, ends up as a philosopher's use of poetry's gifts to think and a fuzzy claim about Poetry as some mystical language close to Being. I chose the phrase "thinking through" to avoid that and point to something rather different: how poetry's liberty of association and analogy enabled representations of order that would have been almost impossible to achieve in Chinese prose of the period. In the sequence of quatrains we will read, poetry not only shapes the process of thought but becomes the object of thought. Thus the phrase "thinking though" has a double sense. The emphasis is not on a product, "thought," but on a process that is underwritten by Tang categorical terms, indeed the very terms that guide parallel exposition. The "difference" in Du Fu is a complexity of overlapping parallel terms that lead the poet into truly new territory.

The premise is that "thought" is not a disembodied universal—as mathematics may be—but occurs in and through a historically constituted language. Moreover, it occurs in and through a certain subset of procedures used in that language. When you understand a language historically, it is easy to see a metaphor repeated so often that it becomes an "extended meaning" and eventually an "idea," with only the foggiest memory of its origins. All this is not news; it is Nietzsche followed by a long tradition of twentieth-century thought on language. It is also hard to argue against.

This becomes interesting again when—by the evolution of one language or looking at the language from the outside—once-daring adventures in the language come to seem like digressive wanderings. Then we need to take the "terms" the author had available seriously and to see his procedures not as pure fancy but as having a certain order, with intellectual weight.

In the famous "Song of a Painting: Presented to General Cao Ba" ("Danqing yin" 丹青引贈曹將軍霸), Du Fu begins by referring to the ancestry of the court painter Cao Ba.[1] His ancestor, Cao Cao 曹操 (155–220), combined both *wen* 文 and *wu* 武, artistic and military talents. The artistic, *wen*, legacy survives in the court painter Cao Ba—even though he bears the Tang title of general, an honorary guard office. In the context of

---

1. Owen, *The Poetry of Du Fu*, vol. 3, 393–97.

Du Fu's poem, Cao Ba's military title becomes intensely ironic. We move to Cao Ba's first great commission from Emperor Xuanzong 玄宗 (r. 712–756), which is touching up the portraits of the generals and ministers who aided the Tang founder, Taizong 太宗 (r. 627–649); we note a remarkable parallel between once-active talents replaced by their representations and the active emperor, Taizong, compared to his descendant Xuanzong, who worries about the paintings of those earlier active men. The repair work is carried out by the painter-descendant of one of the most active generals in Chinese history. This is no accident: the conventional opening in which Du Fu refers to the recipient's family history sets off a process that guides the poem: the interplay of *wen* and *wu* and partial legacies. Following Cao Ba's restoration of the portraits, we have the culminating commission for Cao Ba, in which Xuanzong's favorite horse, Yuhua, is led into the courtyard and painted by Cao Ba, after which the emperor Xuanzong favors the painting more than the real horse—indeed the painted representation is referred to by the horse's name. Something peculiar is going on here. Written in the aftermath of the breakdown of effective government and the An Lushan Rebellion (755–763), the significance of the pattern is hard to miss. Succession on various scales involves *wen*, cultural values and achievements, replacing *wu*, active military values. The real horse is replaced in Xuanzong's favor by the painting of the horse. Lest we miss the pervasiveness of the pattern, Du Fu next turns to Cao Ba's disciple Han Gan 韓幹: Cao Ba could paint both the flesh and bone of a horse, but Han Gan can paint only the flesh. Flesh is the outward, *wen*, aspect; what is missing are the bones, the hard strength within, elusively visible on the surface. In lineage one receives only half of the predecessor's qualities.

This may be an unpersuasively pessimistic way of thinking about lineage, but it was a way of thinking about what had happened to the dynasty, why the theatrical splendor of Xuanzong's reign failed so disastrously. We need not agree with the conclusion, but I would like to argue that this is indeed thinking: seeing a conceptual pattern in history and verifying it in multiple frames of reference. What is not explicitly stated but comes out very clearly in the context is that the active world intrudes on and destroys those who are the lovers of representation.

These procedures are even clearer in regulated poems and can become complicated in poetic sequences. This is the very stuff of Chinese formal criticism of poetry, such as that of the seventeenth-century critic Huang Sheng 黃生. No reader of Du Fu's "Stirred by Autumn" ("Qiuxing bashou" 秋興八首) can fail to notice the patterns of opposition: near and far, here and there, present and past, "in heaven" (also the court) (*tian shang* 天上) and in the mortal world (*renjian* 人間). On these oppositions are built the recurrent forms that give the tapestry coherence: dew on the maple trees, the bronze immortal's dew-pan, the dew on the lotus pod; the beating autumn clothes against the backdrop of White Emperor Castle in the growing darkness, the war drums beyond the barrier passes; and so on.

In "Stirred by Autumn" the processes are obvious, and we are caught up in the sheer density of the whole. In other cases in the same period the processes are the same, but they have become less visible. The case that I want to discuss at length is the set of twelve quatrains entitled "Getting Rid of the Blues" ("Jie men" 解悶). These poems seem to be grouped in apparently unrelated clusters, but there are so many links and parallels among these clusters that a process of association is clearly at work, a process that becomes visible if we refer the poems to basic "terms" of exposition. These terms are very general, and we have to "reaggregate" terms that have become disaggregated in vernacular Chinese as distinct "meanings." We have no difficulty in "Stirred by Autumn" seeing that the "distant" (*yuan* 遠) applies equally to time and space: from Du Fu in Kuizhou, Chang'an is "far" in space and in time. These categories are broad, but they invite the poet to group apparently distinct phenomena together and in that process to reveal a basic coherence that would be hidden in more habitual thought.

It is easy to see how simple categories like the "close" and the "distant" can attach themselves to interesting questions, like the empire and the local, what goes far and "circulates" in the empire, as opposed to that which can belong only to the local, such as a fish—or a fruit.

I should add a word about the title, "Getting Rid of the Blues." It is not at all clear how the content of the poems serves the purpose asserted in the title. Du Fu often claims to use poetry to dispel various terms of unhappiness, but it often seems to follow from the act of composition rather than from the content of the poem. The particular form of unhappiness here, *men* 悶, translated as the "blues," deserves some comment. Unlike more common terms such as *you* 憂, "worry," *men* cannot serve as a verb with an object. In other words, it is a state of being without a specific problem that occasions unhappiness. *Chou* 愁 and *you* are to be unhappy about something or to worry about something; even the more extreme *chouchang* 惆悵 is to be depressed about something. *Men*, however, is a state of being without any easily identifiable concern that causes *men*; hence, "the blues."

Du Fu begins in Kuizhou with the scene before his eyes, a sudden storm and a rustic idyll.

I

草閣柴扉星散居	Thatched pavilions, ramshackle gates, dwellings scattered like stars,
浪翻江黑雨飛初	waves roll, the river blackens, the rain begins to fall.
山禽引子哺紅果	A mountain bird brings its chicks to feed them red berries,
溪女得錢留白魚	the girl by the creek gets a coin and leaves a white fish.[2]

The quatrain is built on the familiar categories of poetic representation. There is a scene of land (which around Kuizhou means "mountains," *shan* 山) and a scene of the river (*shui* 水); in other words, it is a "landscape," *shanshui* 山水. The second couplet recapitulates that opposition with a "mountain bird" and a "girl by the creek."[3] As with many quatrains, the first couplet is the "ground" or background, while the second couplet moves to figures in the foreground. The visual detail in the second couplet makes this not simply figures on a ground but focusing from a far scene to details that

---

2. For this poem sequence, see Owen, *The Poetry of Du Fu*, vol. 4, 368–75.
3. Both Wang Zhu's 王洙 (997–1057) *Song ben* 宋本 edition and the Guo Zhida 郭知達 (fl. twelfth century) edition read *you* 友 for *nü* 女, with *nü* 女 as an early variant (the variant certainly in the *Song ben* edition). *Song ben Du gongbu ji*, 290; Guo Zhida, *Xinkan jiaoding, juan* 30. Most later editions prefer *nü*. As we will discuss later, Du Fu clearly has Meng Haoran's 孟浩然 (ca. 689–740) "Written at the Pool by Mount Xian" 峴潭作 in mind, with the line "The fair girl speeds the metal knife" 美人騁金錯. Meng Haoran, *Meng Haoran shiji*, 29. The source line in Meng Haoran makes *nü* the more likely correct reading.

are close at hand, like a movie camera moving from a wide-angle shot to a close-up. Such close-ups bear the interest of the poem: they are what catch the poet's attention. Both are scenes of feeding: one scene is immediate and belongs to the natural world; the other is mediated and displaced and belongs to the human world.

Normally the second couplet of the quatrain would not be parallel, especially in a quatrain in the seven-syllable line. Du Fu could not resist it: parallelism calls attention to the couplet. The last line is the surprise. The parallel leads him to represent just what he sees, with a visual innocence. He does not say that the girl sold the fish or someone bought the fish—perhaps the poet himself—he tells what he sees, not what he infers from what he sees. Part of the interest of the line is the obvious difference between *our* understanding of the transaction and its purely visual representation. Our knowledge calls attention to the *difference* between the human world and the natural world.

Keeping the scene purely visual calls attention to an object that would be invisible if the poet simply said, "The girl sold a fish." Everything else is natural, local, part of the scene at hand. There is only one thing in the scene that comes from far away and will go far away: this is the *qian* 錢, the coin. If you read a lot of Tang poetry, you will find *qian* as the round growths of moss or lichen, as the round spots on a horse, and only occasionally as "money." But this is a rare case in Tang poetry in which a coin is physical presence in a purchase.[4]

The coin is the token of empire; it circulates, *tong* 通, which is written right on it. In many ways it defines the empire. Perhaps it is used on the margins of the empire, but beyond the empire it is not *tongbao* 通寶, circulating value, but just copper; and its value is that of the metal. Within the empire the coin often mediates between getting food and eating it. The *qian* means two things: in the visual world, the world that Du Fu sees, it is a coin, an object; it has meaning as part of a system, in which case it means "money." As the coin can circulate through the empire, its meaning is everywhere the same—even if the price of commodities differs.

Am I reading too much into this simple scene? Is this too complicated for Du Fu? Or is he thinking of the same question in his own way? Perhaps he surprised himself by using that word in such a crass, unpoetic way, however visually satisfying—that one perfect circle and square in nature's more complex asymmetries. But when we look at the second poem, it turns out that we are not at all reading too much into the scene:

II

商胡離別下揚州	A Hu merchant takes his leave going downstream to Yangzhou,
憶上西陵故驛樓	I recall once climbing to the upper story of the old post station at Xiling.
為問淮南米貴賤	Find out for me in Huainan whether rice is dear or cheap—
老夫乘興欲東遊	following his whim, this old fellow wants to go roaming east.

The geography of the poem extends now beyond Kuizhou into the empire, to human travelers and the great grain barges that were the life of the empire. It extends from the immediate present into the world of memory and speculative planning for

---

4.   In "Empty Purse" 空囊, Du Fu refers to a coin. See Owen, *The Poetry of Du Fu*, vol. 2, 182–83.

the future. Commerce and the variable price of carbohydrates are not hidden here. As money circulates from afar, so do people. This is the Tang; foreigners are everywhere. A Huren, a non-Han, perhaps a Persian of the Yangzhou merchant community, comes to Kuizhou on his way downriver to Yangzhou. Du Fu considers going off to Yangzhou himself if he learns that rice is cheaper there. Coins, food, and people circulate following differentials in prices: this is empire. Or, perhaps, an empire is nothing more than a system for moving a surplus of carbohydrates from one place to another. The Tang survived random violence and misrule, invasion, rebellion, and countless separatist uprisings. But the Tang was not destroyed until the grain-producing areas of the lower Yangzi delta fell apart, along with the transport and distribution system.

Just as the last line of the first poem—"The girl by the creek gets a coin and leaves a white fish"—at once hides and calls attention to commercial exchange, here Du Fu humorously hides and exposes his motives for considering travel. As any gentleman should, he proposes to travel "following his whim" (chengxing 乘興). His "whim" is stirred by his memory of visiting Xiling in his younger days.[5] But a gentleman does not worry about the cost of rice. Du Fu playfully adopts a gentleman's insouciance while undermining it with practical concerns. Other poets like Li Bai 李白 (701–762) and Meng Haoran 孟浩然 (ca. 689–740) adopted the role of the insouciant free spirit as they traveled through the richest parts of the empire, from patron to patron. Du Fu reminds us of limits and what is necessary to survive. We can better understand the poetic discourse of freedom if we understand that it hides necessity.

The coin has infected the "natural" world of the first poem, and we are in imperial space and an economy with coins and carbohydrates going far. Memories and the price of grain can lead to travel. In turn the poem sequence begins to go far, turning to Du Fu's memories of friends and poets, who initially are all associated with food. Toward the end of the sequence we come back to food imperfectly circulating in the empire—in this case not durable rice but delicate fruits like the berries of the first poem, fruits that belong to the local world and elude the empire.

Food keeps returning in these poems, if only as a name. Name/reputation is something else that travels far, as do memories.

III

一辭故國十經秋	Since leaving my native region I have ten times passed the autumn,
每見秋瓜憶故丘	and whenever I see autumn melons I recall my native hills.
今日南湖采薇蕨	These days by the southern lakes he gathers beans and bracken,
何人為覓鄭瓜州	who will go seek out for me Zheng of Melon Isle?[6]

---

5. Xiling 西陵, literally "West Mound," has been variously identified as being in Hangzhou or Kuaiji, both a good distance from Yangzhou. In *Dushi shuo* 杜詩說, Huang Sheng judiciously observes that there were "Xilings" in many places, and that the natural reading of the quatrain places this one in Yangzhou. Cited in Xiao Difei, *Du Fu quanji*, vol. 9, 17.4943. "Following whim" comes from the famous Wang Huizhi anecdote in the fifth-century anecdotal collection *Shishuo xinyu* (see Chapter 1, note 23), but its use in Tang poetry is so common that it does not necessarily invoke the anecdote, except in the aura of insouciance.

6. There is some debate whether this is "Melon Isle Village," not too far from Du Fu's home in Chang'an, or the Tang prefecture of Guazhou 瓜洲. The former is more persuasive. The graphic variance of 洲 and 州 is insignificant in the Tang.

The sequence gradually extends its scope, from the immediate present to a moment of memory and here to an interval, the ten years he has been away from Chang'an and, presumably, last saw his friend Zheng Shen 鄭審, once director of the Imperial Library and now in exile in Jiangling. The stimulus of memory is the melon, which recalls Melon Isle Village, where Zheng Shen lived. In Jiangling, however, he is eating neither melons nor the rice of Huainan but gathering "beans and bracken," the food of extreme poverty. *Tong* is "circulation," but it is also "getting through" or, in the English idiom, "getting ahead" in one's political career. Being director of the Imperial Library was *tong*; exile in Jiangling was being "blocked," displaced to the local margins of the intercourse of empire. Those displaced become gatherers and fishermen.

IV

沈范早知何水部	Shen Yue and Fan Yun recognized He of the Bureau of Waterways;
曹劉不待薛郎中	Cao and Liu did not wait for Director Xue.
獨當省署開文苑	Alone in the Secretariat offices he began a garden of letters;
兼泛滄浪學釣翁	he also drifted at Canglang emulating an old fisherman.

From one old friend not particularly well known for his poetry, Du Fu moves to the poets, in this case Xue Qu 薛璩 (731 *jinshi*). We are moving back further in time, invoking talent and recognition of talent, both the successful case of He Xun 何遜 (ca. 466–ca. 518), whose talent was recognized by Fan Yun 范雲 (451–503) and Shen Yue 沈約 (441–513), and the failed case of Xue Qu, who was born too late to be recognized by the most appropriate earlier poets, Liu Zhen 劉楨 (d. 217) and Cao Zhi 曹植 (192–232). The link between Xue Qu and He Xun may seem as arbitrary as the link between melons and Zheng Shen: both held posts in the Board of Waterworks. Yet, in one standard mode of address, they would have the "same" name: "He of the Board of Waterworks" and "Xue of the Board of Waterworks."

But in the discourse of *tong*, both "getting through" or "circulating" and being "successful," we have a widening sphere of empire, stretching back into the past and circulating not only rice but also names, stories, and poems. This includes stories and poems about circulation and encounter with those who appreciate talent, a community—indeed a community across time, as we will see in the following poem. But there is also failure, like Zheng Shen being sent to the margins; in Xue Qu's case it is not "picking beans and bracken" but becoming the "old fisherman." Xue Qu began in the imperial center establishing a "garden of letters," writing to form community, and he ends up as another "hunter-gatherer," in this case a figure associated not with misery and poverty like Zheng Shen but rather with freedom from care.

Xue Qu found his counterparts among the poets of the Jian'an 建安 era (196–220); Meng Yunqing 孟雲卿 (705–781) goes back even further and through poetry continues that ancient community of poets.

V

| 李陵蘇武是吾師 | "Li Ling and Su Wu
are my teachers" — |

孟子論文更不疑	of Master Meng's discussion of letters 　　there is no further uncertainty.
一飯未曾留俗客	He never once had a worldly guest 　　stay for a meal,
數篇今見古人詩	and in several works we see in our times 　　poems of the ancients.

If the attempt to form community was unsuccessful for Xue Qu and his early third-century predecessors, community comes back in Meng Yunqing's reception of the oldest classical poets and farthest exiles, Li Ling 李陵 (d. 74 BCE) and Su Wu 蘇武 (d. 60 BCE). Li Ling was a Han general who surrendered to the Xiongnu, the enemy of the Han, and spent the rest of life outside the borders of China. Su Wu was a Han emissary detained among the Xiongnu for twenty years. He became a friend of Li Ling; and, when Su Wu was allowed to return to the Han in 80 BCE, they had a famous farewell. A body of classical poems attributed to these figures was in circulation in the third century CE (and perhaps earlier).

For Meng Yunqing these poets are his teachers across eight centuries. Food returns once again, but in this case it is a meal to be shared or not shared with another person, depending on that person's worth. But the community with his "teachers" is reasserted across time as the "poems of the ancients" reappear in Meng's poems. After his capture, Li Ling's loyalty was doubted by Han Emperor Wu, who had his entire family executed; Emperor Wu's successor invited Li Ling back, but with his family gone there was nothing to return to. He was forever "blocked," but the empire also became the means by which his poems have circulated through time.

Poetry comes from afar and circulates through the empire. Like the coin, it has value but a distinct kind of value. From friends and poets he has known, Du Fu turns next to a poet whom he never met but whom he knows through poems—with special attention to one specific poem that brings us back to the first poem of Du Fu's own sequence. Zheng Shen, Xue Qu, and Meng Yunqing were all in the area of Jingzhou, downstream from Kuizhou. Meng Haoran's native Xiangyang was also near Jingzhou.

VI

復憶襄陽孟浩然	I also recall Xiangyang's 　　Meng Haoran,
清詩句句盡堪傳	line after line of lucid poems, 　　all worth handing on.
即今耆舊無新語	These days among the gaffers 　　new phrases are no more,
漫釣槎頭縮頸鯿	they merely fish by a log 　　for the neck-contracting bream.

Poetry circulates, and poetry's "new phrases," *xinyu* 新語, forever fresh, can carry the representation of freshly caught fish throughout the empire, even though the fish themselves remain a local product that cannot be transmitted. The "gaffers" of Xiangyang have their famous "neck-contracting bream" but cannot find words to represent it anymore.

Du Fu has one particular poem by Meng Haoran in mind: "Written at the Pool by Mount Xian" ("Xian tan zuo" 峴潭作).[7]

石潭傍隈隩	The rocky pool lies by a secluded cove,
沙岸曉貪緣	in morning I wend my way along the sandy bank.
試垂竹竿釣	I try casting a hook with a bamboo pole
果得槎頭鯿	and finally catch a bream by a log.
美人騁金錯	The fair girl speeds the metal knife,
纖手膾紅鮮	under slender hands the pink sashimi is fresh.
因謝陸內史	So I beg to differ with Administrator Lu Ji—
蓴羹何足傳	how can water-spinach broth be worth handing on?

Meng Haoran's allusion takes us back one more layer in the past: we come to an anecdote about the Western Jin poet Lu Ji 陸機 (261–303), a native of Wu, who was asked what there could possibly be to compare to the northerner's sheep-milk yogurt, *yanglao* 羊酪. Lu Ji countered that they had the water-spinach broth of Thousand League Lake.[8] Meng Haoran counters Lu Ji's local pride with his own local specialty, a species of local bream.

Before returning to local food, we need to take note of the line that gives Du Fu the memorable last line of his own first quatrain. The "metal knife" of the fifth line in Meng Haoran's poem is *jincuo* 金錯, short for *jincuo dao* 金錯刀, a small knife, here being used to cut sashimi. It is a not uncommon usage in Tang poetry and probably refers to any small knife, but Du Fu clearly knows what kind of knife it originally was. At the end of the handle was a circle of bronze with a square hole; it was a kind of coinage, and the form of the handle became the shape of a copper coin.

The scene of the girl cutting sashimi in Meng Haoran has metamorphosed into the fisher-girl exchanging the fish for a coin. Cutting sashimi is immediate; as a coin of the empire rather than a sashimi knife, the *jincuo* introduces mediation, circulation, and duration. Both scenes become images in lines "of lucid poems all worth handing down." Meng Haoran's earlier consumer eats the fish immediately; Du Fu's later consumer buys. The beautiful line of poetry replaces the local fish that cannot circulate and "go far"—it must be eaten quickly. Fishing for the "neck-contracting bream" continues but "merely," or perhaps in this context this line means they can do no more than fish for the local bream.

No less telling is the use of *chuan* 傳, translated as "handing on." In this world of things that circulate and things that do not or should not circulate, the lines of Meng Haoran should be handed down, lines that tell of the fresh food of the moment, the bream sashimi, compared to which the reputation of Lu Ji's water-spinach broth does not deserve to circulate. Lu Ji's lines were, incidentally, understood as expressing his longing for his native Wu, just as Du Fu thinks of his home when he sees autumn melons.

Du Fu places Meng Haoran and himself at the middle of the sequence, first the poet who has already achieved those lucid lines and, second, the later poet who works at it. The following is the best-known poem of the sequence and often the only one read.

---

7. Meng Haoran, *Meng Haoran shiji*, 29.
8. Liu Yiqing, *Shishuo xinyu*, 2.26.

VII

陶冶性靈存底物	To fire and smelt my spiritual nature what have I got?—
新詩改罷自長吟	finished revising my new poems, I chant them long to myself.
熟知二謝將能事	Well versed in the two Xies I'm getting pretty good;[9]
頗學陰何苦用心	really trying to learn Yin Keng and He Xun, I concentrate terribly hard.

When Du Fu turns to his own poetry, the style changes abruptly to something far closer to "Six Quatrains Playfully Done" ("Xi wei liu jueju" 戲為六絕句) than to anything else in "Getting Rid of the Blues."[10] The poem also presents problems of interpretation similar to the "Six Quatrains." The first line is a remarkable mix of registers. First we have the grand artisanal metaphor of "firing and smelting my spiritual nature" (taoye xingling 陶冶性靈), in literature tracing back to *Gradations of Poetry* (*Shi pin* 詩品), by Zhong Rong 鍾嶸 (d. 518), who refers to Ruan Ji's 阮籍 (210–263) poetry as "firing one's spiritual nature" (*tao xingling* 陶性靈), and to the chapter titled "Literary Writings" (*Wenzhang* 文章) in *Family Instructions for the Yan Clan* (*Yanshi jiaxun* 顏氏家訓), by Yan Zhitui 顏之推 (531–ca. 591), who talks about "firing and smelting one's spiritual nature."[11] "Firing" is the metaphor of a potter; "smelting" is the metaphor of a blacksmith. Clearly this is achieved by literary composition, but the question is whether writing is the mere means or also the product, what remains of the process. Uncertainty on this point makes me constantly change my own translation. Certainly it is the means, as Du Fu writes in "Writing My Feelings in Kui on an Autumn Day" ("Qiuri Kuifu yonghuai" 秋日夔府詠懷): "For firing and smelting my spirit, I rely on my poems" 陶冶賴詩篇.[12] The larger question is the nuance and tone of *cun diwu* 存底物. I cannot recall poetry being called a *wu* 物 before. Is poetry what he has to "fire and smelt my spiritual nature," or is this the object created through and what remains after the process of composition? The dramatic change in register between the first and second hemistich is between lofty and low, "far" and "near." Poetry seems to be what he has left from that fiery process, the product of the process. The further question is whether the process is composition or, in this case, revision. The latter, revision, is announced to be over. Then he chants and in the second couplet seems to contemplate what chants.

Here we are even deeper into the language of "Six Quatrains Playfully Done." We do not know how strongly to read the caesura in the third line here. We need to think of the opening line of the fifth of the "Six Quatrains": "不薄今人愛古人."[13] Because we do not know to whom the "moderns" or the "ancients" refer, this could be "I don't belittle the moderns but adore the ancients," or it could be "I don't belittle the modern's

---

9. The early Song imprints read 孰知. *Shu* 孰 and 熟 are exact homophones, and it was common to omit the radical in manuscripts. The twelfth-century scholar Zhao Cigong 趙次公 interprets 孰 as 熟, and this makes the best sense. Otherwise we would take 孰知 as "who understands?" Cited in Xiao Difei, *Du Fu quanji*, vol. 9, 17.4949.

10. Owen, *The Poetry of Du Fu*, vol. 3, 112–15.

11. Zhong Rong, *Shi pin jizhu*, 123. Yan Zhitui, *Yanshi jiaxun*, 221.

12. The full title is "Writing My Feelings in Kui on an Autumn Day, Respectfully Sent to Director Zheng and Li, Advisor to the Heir Apparent: One Hundred Couplets" 秋日夔府詠懷奉寄鄭監李賓客一百韻. Owen, *The Poetry of Du Fu*, vol. 5, 192–211.

13. Owen, *The Poetry of Du Fu*, vol. 3, 114.

adoration of the ancients." Either case can be argued from earlier poems in the series. In the third line here, with a strong caesura we would read as translated above, but with a weaker caesura the line would be "I fully understand that the two Xies were close to being really good." The fourth line would then read, "I try really hard to study Yin Keng's and He Xun's intense efforts."

In a larger sense Du Fu places himself in the community of poets, with a decided preference for the fifth and sixth centuries, as opposed to Meng Yunqing's commitment to the earliest classical poems.

It is tempting to take this as his poems being the enduring product of his efforts because he places himself between two deceased poets of his own age who survive, *cun* 存, through their poems; that is, he makes something hard (fired or smelted) that will survive when he is gone. Wang Wei 王維 (ca. 699–ca. 761) leaves a landscape with wintry vines and not fruit.

VIII

不見高人王右丞	I do not see that lofty man Wang, Assistant Director of the Right,
藍田丘壑漫寒藤	the hills and gullies of Lantian spread with wintry vines.
最傳秀句寰區滿	Most handed on are his striking lines, the whole world is full,
未絕風流相國能	a panache never ceasing, the capabilities of a minister.

If "line after line of [Meng Haoran's] lucid poems [are] all worth handing on" 清詩句句盡堪傳, "the whole world is full" of Wang Wei's striking lines. The poet is gone, but the lines still circulate. Wang Wei never became minister (as his brother Wang Jin 王縉 did). Du Fu tells us that the last line refers to Wang Wei's brother, suggesting that he carries on Wang Wei's "panache" (*fengliu* 風流).

Du Fu celebrates poetry in a system of circulation that is no longer purely imperial but cultural; in contrast to the conclusion of the poem for Meng Haoran, with its idyllic vision of Xiangyang bereft of its poet, the poem for Wang Wei ends with a bleak, cold-weather landscape filled with vines. The man is gone, not to be seen; the world is filled with his fine lines of poetry; and what continues is the lineage of qualities—strangely linking a poet's "panache" to the "capabilities of a minister."

Empire and poetry are uncomfortably reunited. In the last poems of the sequence, Du Fu turns back to the local things that cannot circulate. This is what the empire and the emperor cannot have, except in representation. The emperor and his consort can *never* taste the Guangdong or even the Fuzhou lychee at it freshest and best; they can only imagine it through its representation as the "best." Some things are local and do not go far: the fish of Kuizhou bought by a coin, the freshly caught "neck-contracting bream" made into sashimi and consumed immediately. He turns to the most famous example of the local food that frustrates imperial desire to possess it: Lady Yang's lychees. The only way you can enjoy them is by "being there." In trying to possess it from afar, the fruit deteriorates, and the system of imperial circulation, *tong*, is itself corrupted.

IX

先帝貴妃今寂寞	The Late Emperor's Noble Consort 　　now lies in mournful silence,
荔枝還復入長安	and once again the lychees 　　are entering Chang'an,
炎方每續朱櫻獻	From hot regions they always follow 　　the offerings of red cherries—
玉座應悲白露團	I'm sure the jade throne must grieve 　　at these orbs of white dew.

It is important here to recognize the role of representations in desire. As Lu Ji had celebrated his local water-spinach and Meng Haoran celebrated his "neck-contracting bream," Zhang Jiuling 張九齡 (678–740), Xuanzong's capable minister, gifted with a poet's panache, celebrated the lychee of his native Guangdong in his "Poetic Exposition on the Lychee" ("Lizhi fu" 荔枝賦).[14] In his preface he says that that he praised the lychee to the gentlemen serving with him, but they were all ignorant of it. And he concludes, prophetically, that it could be brought only by the imperial courier system. Li Zhao's 李肇 *Supplements to the Dynastic History* (*Guoshi bu* 國史補) from the early ninth century tells us that Lady Yang, a native of Shu, loved her local lychees but that the lychees from Guangdong were even better. Therefore, every year the imperial courier system would bring the fruit from Guangdong to Chang'an. Li Zhao adds that, when they were ripe, they would start to rot overnight.[15]

This famous story raises an interesting problem that is woven into Du Fu's poems. If the lychees lose their flavor overnight, how could anyone know that, when fresh, they were even better than the lychees of Shu? Some semblance of comparison could be made by someone who had been in both Shu and Guangdong when the lychees were ripe, but the memory of comparative flavor is an elusive faculty at best. Comparative tasting side by side would be better, but the transportation system of the Tang made that impossible. The better answer is that the reputation of the superiority of the Guangdong lychee was thanks to Zhang Jiuling's poetic exposition.

Despite their loss of flavor, Guangdong (the "hot regions") lychees were still being sent as tribute—perhaps more for their rarity than for their flavor. If the empire is a means of transporting food, this is a frivolous use of the system, trying to make what is properly close at hand into something that goes far. I take "jade throne" as the throne for the spirit of a deceased ruler, in this case obviously Xuanzong. Yet Du Fu does not tell us whether the soul of Xuanzong would be grieved by the reminder of Lady Yang or of the ruin brought about by imperial excess.

Among Du Fu's remembrances of travels, home, and friends, the lychees call to mind a more recent memory of his travels in eastern Sichuan, picking lychees straight from the tree.

---

14. See Kroll, "Zhang Jiuling and the Lychee."
15. Li Zhao, *Guoshi bu*, 19. The "Biography of Lady Yang" 楊貴妃傳 in *Xin Tang shu* 新唐書 attempts to repair this failure of imperial power by claiming that the flavor of the lychees had not changed by the time they reached Chang'an. That raises the question how anyone could tell. *Xin Tang shu* 76.3494.

X

憶過瀘戎摘荔枝	I recall passing Luzhou and Rongzhou and picking lychees,
青楓隱映石逶迤	half-hidden among green maples, winding off into the rocks.
京華應見無顏色	In the capital I'm sure they would be lacking all beauty—[16]
紅顆酸甜只自知	the red berries' sweetness or bitterness can be known by oneself alone.

In contrast to the transported tribute lychees from Guangdong, Du Fu recalls tasting the local lychee just off the tree, just as the bird in the first poem led its young to eat the red berries. We are back to the immediacy of local experience, before the coin introduced mediation and circulation—but immediacy returns only as memory written into a poem. The perfection of the lychee can be fully known only directly and in the moment—though that experience and the meditation on limitations *can* itself be represented in a poem.

XI

翠瓜碧李沈玉甃	The azure melon and sapphire plum are immersed in jade well tiles;
赤梨葡萄寒露成	the russet pear and the grape are perfected by cold dews.
可憐先不異枝蔓	Too bad they had not from the start thought such vines and branches rare—
此物娟娟長遠生	this thing, so lovely, always grows far away.

From celebration of the lychee, Du Fu turns to what the court itself has nearby—melon, plum, russet pear, and grape—all no less wonderful fruits but not prized precisely because they are so common and easily had. Chilled in cold water, they are good antidotes to summer's heat. The lychee, however, has value precisely because it is hard to obtain—not simply rare but remote and available in Chang'an only because of the courier system of the empire.

XII

側生野岸及江浦	It grows off to the side on wild slopes and by the shores of rivers,
不熟丹宮滿玉壺	it will not ripen in the cinnabar palace compound, filling jade pots.
雲壑布衣鮐背死	Commoners of cloudy valleys, blowfish-backed with age, died;
勞人害馬翠眉須	people put to hardship and horses harmed to meet the demands of dark brows.

---

16. This is one of the cases where I do not follow the *Song ben* and the Guo Zhida edition, which read *jun* 君 for *wu* 無. Qian Qianyi 錢謙益 (1582–1664) reads *wu* 無, and scholars now generally credit his claim to have had a Southern Song version of the Wu Ruo 吳若 edition. For one example of the controversy surrounding Qian Qianyi and the Wu Ruo edition, see Zhang Zhongwang et al., *Du ji xulu*, 228. *Wu* is the more obvious reading and consistent with contemporary lychee lore in that the appearance of the fruit is one of the first things to change once it is picked.

It grows far away, and, despite all the emperor's wealth and power, it refuses to ripen in the palace in Chang'an. At last Du Fu refers to the story that the couriers, hurrying to bring the lychees to Lady Yang, trampled people to death in the fields. The last word, *xu*, translated as "demands," most commonly appears in this way in Du Fu's poetry as *jun xu* 軍須, "military demands," the curse of the 760s. But these are "dark brows' demands," not for the commonweal but the emperor's fondness. The emperor's thoughts do not "go far"; they are absorbed in what is close at hand: Lady Yang frowning because she misses her fresh lychees.

The harmed horses are both literal and figurative, echoing the *Zhuangzi* story in which the Yellow Emperor asks a herd boy about governing the empire. The herd boy responds, "Get rid of whatever harms the horses."[17] Xiangyang's gaffers may have plenty of bream but no poets, but the old men on the courier route are trampled to death because of a poetic image of the exquisite flavor of fresh Guangdong lychees.

This is "thinking through poetry" without clear conclusion, and yet it resonates with many of Du Fu's other Kuizhou poems. There were few locales in Tang China that would so readily invite such thoughts. Kuizhou was perched on mountain slopes facing the Yangzi River, with its constant traffic of officials, merchants, and armies going upstream and downstream. Du Fu constantly celebrates this traffic, especially on call from the prefect-commander of the garrison to entertain passing dignitaries, both civil and military. Like Qinzhou, Kuizhou also seemed a permeable border between the Han world and the non-Han, with the river of empire running through it. Du Fu wrote often of what a strange place it was—beginning very early in the Kuizhou poems when he discovered that Kuizhou has no wells and that potable water was a problem. Kuizhou's customs were strange, shamanistic: with effigies of dragons and whipping shamans to end drought, burning the mountain forests, threatening the local dragon to bring rain.[18] Du Fu also bears witness to the local fish and gathered foods. Unlike other poems from poets of the heartland who fled south after the An Lushan Rebellion, Du Fu learns the locale, Kuizhou, even if he cannot be entirely at home in it.

Du Fu knows what represents the world of the empire, and he worries about it: this is the Du Fu we know from Song dynasty critical cliché. He also thinks of "circulating" himself, going downriver to the "happy land" that he always imagined was awaiting him at his next destination. At other times, however, he looks with the eyes of a local on the foolish waste of empire. The lychees were tribute transport, and in one of his strangest Kuizhou poems he sees the transportation of tribute again—not with indignation at old men trampled to death by heedless couriers but with a strange lightness as the heavily laden tribute ship goes under in the treacherous currents of the Wu Gorge. These are the two poems entitled "Capsized Boat" ("Fu zhou" 覆舟), of which I will here give the first.

巫峽盤渦曉	A dawn of whirlpools in the Wu Gorge,
黔陽貢物秋	autumn for sending tribute items from Qianyang.
丹砂同隕石	The cinnabar pebbles were like falling meteors,
翠羽共沈舟	kingfisher feathers joined the sunken boat.
羈使空斜景	The envoy on his mission, gone in the sinking sunlight,
龍宮閟積流	the dragon palace, closed tight under massed currents.

---

17. *Zhuangzi jishi*, 8.833.
18. See "Thunder" 雷 and "Fire" 火. Owen, *The Poetry of Du Fu*, vol. 4, 154–59.

篙工幸不溺   Fortunately the boatman did not drown,
俄頃逐輕鷗   in an instant he goes off with the light gulls.[19]

Du Fu begins as he began the first poem of "Getting Rid of the Blues," setting the large natural scene against which we see the alien thing of empire appear. The currents of the Wu Gorge were notoriously treacherous for boats, no more so than in autumn's high waters, which hid the dangerous rocks, and no more so than that day, with whirlpools forming.

The second couplet is the memorable description of the boat turning over, spilling its load of cinnabar pebbles like a meteor shower, with the lighter kingfisher feathers going under with the boat. The poetic balance of red and blue-green, the heavy and the light, aestheticizes what should not be aestheticized. That incongruity between the representation and the represented event, which calls for gravity, shock, and lament, is uncomfortable and almost comic. It is a "lightness" (*qing* 輕, also "to make light of") that becomes a literal "lightness" in the final couplet.

The envoy overseeing the tribute delivery, perhaps weighed down by an official gown, is invoked as an absence in the afternoon sun; he too does not belong to the place. All goes under to the dragon-king's palace, where it is closed off forever.

The poem closes with a counterbalance of lightness, what floats when all else sinks (*chenfu* 沉浮, "sinking and floating," is a standard figure for "ups and downs" of life). This is the boatman, the man of the great river and perhaps a river guide from Kuizhou. He bobs up and continues a forward floating motion with the gulls. The boatman is linked to the natural world, specifically to the natural world around Kuizhou. The cinnabar pebbles were used to extract mercury, used (improbably) in elixirs of immortality; the kingfisher feathers were to meet the "demands of dark brows." These were luxury goods, now destined for another palace and, now, for a more important local underwater ruler who can bring rain if he is pleased. Of the human agents of imperial transportation, only the boatman, who knows the local river, survives.

---

19. Owen, *The Poetry of Du Fu*, vol. 5, 56–57.

3
History Channels

Commemoration and Communication in Du Fu's Kuizhou Poems

Gregory Patterson

Du Fu's association with historiography is so firmly established that it can be easy to overlook the importance of place and locality in his work. After all, the same arrangement of his collection that gave us the first chronological life in poetry also gave us that life as a spatial itinerary or travelogue.[1] Du Fu the "poet historian," the chronicler of his life and times, was also Du Fu the geographer, the traveler through a series of locales: Chang'an, Huazhou, Qinzhou, Chengdu, Kuizhou, and Changsha. He wrote in such unprecedented detail about the unique landscapes, cultures, and histories of these temporary "perches" that they form distinct identities within his larger corpus, like semi-independent provinces within the empire of the collected works. Such strong local influences are an important manifestation of Du Fu's irreducible "multiplicity," his centripetal resistance (and invitation) to unifying modes of interpretation.[2]

The poems from Kuizhou, more than 400 of them written between 766 and 768, are especially useful for thinking through questions of locality in Du Fu.[3] This is not only because they record a wealth of information about the topography and culture of the Three Gorges region[4] but also because they approach Kuizhou as epitomizing the distinctness and disconnection that defines "the local" as a part existing in some mutually constitutive relation to a larger whole, in this case the imagined community of empire. Like all communities, empires are based on communication, and in Kuizhou thinking about communication was unavoidable. This was largely a function of geography. Located on the empire's far southwestern border, cut off from the outside by towering mountains, Kuizhou was doubly remote; and yet it was also a major transportation hub

---

1. The earliest known *nianpu* was created for Du Fu by Lü Dafang 呂大防 (1027–1097) and was called *Zimei shi nianpu* 子美詩年譜, or *Du shi nianyue* 杜詩年月. See Zhang Zhonggang et al., *Du ji xulu*, 19–20.
2. On the layered multiplicity of Du Fu's corpus, voice, and style, see Owen, *The Great Age*, 183–224.
3. For discussions of the Kuizhou poems in English, see, for example, McCraw, *Du Fu's Laments*; Owen, *The Great Age*, 211–16; Chou, *Reconsidering Tu Fu*, esp. 174–79; Hung, *Tu Fu*, 219–54. In Chinese, see especially Chen Yixin, *Du Fu pingzhuan*, 768–931; Mo Lifeng, *Du Fu pingzhuan*, 172–93; Jiang Xianwei, *Du Fu Kuizhou shi*; Fang Yu, *Du Fu Kuizhou shi*; and Feng Ye, *Du Fu Kuizhou shi*. The list is of course highly selective, and necessarily so.
4. Zhou Jianjun, *Tangdai Jing Chu*, esp. 184–212. On local cultures in Tang poetry more generally, with emphasis on the Chu and Shu regions, see Dai Weihua, *Diyu wenhua*, esp. 70–81, 114–19.

on the primary river highway linking the macro-regions of Shu and Chu. It was most widely known as the entrance to the Three Gorges, a narrow, perilous channel through which the river rushed, swirling around boulders, shoals, and other shipwreck hazards. Travelers dreaded the Gorges; they prayed to pass through quickly, but dangerous conditions left many stranded, hesitating before the river's mysterious traffic signals.[5] Standing at the gateway to this vital yet treacherous channel, Kuizhou combined isolation with the promise of connection, frustrating communication and thereby thrusting it into view as a problem and a desire.

In early literature about the Three Gorges, desire for communication is already the defining theme: the marooned traveler longing for home; the Chu king dreaming of an ethereal, evaporating goddess.[6] It was also associated with times of warfare and political disunion—the Han interregnum (9–23 CE) and the Three Kingdoms period (220–280 CE) in particular—when its singularly *xian* 險 ("perilous," "steep") landscape and strategic location made it a formidable military stronghold, one of many barriers stopping up the empire's circulatory system. As a displaced traveler in another age of blockage in the body politic, whose own debilitated body detained him at the Gate of Kui 夔門, Du Fu was uniquely attuned to Kuizhou's symbolic resonances. Awaiting his opportunity to "get through" (*tong* 通), he responded by switching modes of transport. Poetry became a vehicle with which to travel the "paths of birds" (*niao dao* 鳥道).

Many of these flights of memory and imagination returned Du Fu to the peaceful prewar capital of his youth.[7] However, the same wanderlust lured him down the earthbound paths of Kuizhou's history. Like countless other traveling poets of medieval China, he sought the meanings of his locale in its "ancient traces" (*gu ji* 古跡), its monuments and the History behind them.[8] He wrote *huaigu* 懷古 ("meditations on the past") and related kinds of poems on these *lieux de mémoire*, some of which, like White Emperor City 白帝城, had already been put on the literary map by such luminaries as Li Bai 李白 (701–762) and Chen Zi'ang 陳子昂 (661–702).[9] Others, however, had not. Hardly any previous poet had, for example, represented Qutang Gorge 瞿塘峽 as the creation of the ancient sage king Yu the Great 大禹; nor, surprisingly, had anyone felt compelled to pay tribute to the local temple of Zhuge Liang 諸葛亮 (180–234), the loyal minister of Shu-Han 蜀漢, whose name would become associated with the region mostly

5. Fan Chengda 范成大 (1126–1193) put it succinctly: "This is probably the most dangerous place in the entire world." See Hargett, *Riding the River Home*, 135. For Du Fu's poems on the most famous of these traffic signals, "Hesitation Rock" 灧澦堆, see Owen, *The Poetry of Du Fu*, vol. 4, 138–39, and vol. 5, 134–35; Xiao Difei, *Du Fu quanji*, vol. 7, 13.3737–740, and vol. 8, 16.4620–627. These two recent landmark works will be my primary references for Du Fu's poems.
6. This was of course the Goddess of Wu Mountain 巫山神女, by far the region's most prominent representative in medieval poetry. See "Rhapsody on the Gaotang Shrine" 高唐賦 and "Rhapsody on the Goddess" 神女賦, attributed to Song Yu 宋玉 (fl. third century BCE), in Xiao Tong, *Wen xuan*, 19.875–92. For translations see Knechtges, *Wen xuan*, vol. 3, 325–27. For a useful collection of premodern poems on the Three Gorges, see Yan Qilin, *San xia shihui*.
7. Indeed, as Eva Shan Chou has written, "Chang'an acquired an antonym in Kuizhou . . . each comes to depend on the other for definition." See *Reconsidering Tu Fu*, 175.
8. The capital *H* underscores that the past in question is that of the "high" written tradition. That is, it was the shared past of the literate, capital-based elite. Writing and circulating poetry on local sites was itself a powerful means of inscribing localities within the historical narrative of the empire. All *huaigu* participated in this process, but Du Fu's Kuizhou *huaigu* did so with remarkable self-consciousness.
9. See, among many other examples, Chen's "Yearning for Antiquity at White Emperor City" 白帝城懷古 and Li's "Departing Early from White Emperor City" 早發白帝城. See *Quan Tang shi*, 84.912, 181.1844. For a discussion of Du Fu's six poems on the city, see Jiang Xianwei, *Du Fu Kuizhou shi*, 48–59.

through Du Fu.[10] In writing on these obscure (if not undiscovered) local traces, Du Fu was opening new lines of communication with "the ancient" (*gu* 古), giving Kuizhou a poetic past it did not yet have. This quasi-archaeological effort of forging new historical connections trained his attention on the vehicles and channels that allowed communication across distances of time as well as space.

In what follows I will argue that Du Fu's poems on the traces of Yu and Zhuge Liang respond to Kuizhou's special communicative situation through a shared concern with what I am calling commemorative form. This refers, first of all, to the materiality of traces, the physical substances and their configurations that store historical messages and convey them into the present. Du Fu presents a double vision of monumental matter: on the one hand, he treats it as productive raw material for the creation of channels; on the other, he visualizes it as entropy and decay — the channel threatening to close down and consume the message. This delving into the stuff of monuments, that which roots them to the local land, is joined with a contrasting tendency to imagine them extending their influence outward, beyond the confines of Kuizhou. In this second orientation, with its accompanying gestures of self-reference, we might glimpse the poems signaling their own special capacity to translate site-specific traces into circulating signs, representing the empire to itself through communicative commemorations.

Yu and Geological Form

There is no better illustration of Du Fu's approach to commemorative form than "Meditation on the Past at Qutang Gorge" ("Qutang huaigu" 瞿塘懷古), in which the Gate of Kui becomes a portal into the deep history of Kuizhou and of the channels connecting it with the world. Before proceeding to the poem itself, it will help to recall the famous story of Yu the Great, also known as Yu of Xia (Xia Yu 夏禹), or the Lord of Xia (Xia Hou 夏后): sage king, founder of the Xia dynasty, and one of the figures Du Fu most closely associates with the Three Gorges.[11] Yu was credited in a number of early texts with quelling a great flood by dredging the rivers, causing the floodwaters to recede and flow along deepened channels to the sea. The same act not only gave archetypal shape to the imperial state, as the newly cleared rivers formed the boundaries of the Nine Provinces (*jiuzhou* 九州); it also determined the archetypal economy, because the rivers served as channels of communication and commerce. Yu traveled along them, assessing the character and productivity of each province and delivering samples as "tribute" (*gong* 貢) to the centrally located court. Finally, as David Schaberg has shown, the act of channeling applied to textual production as well, specifically to the politically instructive (because rhetorically well-structured) "channeled speech" of bottom-up remonstrance.[12] In the Yu myth, then, the clearing of channels constitutes and configures the empire as a political, economic, and linguistic system.

---

10. Wang Ruigong, *Zhuge Liang yanjiu*, 892–95. The paucity of surviving poems on Zhuge Liang prior to Du Fu is noted by Hoyt Cleveland Tillman in his "Reassessing Du Fu's Line," 297–98.
11. On the many meanings of the Yu myth, see, for example, Lewis, *The Flood Myths*; Schaberg, "Travel, Geography, and the Imperial Imagination"; Teiser, "Engulfing the Bounds of Order."
12. "All textual production from below is to circulate smoothly upward both for the betterment of the government and for the therapeutic leeching of popular criticism. This is not incoherent speech, the textual equivalent of a flood. . . . Rather, it is speech crafted into poems and other textual structures." Schaberg, "Travel, Geography, and the Imperial Imagination," 168.

Du Fu knew this story well, of course, and he connected it with the Three Gorges region in particular. As "Yu's Temple" ("Yu miao" 禹廟) from 765 makes clear, it had influenced his conception of the area even before he arrived in Kuizhou:

禹廟空山裏	The temple of Yu is in the empty mountains,
秋風落日斜	in the autumn wind the setting sunlight slants.
荒庭垂橘柚	Oranges and pomelos hang down in the desolate courtyard;
古屋畫龍蛇	old rooms are painted with dragons and snakes.
雲氣虛青壁	Cloudy vapors breathe forth from green walls,
江聲走白沙	as the sound of the river runs along white sands.
早知乘四載	I learned long ago of his riding the "four vehicles,"
疏鑿控三巴	channeling and carving to take control of the Three Ba.[13]

Entering this temple in Zhongzhou 忠州 (modern Zhong County 忠縣, Chongqing municipality), Du Fu discovers objects and images that recall Yu's founding deeds. The fruit trees in the courtyard evoke the tribute system; the dragons and snakes painted on the walls represent the harmful creatures of the flood. Under the poet's understanding gaze the images, which seem to depict the landscape of the Three Gorges, come to life in sound and motion. Du Fu closes the poem by declaring his long familiarity with Yu's travels and the labors of "channeling and carving" (shu zao 疏鑿) by which he "took control" (kong 控) of the Ba region. On a general level, then, we see that, as alien as the Three Gorges may have been to Du Fu, he also associates it with the very origins of Chinese civilization as represented in the Yu myth.

It is worth dwelling on the last couplet of "Yu's Temple" for a moment, as it points to aspects of the story that likely made it a mirror and source of identification for Du Fu as he made his way toward Kuizhou. First of all, it identifies Yu, like Du Fu, as a traveler to distant lands, the rider of the "four vehicles" (si zai 四載) who stayed so long away from home. Second, it presents Yu's "channeling and carving" as an act of subduing or civilizing a far-flung region. This same phrase appears in Guo Pu's 郭璞 (276–324) "Rhapsody on the Yangzi River" ("Jiang fu" 江賦) and in Li Daoyuan's 酈道元 (d. 527) Commentary to the Classic of Waters (Shuijing zhu 水經註) to describe Yu's creation of the Gorges.[14] However, Du Fu seems to have been the first shi poet to portray this founding act in verse, perhaps because, while many had preceded him as travelers, he was the first we know of to have actually settled there for any length of time. During the Tang, towns like Zhongzhou and Kuizhou were situated along the empire's southwestern border, a colonial frontier where Chinese settlers coexisted uneasily with a multiethnic indigenous population. In his study of the "civilizing" of this frontier under the Song, Richard von Glahn has shown that Yu was a patron saint of settler communities, his dredging of the rivers symbolic of their own attempts to "take control" of a barbarian

---

13. Owen, The Poetry of Du Fu, vol. 4, 72–75; Xiao Difei, Du Fu quanji, vol. 6, 12.3415–418. See also McCraw's translation in Du Fu's Laments, 183. Unless noted otherwise, all translations are my own, though they are of course informed by the renderings of others. I would like to acknowledge my particular debt to Stephen Owen's Poetry of Du Fu, an invaluable resource to which I have referred throughout. The text and translation of the tricky fifth line of "Yu's Temple" follow Owen.

14. "The gorges of Eastern Ba were channeled and carved by the Xia Descendent" 巴東之峽, 夏后疏鑿 (Guo Pu); "Guangxi Gorge is at the head of the Three Gorges; it must come from Yu of Xia's channeling and carving to let the river pass through" 廣谿峽乃三峽之首, 蓋自夏禹疏鑿而通江者 (Li Daoyuan). Quoted in Qiu Zhaoao, Du shi xiangzhu, 1226, 1265. For a translation of the "Rhapsody on the Yangzi River" see Knechtges, Wen xuan, vol. 2, 321–51.

wilderness.[15] Himself a reluctant settler for three years, Du Fu would have identified with Yu on this basis as well and perhaps imagined opening channels of his own.

It was in Kuizhou that Du Fu found the Yu myth most vividly represented, though not in the commemorative forms one might expect. As we are told at the end of the poem he wrote upon arriving, Yu spoke to him not from a temple but through the very stones that littered the riverbanks:

| 禹功饒斷石 | From the deeds of Yu, a surplus of broken rock; |
| 且就土微平 | proceeding further, the land is slightly level.[16] |

As these lines suggest, Du Fu approached Kuizhou's "natural" landscape itself as a kind of historical monument. Its boulders and slabs stretching from the foothills out into the river — the distinctive geological features of this part of Eastern Sichuan — presented themselves to him as debris left over from Yu's "channeling and carving."[17] Here is a first example of how Du Fu foregrounds the materiality of ancient traces in Kuizhou, in this case by the very nature of the traces he identifies as ancient. The local stones were not given as historical in the way a temple, stele, or city was. Du Fu, under the influence of Guo Pu and Li Daoyuan no doubt, made them so. Insofar as the reader perceives this as surprising — as an act of imagination — the historicizing of the stone has the simultaneous effect of emphasizing its "stoniness," the raw material on which the poet's transformative vision works.

Du Fu pursued this reading of Kuizhou's geology furthest in "Meditation on the Past at Qutang Gorge," a remarkable five-character regulated verse in which he traces the origins of the massive landform to Yu's labors. The poem plunges into deep time, imagining the act of channeling and carving and its transformation of matter into meaning, chaotic flux into ordered space.

西南萬壑注	From the southwest, myriad valleys pour forth;
勁敵兩崖開	formidable opponents, two cliffs open.
地與山根裂	The earth and the mountain's roots split;
江從月窟來	the river arrives from the moon cave.
削成當白帝	Sheared completely, it faces White Emperor,
空曲隱陽臺	and its empty folds hide the Sunlit Terrace.
疏鑿功雖美	While the deed of channeling and carving is lovely,
陶鈞力大哉	how much greater was the force of the potter's wheel![18]

---

15. "The apostles of Han civilization sought to civilize the frontier by propagating secular cults which linked the conquest of both nature and savage to the invincible might of the great Han demiurges, from the mythical Great Yu to apotheosized historical figures such as Li Bing and Zhuge Liang." Von Glahn, *The Country of Streams and Grottoes*, 13.

16. "Moving My Dwelling to the Outskirts of Kuizhou" 移居夔州郭. Owen, *The Poetry of Du Fu*, vol. 4, 121; Xiao Difei, *Du Fu quanji*, vol. 6, 12.3529–531. The translation of the title follows Owen. Du Fu's association of Yu's deeds with *ping* and habitability may derive from *Mencius*, in which the taming of the flood results in the land becoming fit for human life and inaugurates a history of civilizing figures in which Mencius includes himself. *Mengzi zhushu*, 6.117–18.

17. This was not a passing flight of fancy. In two other poems Du Fu describes the Yangzi River as "opened and cleared" 開闢, alluding to the same origin story. See the first of the "Songs of Kuizhou: Ten Quatrains" 夔州歌十絕句, and "The Mouth of the Gorges: Two Poems" 峽口二首. Owen, *The Poetry of Du Fu*, vol. 4, 162–69; vol. 5, 16–17. Xiao Difei, *Du Fu quanji*, vol. 7, 13.3747–749; vol. 8, 15.4224–226. David McCraw puts it well: Du Fu's "mental eye seems to intuit the geological inscape underlying the Yu myth." McCraw, *Du Fu's Laments*, 53.

18. Owen, *The Poetry of Du Fu*, vol. 5, 21. Xiao Difei, *Du Fu quanji*, vol. 8, 15.4244–248. Also translated in McCraw, *Du Fu's Laments*, 52.

The first half of the poem presents a dramatic clash of elements: the river gushes forth; great masses of rock are sundered apart. Each of the first four lines ends with a verb— "pours," "opens," "splits," "arrives"—underscoring the dynamism of this "geogony."[19] In the poem's second half, the action stops, and Qutang Gorge stands amid other local landmarks as a made thing, a "lovely" (*mei* 美) work of art. However, this aesthetic appraisal is explicitly contrasted, in the exclamation of the final line, to a more adequate interpretation: "How much greater was the force of the potter's wheel!"

"Meditation on the Past at Qutang Gorge" is remarkable for several reasons, first of all for being a *huaigu*, a "meditation on the past." In such a poem, as Stephen Owen has shown, one might anticipate an account of a visit to a monument or a view from a height, perhaps an overview of a famous city.[20] Within the general scene, sites would be singled out, the histories behind them recalled, leading very probably to a reflection on principles of rise and fall or a lament for impermanence more generally. At the very least we expect the *huaigu* poet to survey the scene and wonder, "[Their] valiant plans— where are they now"?[21]

"Meditation on the Past at Qutang Gorge" does share some features with conventional *huaigu*. It records an imaginative, affective response to a *lieu de mémoire* (though one not easily recognized as such). Like the minister of Zhou gazing upon the millet field, the model for so many later *huaigu* poets, Du Fu peers beneath the apparent surface of the scene to reveal a hidden history.[22] However, everything else in the poem exceeds horizons of expectation, just as its subject punctured the actual horizon of Kuizhou. There is little of the melancholy associated with the subgenre. Difficult as it is to see Qutang as a historical monument, it is even harder to see it as a ruin, and the poem describes not a process of decline or decay but of founding and formation, which leads to a practical question: How does one begin a *huaigu* on the creation of place? Du Fu cannot start in the typical way, by setting the scene, because in the history of this monument there is nowhere to begin. Ingeniously, he finds his way through this aporia by beginning with cracking rock and gushing water instead of the usual opening scene or sentiment. Tracing the history of Qutang leads him back to the raw materials of the trace itself.

However, the counterpart to this focus on materiality in the first half is a shift of perspective in the second, an expanded view that takes in the finished monument and contemplates its effects. In the third couplet, Du Fu pictures Qutang Gorge standing in relation to Kuizhou's other most prominent landmarks: it "faces White Emperor" (*dang Baidi* 當白帝) and "hides the Sunlit Terrace" (*yin Yangtai* 隱陽臺). Not merely one among others, the gorge is the defining site that orients the rest, ordering their relations. It is the point around which everything gathers and finds its place. This in turn reminds us of its original role as a channel, structuring and informing communication between provinces and court. Leading us outward, its commemorative form calls to mind the network that connected Kuizhou to the empire at large.

---

19. McCraw, *Du Fu's Laments*, 53.
20. Owen, "Place," 417–57; Owen, *Remembrances*, esp. 16–32; Owen, *The Poetry of the Early T'ang*, especially 38–40, 206–9. On the early development of *huaigu*, see Knechtges, "Ruin and Remembrance," 55–89. See also Frankel, "The Contemplation of the Past in T'ang Poetry," 345–65; and Zhang Runjing, *Tangdai yongshi huaigu shi yanjiu*.
21. The *ubi sunt* theme discussed in Owen, *The Poetry of the Early T'ang*, 209.
22. Owen, *Remembrances*, 20–22.

The first three couplets of "Meditation on the Past at Qutang Gorge" thus proceed from the monument's material composition to a vision of how it reaches beyond itself and transforms its surroundings. This, in turn, leads in the final couplet to the question of the implied relation between the poet/speaker and the commemorated hero. In "Yu's Temple," as I noted above, Du Fu seems to identify with Yu as a traveler and settler in strange lands. What basis for identification do we find in "Meditation on the Past at Qutang Gorge"? An intriguing solution is suggested by the enigmatic final couplet, which praises the "beauty" of the carved channel only to shift attention to the apparently more admirable "force of the potter's wheel" (taojun li 陶鈞力). As the potter's wheel was a byword for zaohua 造化, the meanings of which could range from a natural process of "transformation" to a quite anthropomorphic Fashioner, Du Fu portrays Yu as working in concert with the great creative powers of the cosmos.[23] As he put it in another Kuizhou poem:

禹功翊造化　Yu's deeds assisted zaohua;
疏鑿就欹斜　channeling and carving, he ventured into uneven lands.[24]

"Assisting zaohua" or borrowing the "force of the potter's wheel" was not only a way of describing deeds of ancient sages, however. Similar expressions were commonly used to praise a variety of cultural accomplishments, as when Du Fu wrote of himself that "In court debates I responded to zaohua" 廷爭酬造化, and to a friend that "Your deeds are fit for the furnace of zaohua" 功安造化爐.[25] Indeed, Liu Xie's 劉勰 (ca. 465–522) Wenxin diaolong 文心雕龍 employs the potter's wheel as a metaphor for literary composition: "Therefore, for the sculpting [tao jun] of literary thought, what is valuable is to be empty and quiet" 是以陶鈞文思，貴在虛靜.[26] Du Fu's conclusion to "Meditation on the Past at Qutang Gorge" thus praises Yu's channels in language that could have applied to poetry as well.

Though this reading remains somewhat speculative, I would suggest that here Du Fu is identifying with Yu as an artificer or fashioner (much as many mid-Tang poets allied themselves with zaohua) and with Yu's deed as a counterpart to the act of writing. On this interpretation the poem ends by referring to itself: the "channeling and carving" of the gorge becomes a mirror for the poem that traces its history, both comparable acts

23. Traceable to the "Great Ancestral Teacher" 大宗師 chapter of Zhuangzi, zaohua and its kin were regularly invoked in Tang poems on mountains, and, especially on marvels located in far-flung regions of the empire. See Schafer, "The Idea of Created Nature in T'ang Literature," 155. Du Fu's poem can be read as a hybrid mixture of huaigu and a poem on "created nature." The key difference from the latter is his insertion of Yu as a historical intermediary between the gorge and the ahistorical zaohua. On zaohua as an image for the poet in mid-Tang verse, see Shang Wei, "Prisoner and Creator," 19–40.
24. In "Brushwood Gate" 柴門. Owen, The Poetry of Du Fu, vol. 5, 124–29. Xiao Difei, Du Fu quanji, vol. 8, 16.4566–572.
25. The first line is from Du Fu's poem on departing from the Three Gorges, "In Spring of the Third Year of the Dali Reign Period, at White Emperor City, I Set Out by Boat through Qutang Gorge. I Have Lived in Kuifu a Long Time But Am Going to Drift Around in Jiangling, And Composed a Poem of Forty Rhymes in All" 大曆三年春白帝城放船出瞿塘峽久居夔府將適江陵漂泊有詩凡四十韻. Owen, The Poetry of Du Fu, vol. 5, 398–407. Xiao Difei, Du Fu quanji, vol. 9, 18.5434–452. The second is from "Mourning for Revenue Manager Zheng of Taizhou and Vice Director Su" 哭台州鄭司戶蘇少監. Owen, The Poetry of Du Fu, vol. 4, 30–33. Xiao Difei, Du Fu quanji, vol. 6, 11.3312–319. For similar uses by other Tang poets, see Schafer, "The Idea of Created Nature in T'ang Literature."
26. Liu Xie, Wenxin diaolong, 396.

of "assisting *zaohua*."[27] This mirror highlights two aspects of the poem in particular. First, it calls attention to the surprising interpretation of the landform: the imaginative "fashioning" of stone into a site of history echoes Yu's carving of ordered space out of the flood. Second, it evokes the poem's role as a circulating medium, which, like the channels that are its native element, defines and structures the identities of places by communicating across distances. If the allegory is allowed, "Meditation on the Past at Qutang Gorge" can be read as taking on or transposing the commemorative form of its monument, channeling the history of channels.

Zhuge Liang and Architectural Form

While the story of Yu and its embodiment in Qutang Gorge no doubt guided Du Fu's approach to commemorative form in unique ways, we find intriguing similarities in his poems on Zhuge Liang's monuments. These are also characterized by a striking emphasis on the material conditions of the channels through which history is transmitted and accessed. However, whereas in "Meditation on the Past at Qutang Gorge" matter figures as raw material to be fashioned by sages and poets, in the poems on Zhuge Liang it is primarily associated with the reverse processes of erosion and entropy. And yet here as well the focus on matter is paired with expanded views of connected spaces and accompanying gestures of poetic self-reference.

Zhuge Liang is unique among the various figures Du Fu memorialized in Kuizhou. The poems dedicated to him stand alone both in number and in their remarkable formal variety, which ranges from the quatrain to regulated verse and the old-style ballad, as if Du Fu sought to lodge his memory in every poetic structure available. One of the defining characteristics of these poems, taken as a group, is the prominence they give to monuments (temples, portraits, trees). Much more than backdrops for reflections on exemplary deeds, mere triggers for the proper subject of remembrance, they become subjects in their own right. As Du Fu writes in the tenth "Song of Kuizhou: Ten Quatrains" ("Kuizhou ge shi jueju" 夔州歌十絕句): "The Warrior Count's shrine hall must never be forgotten" 武侯祠堂不可忘.[28] Notice that here it is not Zhuge Liang himself but the temple that is to be remembered. This may seem a slight distinction, but it is an instance of a larger pattern in which the commemorated subject is all but displaced by the material media of commemoration.

This approach to Zhuge Liang's monuments was certainly informed by the story of his life, in which Kuizhou had a special significance. Kuizhou was where Liu Bei 劉備 (161–223), the First Lord (Xianzhu 先主) to whom he was so legendarily devoted, died in 223 after a failed campaign against the kingdom of Wu. Before his death, Liu Bei appointed Zhuge regent to his young heir, Liu Shan 劉禪 (207–71), and Zhuge went on to serve the Later Lord (Houzhu 後主) until his own death ten years later.[29] In the hindsight of history, the passing of the virtuous First Lord signaled the shifting of heaven's favor and with it any hope of Shu winning the empire. Precisely because

---

27. The seventeenth-century critic Huang Sheng 黃生 comes close to saying this in his commentary, which explicitly likens poem and gorge as products of "carving": "This poem's exquisitely craggy lines are indeed like something the Five Strongmen carved out" 此詩奇險之句亦若假鑿於五丁者. Quoted in Qiu Zhaoao, *Du shi xiangzhu*, 1558–559.
28. Owen, *The Poetry of Du Fu*, vol. 4, 169. Xiao Difei, *Du Fu quanji*, vol. 7, 13.3759–760.
29. Zhuge Liang's official biography is found in *Sanguo zhi*, comp. Chen Shou 陳壽 (233–297), 35.911–28.

of their futility, however, his efforts took on symbolic value as tribute to his patron's memory. In Kuizhou Zhuge became a figure of persistence, endurance, and memory, committed to a dead ruler and a hopeless cause, a living monument struggling against inevitable decay.

But it is an episode from Zhuge Liang's afterlife that best illuminates Du Fu's preoccupation with and perspective on the temple in particular. As Hoyt Tillman has observed, during Du Fu's time Zhuge Liang was not the universally acclaimed hero he would later become.[30] He was, however, "loved by the people of Shu," as Du Fu put it in a poem commemorating his own patron, Yan Wu.[31] Like Yu the Great, he was the object of a local cult, the popularity of which is indicated by an anecdote from the *Record of Xiangyang* (*Xiangyang ji* 襄陽記) included in Pei Songzhi's 裴松之 (372–451) commentary to his *Sanguo zhi* 三國志 biography.[32] After Zhuge Liang's death, we are told, Liu Shan's administration was flooded with requests to build temples to his memory. Fearing a threat to his clan's authority, the Later Lord refused but to no avail. Zhuge Liang's followers made their offerings en masse and outside sanctioned places of worship, "on the roads and paths." In response, the state finally permitted them to erect a temple in Mianyang 沔陽 near Zhuge Liang's burial site and at a safe remove from the Liu ancestors in Chengdu. In this account, temples, and more specifically their locations, take on significance as expressions of the people's love and their desire to see Zhuge Liang reunited with the ruler he so loyally served. As we will see, the same issue reappears at the center of some of Du Fu's most interesting commemorative poems.

But let us begin with the images of ruination that characterize the poems on Zhuge Liang's Kuizhou temple. The following short and rather neglected poem vividly illustrates the theme.

上卿翁請修武侯廟遺像缺落時崔卿權夔州
Respectfully Sent to Old Qing Requesting the Repair of a Damaged and Decayed Portrait in the Temple of the Warrior Count, When Cui Qing Had Charge of Kuizhou

大賢為政即多聞	Since the Great Worthy's governance is heard so much of,
刺史真符不必分	the Prefect's "true tallies" need not be divided.
尚有西郊諸葛廟	Still, in the western outskirts, there is Zhuge's temple.
臥龍無首對江濆	the Sleeping Dragon, headless, faces the river's spray.[33]

A petition to Du Fu's uncle on his wife's side, the poem employs equal measures of flattery and shock to spur its addressee to action. On the one hand there is Old Qing, whose reputation is so secure that he is not required to use "true tallies," which were split between emperor and minister and rejoined upon completion of a mission. On the other there is Zhuge Liang, whose decapitated image is succumbing to the corrosive elements. The unstated implication is that, unlike Old Qing, who is "heard so much of," Zhuge Liang's good name is still dependent on silk, ink, and other fragile material supports. Without the intervention of men like Du Fu and his uncle, who can spread the

---

30. Tillman, "Reassessing Du Fu's Line," 297–98.
31. "Like Zhuge, loved by the people of Shu" 諸葛蜀人愛. From "Lord Yan Wu, Posthumously Made Vice-Director of the Left, Duke of Zheng" 贈左僕射鄭國公嚴公武 (following Owen's translation of the title). Owen, *The Poetry of Du Fu*, vol. 4, 248–55. Xiao Difei, *Du Fu quanji*, vol. 7, 14.3981–996.
32. *Sanguo zhi*, 35.938–39. See discussion in Henry, "Chu-ko Liang," 607–10. For a translation of the *Xiangyang ji* anecdote, see Chittick, "Pride of Place," 187.
33. Owen, *The Poetry of Du Fu*, vol. 5, 316–17. Xiao Difei, *Du Fu quanji*, vol. 9, 17.5247–248.

word via poems and other mobile messages, Zhuge's faceless image will continue to decompose, yielding to the river's oblivion.

Although the headless portrait is perhaps a uniquely vivid example, the theme of historical traces under threat by a decomposing medium appears prominently in other poems as well. In the famous "Diagram of the Eight Formations" ("Ba zhen tu" 八陣圖), Du Fu praises Zhuge Liang's lithic illustration of military strategy because "the stones do not turn" (*shi bu zhuan* 石不轉), drawing attention to the force of the river current bearing down on them.

功蓋三分國	His deeds covered a kingdom split in three,
名成八陣圖	his fame completed the Diagram of the Eight Formations.
江流石不轉	The river flows on, the stones do not turn,
遺恨失吞吳	a remaining bitterness at his failure to swallow Wu.[34]

The tragic fortunes of the Shu state are reenacted in the elemental struggle of stone against water, the formed carrier of historical meaning against the element of formlessness and forgetting. It is only a matter of time before the river prevails and the stones do in fact "turn," erode, or are submerged. They will be swallowed like Shu, only more slowly, giving them time to express a "remaining bitterness" at the injustices of history. Unlike the more rapidly degrading portrait, which with the help of a persuasive poem may yet be made whole, the stone diagram's defeat is irreversible.

We also find images of corrosion inserted into longer poems on Zhuge Liang's monuments. In "Zhuge's Temple" ("Zhuge miao" 諸葛廟) the memory of Shu's "failure to swallow" their rivals gives way (in lines 9–10) to a vision of the present temple as a site of two kinds of dissolution:

久遊巴子國	Long I traveled in the land of Ba
屢入武侯祠	and often entered the Warrior Count's temples.
竹日斜虛寢	Sun on bamboo slants on his empty shrine,
溪風滿薄帷	creek breeze fills the thin curtains.
君臣當共濟	Ruler and subject then worked together,
賢聖亦同時	a worthy man and sage, living at the same time.
翊戴歸先主	He pledged to support the First Lord,
并吞更出師	he sent the army forth again to swallow the foe.
蟲蛇穿畫壁	Insects and snakes pierce the wall paintings,
巫覡醉蛛絲	a shaman is drunk among spider webs.
欻憶吟梁父	All at once I recall his "Song of Liangfu,"
躬耕也未遲	it's not yet too late to plow my own land.[35]

Here again Zhuge Liang's commemorative materials are being consumed by entropic forces. The unfortunate portrait, already defaced by the river, is being devoured by pests. Moreover, this goes unnoticed by the dissolute and oblivious local holy man, who is "drunk among spider webs" that surround him like a mummifying cocoon. "Zhuge's Temple" thus distills into a single couplet the approach to monumental matter seen in the previous two poems. While it is true that references to decay and dilapidation

---

34. Owen, *The Poetry of Du Fu*, vol. 4, 136–37. Xiao Difei, *Du Fu quanji*, vol. 6, 12.3572–575. The translation largely follows Owen.

35. Translation by Owen, *The Poetry of Du Fu*, vol. 5, 168–69. Xiao Difei, *Du Fu quanji*, vol. 8, 16.4708–710.

were thoroughly conventional in Tang poetic treatments of monuments, Du Fu's deployments of the theme in lines like these transcend the norm in their originality and physical detail. Like his identification of the local geology as a monument to Yu, such images direct us down into the matter of the trace. However, in contrast to the stone of the gorge, which stood for an emergence of form and meaning through the "opening and clearing" of the channels of empire, the materials of Zhuge Liang's monuments are reclaiming the forms they have supported, closing off the channel.

And yet this seems to have only strengthened Du Fu's desire to get through and to discover connections on the other side. Like Zhuge Liang's local followers portrayed in the aforementioned *Xiangyang ji* anecdote, Du Fu was preoccupied with the symbolism of temple location—specifically with the proximity of Zhuge Liang's temple to that of Liu Bei. Consider, for example, the end of the poem on Liu Bei included in the famous series on Kuizhou's historical landmarks, "Singing My Thoughts on Ancient Traces" ("Yonghuai guji" 詠懷古跡):

武侯祠屋常鄰近   The Warrior Count's chapel is always nearby;
一體君臣祭祀同   as a single body, ruler and minister share the sacrifices together.[36]

The commemoration of the First Lord concludes by emphasizing the closeness of his minister's memorial chapel.[37] Being "always nearby," the structure symbolizes Zhuge's unbending loyalty in lasting architectural form, providing a redemptive counterimage to the story of separation that took place in Kuizhou with Liu Bei's death. It is also significant against the backdrop of the efforts described in the *Xiangyang ji* to maintain a distance between temples in order to restrain the power of his local cult. Most fundamentally, it taps into the metaphorical resources through which the seamless, quasi-erotic intimacy between the two men was commonly represented through tropes of dissolving boundaries and merging bodies: they were like fish and water or clouds and wind.[38] Such figures of speech made the relationship an ideal of perfect communication and communion, of distance entirely overcome. Playing on the same trope, Du Fu brings them together in the smoke of sacrificial offerings, which, despite the separation of temples, they share "as a single body."

This image, in turn, works self-referentially to foreground the poem (as distinct from the temples) as the medium through which the connection is established. Just as the geological form of Qutang Gorge threw into relief the imaginative interpretation of it as a historical monument, so the architecture of Zhuge Liang's Kuizhou temples highlights the poetic form in which the spirits of the deceased are brought together. Specifically, it makes meaningful the seamless transition between the poem on Liu Bei and the one on Zhuge Liang that follows it in the series. The proximity of poems replicates and surpasses that of the temples, with the connection articulated by the hinge-like final word, "together" (*tong* 同). If, as Mo Lifeng has argued, Du Fu's Zhuge Liang poems resemble temple hymns in the formality of their prosody and diction, and in

---

36. Owen, *The Poetry of Du Fu*, vol. 4, 364–65; Xiao Difei, *Du Fu quanji*, vol. 7, 13.3854–856. See also Frankel, "The Contemplation of the Past in T'ang Poetry," 360.

37. An "original note" to the poem by the poet provides more specific information: "The palace building [of Liu Bei] is now a temple; his shrine is to the east of the palace compound" 殿今為寺, 廟在宮東.

38. On the subversive development of such erotic implications in contemporary Three Kingdoms fan fiction, see Tian, "Slashing Three Kingdoms," 224–77.

their reverent tone,[39] I would suggest that they also mirror temple structures in their reconfigurations of memorial space.

At stake in the positions of Kuizhou's temples and their poetic representations, then, is the conquering of distance, the communication between separated spaces and bodies. The distance overcome might be that which separated two nearby buildings; however, it also included much wider expanses, as is demonstrated by the inexhaustibly interesting "Ballad of an Ancient Cypress" ("Gubai xing" 古柏行). In this poem, prompted by a giant tree on the grounds of the Kuizhou shrine, Du Fu recalls visiting a Zhuge Liang temple in Chengdu, which stood much closer to the temple of Liu Bei.

	孔明廟前有老柏	In front of Kongming's temple there is an ancient cypress.
	柯如青銅根如石	with a trunk like bronze and roots like stone.
	霜皮溜雨四十圍	Its frosted bark, rain-streaked, runs forty spans around.
4	黛色參天二千尺	its blackened form, level with heaven, stands two thousand feet high.
	君臣已與時際會	Ruler and minister, in their times, already had their meeting.
	樹木猶為人愛惜	but this tree is still loved and cherished by the people.
	雲來氣接巫峽長	Clouds arrive and ethers meet, in Wu Gorge, so long.
8	月出寒通雪山白	the moon comes out, the cold penetrates to White Snow Mountain.
	憶昨路繞錦亭東	I recall where the road skirted east of Brocade Pavilion.
	先主武侯同閟宮	the First Lord and Warrior Count shared a single compound.
	崔嵬枝幹郊原古	Majestically towering, trunks and branches entwined from times most ancient;
12	窈窕丹青戶牖空	secluded and remote, the portraits, doorways, and casements empty.
	落落盤踞雖得地	Shedding leaves, it perches, coiled, and though it's found a place,
	冥冥孤高多烈風	darkly, darkly, alone it towers, in so much violent wind.
	扶持自是神明力	Holding it up can only be the force of shining spirits.
16	正直原因造化功	its true uprightness is due to the feats of the Fashioner.
	大廈如傾要梁棟	If a great hall were to collapse and rafters were required,
	萬牛回首丘山重	ten thousand oxen would turn their heads at such mountainous weight.
	不露文章世已驚	Not even showing its patterning, it would make the world amazed,
20	未辭翦伐誰能送	nor would it refuse to be cut down, but who could transport it?
	苦心豈免容螻蟻	How could its bitter trunk avoid letting in the termites,
	香葉終經宿鸞鳳	but its fragrant leaves have ever given lodging to the phoenix.
	志士幽人莫怨嗟	Ambitious gentleman and recluse—do not sigh in resentment!—
24	古來材大難為用	from ancient times when timber is great it is hard to put to use.[40]

39. Mo Lifeng, "Du Fu dui Zhuge Liang de zansong," 128–38.
40. Owen, *The Poetry of Du Fu*, vol. 4, 228–31. Xiao Difei, *Du Fu quanji*, vol. 6, 12.3575–582. I want to stress that my reading aims only to highlight features of this ultracanonical poem relevant to my particular theme. For the poem's place in the "barren tree" tradition, see Owen, "Deadwood," 157–79. See also translations by Hawkes, *A Little Primer*, 156–64; and Hung, *China's Greatest Poet*, 226. The translation follows Owen closely, especially in the last section.

The first thing to note, in the context of the present discussion, is what makes the Chengdu temple memorable for Du Fu: unlike in Kuizhou, where Liu Bei's shrine stood at a remove from that of his minister, in Chengdu the two men "shared a single compound" (*tong bigong* 同閟宮). Again, as in the poem on Liu Bei in "Singing My Thoughts on Ancient Sites," quoted above, and as in the *Xiangyang ji* account, the focus of concern is the proximity of temples, restoring in death the perfect communion that lord and minister enjoyed in life. And, again, restoring such mutual presence requires conquering distance through an act of poetic imagination. Whereas in "Singing My Thoughts" distance is overcome symbolically, through sacrificial smoke and sequential poems, here it is overcome by remembering an actual (though far more distant) shared space.

Most remarkable, however, is how these conjoined rooms of memory are arrived at by way of a gathering of distant regions into a single panoramic perspective. In the order of the poem's exposition, the personal memory appears as the continuation of a steady enlargement of the visual frame, a "zooming out" that begins with the fantastically enormous tree itself. With a trunk "forty spans around" and a height of "two thousand feet" the cypress already leads our gaze upward and beyond Kuizhou. The fourth couplet broadens the scope further to include more distant landmarks and features images of atmospheric "connection" (*jie* 接) and "penetration" (*tong* 通). It is only then, as we follow the extension of the "blackened form" (*daise* 黛色) outward in space, that we travel back in time to the Chengdu of Du Fu's past. This suggests that Chengdu does not necessarily succeed or supplant Kuizhou on an axis of linear time so much as join it within a temporally ambiguous expanded view, a macroscopic doubling of the conjoined temples. Such a reading would help explain the ambiguity that has made it impossible for commentators definitively to show where the memory passage comes to a close.[41] Does the seventh couplet refer to Chengdu or Kuizhou? And the eighth? But perhaps the demand for an either/or choice between locations is itself misplaced. Perhaps the point was precisely to conceive a perspective that included both places simultaneously, a perspective in which the locales of temples and trees forfeit their distinct identities, as if the Kuizhou cypress somehow reached all the way to Chengdu and intertwined with the cypresses there. The canopy thus formed would connect Zhuge Liang's remote memorial spaces just as such spaces were connected to those of Liu Bei, subsuming distinct parts into a larger whole. Moreover, it would make visible a fame that transcends territorial boundaries and "hangs over the universe" (*chui yuzhou* 垂宇宙), as Du Fu writes of Zhuge Liang in the fifth and final "Singing My Thoughts on Ancient Traces."[42] In "Ballad of an Ancient Cypress," then, we have a singularly vivid example of the connective, communicative side of Du Fu's writing about commemorative form in Kuizhou: a vision of cypress trees branching out like telephone lines across the land, integrating remote regions under a shared veneration for Zhuge Liang.

The cypress is not only an image of fame, however, but also of the medium that enabled it: the spreading "blackened form" of poetry. Like the carved river channels in "Meditation on the Past at Qutang Gorge," Du Fu's cypress was a way of making visible the power of poems to communicate and establish connections across distances

41. For a selection of the differing interpretations of the memory passage's duration, see Pu Qilong, *Du Du xinjie*, 23.298.
42. "Zhuge's great fame hangs over the universe" 諸葛大名垂宇宙. The translation follows Owen, *The Poetry of Du Fu*, vol. 4, 365. Xiao Difei, *Du Fu quanji*, vol. 7, 13.3856–858.

by means of circulation. To imagine distant times and places in a poem was not so different from thinking about where that poem had been or where it would go. "Ballad of an Ancient Cypress" does exactly this, by referencing "Minister of Shu" ("Shu xiang" 蜀相), a poem Du Fu wrote in Chengdu about the temple visit he would later recall.

丞相祠堂何處尋	The Great Minister's shrine hall, where is it to be sought?
錦官城外柏森森	outside Brocade Official City, where the cypresses grow dense.
映階碧草自春色	Shining on stairs, emerald grass is itself the color of spring.
隔葉黃鸝空好音	behind the leaves, yellow orioles sing sweet songs in vain.
三顧頻煩天下計	The repeated effort of the Three Visits— all for strategy to win the empire.
兩朝開濟老臣心	the founding and transitioning of two courts came from an old minister's heart.
出師未捷身先死	That leading the army, and not yet prevailing, he first met with death,
長使英雄淚滿襟	will always cause heroes to wet their robes with tears.[43]

Read after "Ballad of an Ancient Cypress," this poem cannot but appear as its companion piece, as if the Kuizhou piece were reaching back to it across Du Fu's collection, and not only to the experience it describes. Du Fu had this poem with him in Kuizhou, of course, where he reread and edited his works. Although we cannot know whether and to what extent it informed his memory, we do know that in Kuizhou he was remembering the circumstances of its composition while visualizing a medium of connection to Chengdu. Whether or not Du Fu had it consciously in mind, "Minister of Shu," the poem that carried knowledge of Zhuge Liang's Chengdu temple to Kuizhou and beyond was precisely that connecting medium. The canopy of fame was composed of just such traveling texts.

And so it is fitting, after reading "Ballad of an Ancient Cypress," that "Minister of Shu" treats the cypress foliage itself as a scene of telephonic communication. The cypresses appear at the very beginning of the poem, marking the site of Zhuge's temple and drawing the visitor to it from afar. They return in the second couplet as part of the scene the poet encounters as he approaches the monument. In line 4, just before he reflects on Zhuge's story, Du Fu remarks on sounds coming from within the canopy: "Behind the leaves, yellow orioles sing sweet songs in vain" 隔葉黃鸝空好音. Screened by the cypress leaves, the orioles sing to each other, unseen by the poet. The landmark that allowed him to access the site of history, the symbol of connection across vast distances, is now a barrier, dense matter concealing the birds and rendering them present only as disembodied sounds. We are returned to the materiality of commemoration, here expressed neither as formation nor deformation but as the opacity of the media through which remote communication necessarily occurs. As noted by Jin Shengtan 金聖嘆 (1610–1661), one of Du Fu's most insightful commentators, this very much includes communication with history:

43. Owen, *The Poetry of Du Fu*, vol. 2, 298–99. Xiao Difei, *Du Fu quanji*, vol. 4, 7.1930–940; Hawkes, *A Little Primer*, 103–8. Interestingly, Owen interprets the second line as referring to a single tree, reputedly planted by Zhuge Liang himself. This would make for an even closer resemblance to the Kuizhou temple.

> The means by which the oriole seeks its friend is how gentlemen move each other across a hundred generations. They have a desire to befriend the ancients, and yet alas the ancients can never be seen, as if separated by leaves.[44]
> 黃鳥所以求友，君子曠百世相感，有尚友古人之情，而無如古人終不可見，如隔葉也。

In Jin Shengtan's reading, the relation between the orioles models the relation of the poet to the historical past. Just as the birds remain invisible to and remote from each other within the occluding foliage, so the ancients remain occulted behind their monuments and ultimately inaccessible. It is dark inside the canopy, an echo chamber of absence and isolation. And yet these are the conditions under which a community attempts to find itself, through the "sweet songs" emanating from leaves, landmarks, and scrolls.

* * *

Despite manifest differences of subject matter, Du Fu's poems on the ancient traces of Yu the Great and Zhuge Liang display similar approaches to commemorative form. As we have seen, they are characterized on the one hand by a focus on the materiality of monuments, coded either as productive raw material (the rocks and cliffs of the historicized landscape) or "downward-dragging, corroding" decay (the Diagram of the Eight Formations, the ruined temple with its disfigured portrait).[45] On the other hand, they feature prominent images of interconnection (Qutang Gorge orienting the surrounding landmarks, the linked temples of Zhuge Liang and Liu Bei, the cypress spreading across regions). In relation to these latter images, I noted the poems' recurring tendency to self-refer by taking monuments as mirrors in which to display their own capacity to fashion and connect. Like Yu's channels, Du Fu's poems transform Kuizhou's geological environment into a site of history; like the temples of Chengdu, they bring together separated figures in the same commemorative space; and, like the cypress, they communicate across vast spatial and temporal distances.

This treatment of commemorative form was not only a response to the stories encoded in local traces, or to Du Fu's own life circumstances—though of course both of these contexts mattered immensely. It should also be understood as a response to the communicative situation specific to Kuizhou, the gateway to the empire's most perilous channel. The Three Gorges called forth desire for communication and reflection on its means, including communication with history. Kuizhou's traces stood out to him as occluded channels that both invited and obstructed passage, leaving the traveler to linger on the threshold. On the other side he discovered histories of connection and communion—wishful images of a stranded, isolated poet, to be sure, but also emblems of poetry as an expression of communicative desire.

---

44. Jin Shengtan, *Jin Shengtan xuanpi Du shi*, 79.
45. Simmel, "The Ruin," 261.

4

Ironic Empires

Lucas Rambo Bender

Du Fu has for much of the last millennium been thought of as the poet who held together worlds that had otherwise broken apart. His morally exemplary verse, it has often been asserted, proved that poetry had not ultimately lost that primeval connection with ethics and politics that was promised in the "Great Preface" to the *Classic of Poetry* (*Shi jing* 詩經). His sympathy for the suffering people of his time proved that the individual could still speak for the larger empire, the affairs of the state "rooted in the experience of a single person."[1] And his penetrating insight into the true significance of the An Lushan Rebellion proved that there was no unbridgeable divide between individual subjectivity and objective truth, that it remained possible for a poet to feel the world in a way appropriate to its true moral contours.[2] In all of these respects, Du Fu was China's "poet sage" and also its "poet historian," tasked with maintaining poetry's ultimate defensibility throughout a millennium in which the art was often in danger of being seen as shirking political and ethical responsibility in its indulgence in the experience of the individual and in the labyrinths of private subjectivity.

Du Fu has, however, sometimes been seen as almost the diametrical opposite of this synthesizing figure. Stephen Owen, for example, identifies Du Fu as the first poet to write into being a private sphere, constituted by subjective interpretations markedly distinct from the ideologies of the empire.[3] In the mid-Tang, Owen writes, important poets imitated Du Fu in offering

> playfully inflated interpretations of domestic spaces and leisure activities as a discourse of private valuation, articulated against commonsense values. Such values and meanings, offered in play, belong to the poet alone, and they create an effective private sphere distinct from the totalizing aspect of Chinese moral and social philosophy, in which even solitary and domestic behavior are part of a hierarchy of public values.[4]

---

1. See *Mao shi zhushu*, 1.18.
2. For examples of this tendency in traditional and modern Chinese criticism of Du Fu, see Bender, "Du Fu," especially 213–20.
3. Owen, *The End of the Chinese "Middle Ages,"* 89.
4. Owen, *The End of the Chinese "Middle Ages,"* 4.

These sorts of poems were instrumental, Owen suggests, to a larger trend that comes to define much of later Chinese literary culture, whereby "in ways large and small, writers begin to assert their particular claim over a range of objects and activities: my land, my style, my interpretation, my garden, my particular beloved." In these poems, therefore, the relationship between private subjectivity and public values becomes problematic, resulting in new divisions between literary writing and moral thought concerned with the fortunes of the empire. If many critics have seen Du Fu as the poet for whom no private moment failed to open out onto public concern, Owen thus reads him as providing one of the most important templates for escaping imperial responsibility and, ultimately, questioning imperial values.

It might be natural to assume that these two visions of Du Fu derive from different portions of his very large and diverse poetic corpus. In fact, however, the poems that might be most readily identified as laying the groundwork for a poetics of private subjectivity are often among those that provide the most convincing proofs for the traditional claim that Du Fu never forgot the problems of the empire "even for the space of a single meal."[5] These complex poems—written primarily in Kuizhou, on humble, domestic topics—seem to point in both directions at once, both affirming Du Fu's public commitments by importing imperial values into the minutiae of his private life and simultaneously ironizing those values by highlighting the comic incongruity of their application to topics that would normally fall beneath the notice of high-cultural forms like poetry. The poems become jokes, mocking the futility of Du Fu's attempts to apply imperial values to the mundanities of life on the far outskirts of the Tang imperium; at the same time, however, they often cut this humor with melancholy reflections upon his own continued dependence on an empire he begins to see in all its violence. By probing the applicability of public-minded concern within his domestic life, these poems thus break the world apart in Du Fu's desperate attempts to hold it together and reveal perverse interconnections in the ironies of his attempts to escape.[6]

Early Poems on Humble Topics

Du Fu's collection contains a number of poems on humble, domestic topics that are thought to predate his time in Kuizhou. In several cases, these poems offer reasonably solid support for traditional claims that imperial values filter down into even those areas of his life wherein the less virtuous among us might forget them. In poems like "Sick Horse" ("Bing ma" 病馬) and "Palm Whisk" ("Zongfuzi" 椶拂子),[7] for example—generally dated to Du Fu's sojourns in Qinzhou and Chengdu, respectively—Du Fu valorizes the support he has received from the accoutrements of his exile in terms that are clearly meant to parallel ideals of official service to the emperor. Traditional commentators, accordingly, generally understand these poems to be fundamentally about the poet's disappointed loyalty and about the government that has disappointed it, reading his claims to be "moved by the deeper significance" of his loyal horse and to always "carefully wrap up and put away" his palm whisk as suggesting that his own commitment to

---

5. This famous cliché derives from Su Shi 蘇軾 (1037–1101); see *Su Shi wenji*, 318.
6. These poems have also been recently studied by Gregory M. Patterson, both in his dissertation, "Elegies for Empire," 126–48, and in a recent paper presented at the 2016 meeting of the T'ang Studies Society.
7. Xiao Difei, *Du Fu quanji*, vol. 3, 6.1575; vol. 5, 10.2886; Owen, *The Poetry of Du Fu*, vol. 2, 182–83 and vol. 3, 256–59.

the empire has not been rewarded with the same sort of appreciation.[8] There is nothing particularly humorous about these poems: it might, perhaps, be somewhat absurd to speak of the loyalty of a flywhisk, but less so of a horse—and at any rate commentators are nearly unanimous that these topics are mere pretexts for bringing up more serious issues.

It is not until 764 that Owen begins to document real recalcitrance to Du Fu's attempts to elevate his domestic affairs to imperial significance. Owen focuses his discussion on "Deck by the Water" ("Shui jian" 水檻),[9] a poem that describes Du Fu's vacillations as to whether he should repair his ruined hermitage's broken porch. On Owen's reading, "whether to repair a sagging deck had never been a question that was felt to merit serious poetic treatment," and so the basic drama of the poem lies in Du Fu's attempt to justify "why this matters to him and why the serious genre of poetry should concern itself with something so trivial and commonplace"[10] through "an outrageous application of a passage in the *Analects* (XVI.6), in which Confucius enjoins us to 'support what totters,' *fudian* 扶顛."[11] Since Confucius in this passage was speaking about governance, not porches, Du Fu's attempt to apply the precept to his domestic sphere becomes ridiculous, highlighting the disconnect rather than the continuity between his Chengdu hermitage and imperial politics. The poem thus produces an ironic fracturing of the world, demonstrating that the values that pertain to the state do not transfer easily to the domain of domestic life. "No matter how much Du Fu strains to allegorize his domestic structure, it remains stubbornly no more than a deck, ironizing his attempts at interpretation and foregrounding their excess"[12] and leading the poet himself in the end to recognize that his attachment to the porch is not an instance of the sophisticated cultural values he invokes but merely a case of humble familiarity. The porch is simply his, and he cares for it, quite apart from what the empire might value: herein lie the rudiments of a private sphere.

Most of Du Fu's Chinese commentators, however, have read the poem rather differently. Where Owen interprets Du Fu's "fear that he will be laughed at by those who know" as suggesting the poet's discomfort with his overweening application of the *Analects* to his porch, traditional commentators like Zhou Zhuan 周篆 (1642–1706) argue the opposite, that Du Fu fears being laughed at precisely if he *fails* to follow Confucius's injunction even in the domestic sphere, where he could easily succeed.[13] For these commentators, the poem thus represents Du Fu's thoroughgoing commitment to those normative, imperial values that Owen takes him as ironizing. And this ambiguity, I suggest, is not an accident. When we come to the poetry on domestic affairs that Du Fu wrote during the two years he lived in Kuizhou, from 766 to 768, the possibility

---

8. For comments of this sort about "Sick Horse," see, for example, Zhao Cigong, *Du shi*, 350; and the comment attributed to Shi 師 in Huang Xi and Huang He, *Bu zhu Du shi*, 20.23a. For similar comments on "Palm Whisk," see Shan Fu, *Du Du shi* 9.17, and Qiu Zhaoao, *Du shi xiangzhu*, 1031.
9. Owen, *The Poetry of Du Fu*, vol. 3, 360–61; Xiao Difei, *Du Fu quanji*, vol. 6, 11.3155–58.
10. Owen, *The End of the Chinese "Middle Ages,"* 91.
11. Owen, *The End of the Chinese "Middle Ages,"* 92.
12. Owen, *The End of the Chinese "Middle Ages,"* 92.
13. For Zhou Zhuan's comment, see Xiao Difei, *Du Fu quanji*, vol. 6, 11.3156. Note that Shan Fu argues that the poem is an allegory for the empire, with wind and rain standing for the disorder of the rebellion and the porch standing for the state. Shan Fu, *Du Du shi*, 10.17b–18a. Similarly, Weng Fanggang 翁方綱 (1733–1818) suggests that supporting his porch is a veiled reference to Du Fu's attempt to save Fang Guan 房琯 (696–763). See Xiao Difei, *Du Fu quanji*, vol. 6, 11.3157. In these readings, the use of the *Analects* is not out of place at all.

of such alternate readings becomes structurally significant, part of a meditation upon Du Fu's liminal position on the border of the empire and on the edge of the imperial bureaucracy.[14]

Vegetable Allegories

There was, of course, significant classical precedent for writing poetry on the humble affairs of village life out in the provinces. Among all forms of Chinese literature, in fact, poetry might have seemed to Du Fu the most propitious for connecting potentially discontinuous realms of experience. Not only had the Mao Commentary's "Great Preface" to the *Classic of Poetry* promised that "the affairs of a single state" could be observed within the experience and feelings of a single individual; moreover, the same text established what might roughly be termed allegorizing treatment ("comparison," *bi* 比) as one of the Six Principles through which the *Classic* needed to be understood,[15] making it possible, for example, for a "big rat" eating up a peasant family's grain to stand in for a greedy ruler.[16] And according to the legendary origins of that same *Classic*, the poems it contains were collected from among the far-flung populations of the Zhou dynasty's vast domain in order to reveal to the central court the condition of local mores. There was thus nothing inherently unlikely, according to this Classicist vision, about great poetry deriving from a backwater like Kuizhou.

Du Fu, however, seems to have discerned the possibility for bathetic humor in the too-earnest application of these principles. In the following poem, for example, when he claims to be "drawing a comparison" between the bad vegetables that he has received from Kuizhou's public garden and the affairs of the age, he is both aligning his poetic practice with the most august source of the tradition and simultaneously mocking himself for using *Shi jing* poetics to complain about a substandard vegetable delivery.

園官送菜 The Garden Officer Sends Vegetables[17]
園官送菜把，本數日闕，矧苦苣馬齒，掩乎嘉蔬。傷時小人妬害君子，菜不足道也，比而作詩。

The garden officer sends me bundles of vegetables, but he has actually been remiss for several days. Worse, the bitter lettuce and horse-tooth amaranth overwhelm the finer vegetables. I am pained that in this age petty people do harm to gentlemen out of spite: the vegetables themselves are not worth bringing up, but I drew a comparison and wrote this poem.

清晨蒙菜把　　In the clear morning, when I receive my bunch of vegetables,
常荷地主恩　　I always bear the local master's grace.[18]
守者愆實數　　But the one in charge of this cheats on the count,

---

14. For Du Fu's biographical sketch, see the introduction to this volume. For more focused discussions of Du Fu's situation in Kuizhou and Kuizhou's position within the Tang empire, see Patterson, "Elegies for Empire," especially 74–126; Fang Yu, *Du Fu Kuizhou shi*, 9–70; Jiang Xianwei, *Du Fu Kuizhou shi*, especially 60–71, 173–76, and 222–24; and Feng Ye, *Du Fu Kuizhou shi.*

15. *Mao shi zhushu*, 1.15.

16. *Mao shi zhushu*, 5.211.

17. Throughout this chapter, the Chinese texts reproduce as closely as Unicode allows the readings of *Song ben Du Gongbu ji* compiled by Wang Zhu 王洙 (997–1057). The translations are (generally slight) modifications of Owen's in *The Poetry of Du Fu.* This poem is in Owen, *The Poetry of Du Fu*, vol. 5, 116–19; Xiao Difei, *Du Fu quanji*, vol. 8, 16.4546ff.

18. Presumably, Bai Maolin 柏茂林, the local supervisor in chief and Du Fu's patron in Kuizhou.

4	略有其名存	so pretty much only the name remains.
	苦苣刺如針	The bitter lettuce has thorns like needles;
	馬齒葉亦繁	the leaves of horse-tooth amaranth are also many.
	青青嘉蔬色	Green, green, the colors of the better vegetables[19]
8	埋沒在中園	are buried away in the garden.
	園吏未足怪	This garden officer is not worth being upset about,
	世事因堪論	but the situation of the times can be discussed through this.
	嗚呼戰伐久	Alas! Warfare has gone on so long
12	荊棘暗長原	that thorns and brambles darken the long plain:[20]
	乃知苦苣輩	For this reason we know that things like bitter lettuce
	傾奪蕙草根	will overwhelm the roots of sweet basil.
	小人塞道路	And petty men stuff the roads of power,
16	為態何喧喧	how noisy and clamorous their manner!
	又如馬齒盛	This too is like the horse-tooth amaranth, flourishing so
	氣擁葵荏昏	that its aura crowds and shades out mallow and perilla.
	點染不易虞	It's not easy to protect against contamination,
20	絲麻雜羅紈	like strands of hemp mixing with gossamer and damask:
	一經器物內	And once these pass through the cookware
	永掛蟲刺痕	they always leave marks of their coarseness and thorns.
	志士采紫芝	The man of high aims plucks the purple mushroom,
24	放歌避戎軒	singing out while avoiding army carts;[21]
	畦丁負籠至	But I, when fieldworkers come shouldering baskets,
	感動百慮端	am stirred by a hundred sources of care.

Du Fu is anxious here to defray the imagined scorn of his readers, telling us twice that the bad vegetables he has received are too insignificant to write a poem about. These vegetables, he assures us, are not in fact the focus of the verse: instead, they serve merely as a means of discussing the larger political and cultural situation of the age. And for the most part, Du Fu's traditional commentators throughout the centuries have believed him on this point. Yang Lun 楊倫 (1747–1803), for example, writes that even though "the poem starts out with being angry at the garden officer for being greedy with his food, when it enters into a larger indignation, it gets the meaning of the poets of the *Shi jing* when they criticized abuses in the state" 本是憤園官侵剋食料，卻入此大感慨，得詩人諷誠之旨.[22]

The poem's final couplet can, however, also be read to suggest that less exalted concerns may number among Du Fu's "hundred sources of care." Something of the multiplicity implied by this phrase has, in fact, already been enacted by the poem, which jumps between claiming that the vegetable shipment is bad because the garden

---

19. This line may perhaps recall two famous early love poems containing the line "Green, green are the plants on the riverbank" 青青河畔草. See Lu Qinli, *Xian Qin Han Wei*, 192 and 329.
20. This passage alludes to a saying from the *Laozi* 老子: "Where an army camps, there will thorns and brambles grow. After a great war, there will always be years of poor harvest" 師之所處，荊棘生焉，大軍之後，必有凶年. *Laozi yizhu*, 72.
21. This couplet refers to the "Four Hoaryheads" 四皓, who famously retired to Mt. Lantian during the misgovernance of the Qin dynasty. Huangfu Mi's 皇甫謐 (215–282) *Gaoshizhuan* 高士傳 records a song attributed to these famous recluses, in which they speak about their hunger being satisfied by purple mushrooms. See *Taiping yulan*, 507.2442.
22. Yang Lun, *Du shi jingquan*, 16.761. Similarly, Wang Sishi 王嗣奭 (1566–1648) sees the poem as a criticism of the way that military officials are now lording it over civil officers. See his *Du yi*, 7.246.

officer "cheats on the count" (line 3), to intuiting that the bad vegetables are the tangible results of bad governance (lines 11–14), to seeing them as metaphorical figures for a corrupt political culture (lines 15–18)—a sort of overdetermination that may reveal a poet who "doth protest too much" the canonical sanction of writing about bad vegetables. It seems telling, furthermore, that the poem's mouthwatering imagination of the greenness of these better vegetables recalls a paradigmatic line of early five-syllable verse about springtime lust in separation. If the "Great Preface" offers one canonical source for understanding what the poem is about, that is, the echo of this famous line may present another, one more accepting of personal and even sensual interests.

Beyond these hints that Du Fu may not have succeeded at weeding out any concern about the vegetables themselves, moreover, the final couplets explicitly represent a self-conscious reinterpretation of the poem through another sort of poetic precedent: that of the legendary Four Hoaryheads, recluses who sang their "Song of Purple Mushrooms" as they left behind the misgoverned Qin Empire. The poetry of such lofty individuals, Du Fu reflects, contrasts distinctly with his own poem: where they sang happily of lightly picking numinous mushrooms that grew without human labor beyond the imperial world, he is complaining about coarse vegetables that bear down heavily on the backs of the muck-working peasants who are forced to deliver it to him. These vegetable-laden peasants, moreover, recall the language of the poem's first couplet, the word used for their "shouldering" (fu 負) being a synonym for "bearing" (he 荷), which Du Fu had used to elegantly express his gratitude for his patron Bai Maolin's generosity in providing him with food. The implication of this echo seems to be that, unlike the Four Hoaryheads, Du Fu is in fact "weighed down" by his concern with these vegetables, much as the peasants are physically encumbered in delivering them to him. This self-conscious twist may suggest, then, that Du Fu has failed to transcend the petty concerns that he repeatedly tries to disclaim by reference to canonical texts. It may, moreover, revalue his hopes of maintaining connection with imperial values, since he is a beneficiary of precisely the imperial system here, and at the expense of others less fortunate.

Despite its appearance of cantankerous roughness, then, this poem represents a careful condensation of many of the themes that animate Du Fu's verse on humble topics during his Kuizhou years. Seen retrospectively from the poem's conclusion, in fact, this cantankerous roughness would seem itself part of the point, dramatizing the poet as the type of old crank who would write pretentious allegorizing poetry to complain about free food. The poem thus turns back on itself and on its pretensions to import high-cultural significance into domestic affairs, a technique we can see replicated in another vegetable allegory Du Fu wrote in Kuizhou, this time in a register that is less seriously self-critical than humorously pathetic.

種萵苣并序 Planting Lettuce[23]
既雨已秋，堂下理小畦，隔種一兩席許萵苣，向二旬矣，而苣不甲坼，伊人莧青青。傷時君子或晚得微祿，轗軻不進，因作此詩。

It is autumn now that the rains have come, and I have made a small plot by the main hall. There I planted a few beds of lettuce in separate plots.[24] It has been almost twenty days,

23. Owen, *The Poetry of Du Fu*, vol. 4, 218–21; Xiao Difei, *Du Fu quanji*, vol. 7, 13.3686–94.
24. The *Song ben* text (reproduced here) reads "withered lettuce," which makes no sense. This translation follows Zhao Cigong's emendation of 萵/萎. See Zhao Cigong, *Du shi*, 1006.

yet the lettuce has not germinated, and other people's amaranth is growing green.[25] I lament the times, that a gentleman may late in life get a small salary, but the going is rough and he does not advance. Therefore I made this poem.

	陰陽一錯亂	Yin and Yang were topsy-turvy,
	驕蹇不復理	domineering, recalcitrant, no longer in good order.
	枯旱於其中	Dryness and drought were in their midst,
4	炎方慘如爍	and the hot regions were dismal, as if ablaze.[26]
	植物半蹉跎	Half of all plants had missed their time,
	嘉生將已矣	and the possibility of a good harvest was almost gone.
	雲雷欻奔命	Clouds and thunder suddenly sped to command
8	師伯集所使	as Rainmaster and Windbaron gathered their minions.
	指麾赤白日	They directed the reddish-white sun,
	澒洞青光起	and in swirling masses blue light appeared.[27]
	雨聲先已風	The rain sounds were preceded by wind,
12	散足盡西靡	and the scattering drops all slanted west.
	山泉落滄江	Mountain streams fell into the gray river,
	霹靂猶在耳	and peals of thunder were still in my ears.
	終朝紆颯沓	All day long it whirled swirling,
16	信宿罷瀟洒	then after two nights it ceased its briskness.
	堂下可以畦	Beside the hall was a possible garden plot,
	呼童對經始	I called to my boys to start it out it with me.[28]
	苣兮蔬之常	O lettuce! Common among vegetables,
20	隨事藝其子	we went through the process to plant its seeds.
	破塊數席間	We broke up clods in several beds;
	荷鋤功易止	carrying hoes, the achievement was easy to complete.
	兩旬不甲坼	But after twenty days, you did not germinate,
24	空惜埋泥滓	and I, helpless, pitied how you were buried in mire.
	野莧迷汝來	Wild amaranth comes, confusing itself for you;[29]
	宗生實於此	teeming growth is truly right here.
	此輩豈無秋	Though this type of plant must also know autumn,
28	亦蒙寒露委	bearing as well the accumulation of cold dew,
	翻然出地速	In a flash it comes forth from the ground,

---

25. Both Owen and Xiao follow the early texts that report a variant 獨野莧青青, "only the wild amaranthus is growing green." I have followed the *Song ben* reading not only because it is more prevalent in early texts (including texts wherein 獨野 is not given as a variant), but also because it is clearly the *lectio difficilior*, and because the presence of 野莧 in line 25 provides an obvious explanation for the introduction of the variant. It is, moreover, quite likely that Du Fu's neighbors might have planted amaranth (indeed, he received a variety of amaranth, "horse-tooth amaranth" 馬齒莧, as part of the vegetable shipment he complained about in the previous poem).

26. The language of this line recalls the *Shi jing*, "The Banks of the Ru" 汝墳: "The royal House is like a blazing fire" 王室如燬. *Mao shi zhushu*, 1.44. The "hot regions" or "fiery regions" (*yanfang* 炎方) refers to the South.

27. This passage is reminiscent of several poems in the *Chu ci* 楚辭, particularly the *Lisao*'s 離騷 description of its speaker's journey through heaven. See *Chu ci jijiao*, 411–50.

28. The language of this line recalls the *Shi jing* poem "Spirit Terrace" 靈臺: "We started out the Spirit Terrace" 經始靈臺. *Mao shi zhushu*, 16.579.

29. Owen translates this line differently: "You, wild amaranthus, I don't know where you came from." Although Owen's reading is favored by a number of premodern commentators, in the present context Du Fu is probably thinking of the harm of having virtue "confused" with vice. As Confucius had supposedly said, "I hate that which seems to be something, but is not" 惡似而非者. See *Mengzi zhushu*, 14.263.

滋蔓戶庭毀	and lushly spreading, my whole yard is ruined.
因知邪干正	Thus I understand how evil overwhelms right,
32 掩抑至沒齒	suppressing it until it perishes.
賢良雖得祿	Even if the worthy and good get a salary,
守道不封己	they keep to the Way, and do not enrich themselves.
擁塞敗芝蘭	Crowding and blocking ruins holy mushroom and orchid;
36 眾多盛荊杞	thorns and medlars flourish in multitudes.
中園陷蕭艾	When a garden falls to mugwort and artemisia,
老圃永為恥	an old gardener will always feel ashamed.[30]
登于白玉盤	Offered on plates of white jade,
40 藉以如霞綺	spread on figured silks like clouds:
莧也無所施	Yes, amaranth has no place there;
胡顏入筐篚	how does it dare enter the baskets?

If "The Garden Officer Sends Vegetables" relates its allegorical procedures to the *Shi jing*, this poem looks to that other ancient source of the Chinese poetic tradition, the *Chu ci* 楚辭, and the *Lisao* in particular. In the *Lisao*, the speaker allegorizes his virtues as the aromatic herbs that contemporary religious practice seems to have used to entice deities, writing about his careful cultivation of basil and eupatorium in a world where lesser men stink like rotting weeds. Here Du Fu too is a gardener, working to promote the growth of fine plants against his neighbors' cultivation of base amaranth. Yet as hard as this poem works to affiliate itself to the *Lisao*—invoking the figures of the gods that its speaker drove before him in his cosmic travels and even going so far as to use the *Lisao*'s characteristic empty syllable, *xi* 兮, in a crucial line—it can, ultimately, only represent a deflation of that august register. Du Fu is not here cultivating fragrant, god-pleasing plants like basil and eupatorium but rather lettuce, "common among vegetables." The poem's grandiose apostrophe to the plant, "O lettuce!" 苣兮, is thus immediately undercut by the patent inability of such hardy fare to stand in for the rare and fragile virtues of the "gentleman" that it is being tasked with representing. There is something vaguely ridiculous, we must sense, in transplanting the *Lisao* tradition into this sort of garden.

If lettuce has a hard time standing in for virtue here, Du Fu himself also finds it difficult to occupy the role of the "gentleman" that he has set himself at the outset. A failure to grow lettuce, for example, is far from what we would normally expect from the phrase "the going is rough and he does not advance," especially given that this comment is prefaced with the notice that the poet had recently been awarded a "small salary" as a nominal official in the Ministry of Works 工部. As if recognizing this incongruity, Du Fu hints near the end of the poem that, in practice, in Kuizhou he is indistinguishable from an "old gardener" (*laopu* 老圃), the sort of common human vegetable that Confucius scorned in a famous passage drawing a distinction between the menial knowledge that characterizes the underclass and the virtues of the moral elite that should run the empire. Though a gentleman-official of his rank might ideally eat off plates of white jade, spread on figured silks like clouds, Du Fu's tableware in

---

30. The phrase "old gardener" recalls the *Analects*, wherein Confucius responds to being asked about gardening, rather than government, "In that, I am not as good as an old gardener" 請學為圃，曰：吾不如老圃. *Lunyu zhushu*, 13.116.

exile was certainly humbler, and we can imagine there was little obvious incongruity in taking the amaranth grown by his neighbors into his basket.

The poem works, then, to undermine the pretensions it announces, exposing Du Fu's claims of moral superiority by showing that in his straitened circumstances, as a humble farmer planting lettuce, he now matches poorly with the (ultimately aristocratic) pattern of the "gentleman," *junzi* 君子. By the eighth century, of course, the term *junzi* was so thoroughly conventional that its original connection to aristocracy and government—it literally means "son of the lord"—is rarely salient in its use; one wonders here, however, whether Du Fu is not thinking back on the term's etymology. For if the preface labels him a *junzi*, the poem itself describes a series of ineffectual lords, *jun* 君: from the cosmic ruler who allows yin and yang to get confused; to the Tang emperor, who has allowed Du Fu to be confused for an old gardener; and finally to Du Fu himself, who has failed to prevent base amaranth from confusing itself for lettuce in the empire of his garden.[31] Equally salient here is Confucius's conviction—announced in a passage Du Fu seems to have had in mind when he wrote this and similar Kuizhou-era poems—that, much like a lord, the gentleman is supposed to exert a civilizing influence upon his surroundings:

> Confucius wanted to go off to live among the Yi tribes. Someone said, "How will you deal with their baseness?" The Master said, "If a gentleman lives among them, what baseness will remain?"
> 子欲居九夷。或曰："陋，如之何？"子曰："君子居之，何陋之有。"[32]

Yet instead of bringing a civilizing influence down to the barbarous southlands, Du Fu has no choice but to eat his neighbors' coarse food.

Like "The Garden Officer Sends Vegetables," this poem is thus carefully constructed to frustrate the poet's ostensible desire to link his domestic affairs with the ideals of the imperial elite, effectively imposing a discontinuity between the two realms of significance that is unmistakably reminiscent of Owen's reading of "Deck by the Water." Humorous though this self-undermining of the poet's pretensions may be, the fracture that this poem introduces between garden and empire does not result in the carving out of a private sphere wherein the state's claims upon the individual might be attenuated. Instead, Du Fu enunciates his alienation from the empire precisely in his attachment to it, his failure as an "old gardener" manifesting both his debilitating dedication to Confucius' project and his inability to pursue it here in Kuizhou. The same double bind, moreover, is apparent in the poem's appeal to the canonical tradition of the *Lisao*, whose purported author, Qu Yuan 屈原, had lived roughly in the region in which Du Fu found himself.[33] On the one hand, this *Lisao* register is invoked to justify the poet's engagement with the humble task of gardening, serving in the poem as representative of Du Fu's continued investment in the Chinese imperial tradition; on the other, its

---

31. Such "confusion" would have been understood as a paradigmatic failure of government, since according to Confucius, the primary duty of government was to "correct names" 正名 (see *Lunyu zhushu*, 13.115) so that each thing was recognized as itself. And according to the *Yi jing*, it was the duty of a sagely ruler to "correctly observe and manifest the myriad things" 聖人作而萬物覩. For this quote, and a medieval interpretation of its significance, see *Zhouyi zhushu*, 1.15.
32. *Lunyu zhushu*, 9.79.
33. Technically, Qu Yuan was from a region considerably farther east (around modern-day Jingzhou in Hubei). For Du Fu, however, there is little difference between Kuizhou and Hubei, at least culturally: both are on the southern edge of the Chinese world.

adoption here can perhaps equally be read to symbolize the way that Du Fu himself is being colonized by the barbarous southern region in which he finds himself, rather than vice versa. In this way too, therefore, the poem's very language is a paradoxical sign simultaneously of Du Fu's adherence to the empire and also of his estrangement from it.

Poetry for Servants and Children

The paradox that Du Fu's poetry should both enact attachment to and alienation from the empire was, in a certain sense, already built into the institution of eighth-century verse. Poetry was (at least aspirationally) a means of advancement in high society, as it was tested on the *jinshi* exam and often functioned as an accoutrement of elite social life. Yet, however integrated poetry might have been in the lives of the official classes, the most famous poets were not always the highest officials, and successful officials both had less reason and less opportunity to write. From the time of the so-called four outstanding men of the Early Tang (*chu Tang sijie* 初唐四傑) in the late seventh century, the court had largely ceased to be the center of literary activity; instead, poetic talent often provided a way for men of frustrated ambition to claim an authority that had not (yet) been awarded them by the state.[34] As David McMullen has shown, Tang history is marked by a progressive estrangement between the court and the centers of elite cultural and literary production,[35] a process crucial to the early ninth-century development of private subjectivity and private space, which occurred largely in the works of "countercultural" writers on the margins of official power.[36] By that point, claims of adherence to the Chinese tradition could themselves be bold claims of disaffection from the empire as it actually was.

Du Fu, however, was not there yet: as we saw in the last two poems, physical estrangement from the imperial center tends strongly to be conflated in his verse with alienation from high-cultural ideals. Yet the voluminous productivity of his Kuizhou period exerts pressure on the already strained relationship between poetry and the vision of elite community toward which it still aspired, not only because Kuizhou was both culturally and ethnically on the margins of the Chinese imperium[37] but also because it is hard to imagine what audience Du Fu might have had in mind for poems complaining about vegetables. In some of this poetry, therefore, Du Fu comes to reflect almost explicitly upon the issue of audience, writing sometimes to people on or beyond the margins of elite sociality, such as his children and his domestic servants. In these poems, Du Fu generally takes on the posture of the imperial insider, bringing elite Chinese civilization down to the barbarous southlands, including within its ambit his (almost certainly illiterate, and in some cases non-Han) servants and slaves[38] and

34. See Owen, "The Cultural Tang," 300.
35. See McMullen, *State and Scholars*.
36. The idea that now-canonical ninth-century writers like Han Yu 韓愈 (768–824) were part of a "counterculture" can be found in Owen, "The Cultural Tang," 330.
37. For a discussion of Du Fu's poems on Kuizhou's culture, see Patterson, "Elegies for Empire," 74–126.
38. Du Fu's domestic arrangements are difficult to discern with any certainty. He certainly had at least one Liao 獠 (Rau) slave, whom the poet identifies as such in "To Be Shown to My Liao Slave Aduan" 示獠奴阿段 (Owen, *The Poetry of Du Fu*, vol. 4, 128–29; Xiao Difei, *Du Fu quanji*, vol. 6, 12.3546–50). Another slave girl he calls Aji 阿稽 was probably also Rau, given medieval notices on the naming conventions among these southern peoples (see *Wei shu*, 101.2248). The other servants that Du Fu mentions are of less certain

passing its lessons and values on to his sons, Zongwen 宗文 and Zongwu 宗武. And as was the case in "The Garden Officer Sends Vegetables" and "Planting Lettuce," this attempt to maintain a connection between his domestic affairs in faraway Kuizhou and the values of the imperial center stretches those values past the breaking point.

課伐木 Assessing the Cutting of Trees[39]

課隸人伯夷、辛秀、信行等入谷斬陰木，人日四根止，維條伊枚，正直侹然。晨征暮返，委積庭內。我有藩籬，是缺是補，載伐篠簜，伊仗支持，則旅次於小安。山有虎，知禁，若恃爪牙之利，必昏黑撐突。蠻人屋壁，列樹白菊，鏝為牆，實以竹，示式遏。為與虎近，混淪乎無良，實客憂害馬之徒，苟活為幸，可嘿息已。作詩付宗武誦。

I exhorted my servants Boyi, Xingxiu, Xinxing, and others to go into the valley and chop trees on the northern slope,[40] with each of them to cut just four each day, only those with branches and trunks[41] that were straight and standing upright. They went off in the morning and returned at twilight, leaving a pile in the courtyard. I have a fence, and where there are openings there they shall mend. I had them cut bamboo, large and small,[42] using them for supports, and my lodging became a bit more secure. There are tigers in the mountains, but they recognize prohibitions. If they are to depend on the sharpness of their claws and teeth, they must always attack in the murky dark. By the walls of their houses, therefore, the people of Kuizhou plant rows of white chrysanthemums;[43] they make their walls of plaster, and reinforce them with bamboo: by this they demonstrate "fending off."[44] Because of being close to tigers, and mixed up with evil sorts, this sojourner worries about the kind that harms horses,[45] and merely to manage to survive is lucky: one can quietly sigh about this. I wrote this poem and gave it to Zongwu to read out.

---

ethnicity and less certain legal status. The Tang legal categories under which "debased" 賤 laborers were attached to the government or to private individuals are quite complicated, and since we have almost no information on Du Fu's relationship to most of the servants he mentions, there is little reason to go into detail here. Instead of speculating on the ethnicity or legal status of slaves other than those Du Fu identifies outright, therefore, I use the terms "servants" and "slaves" in this paper without any claim to precision. The legal boundaries between different gradations of servitude seem to have been quite porous, what was not porous was the distinction between "debased" and "fine" 良 status. For the Tang system of slavery and servitude, see Li Jiping, *Tangdai nubi*. For the development of the legal categories that defined slaves and servants in the period leading up to the Tang, see Hori Toshikazu's *Chūgoku kodai*. Chu Gansheng's *Nubi shi* contains a number of interesting anecdotes from diverse periods. In English, the institution of non-Han slavery in the Tang is discussed briefly in Schafer, *The Golden Peaches*, 40–47; and in Abramson, *Ethnic Identity*, 133–38.

39. Owen, *The Poetry of Du Fu*, vol. 5, 120–25; Xiao Difei, *Du Fu quanji*, vol. 8, 4556*ff*.
40. According to the *Zhou li* 周禮, one was supposed to cut trees from the north side of mountains in the summer and from the south side in the winter. *Zhouli zhushu*, 16.248.
41. The language here echoes the *Shi jing* poem "Banks of the Ru" 汝墳: "Along the banks of the Ru / I cut down the branches and the slender trunks" 遵彼汝墳，伐其條枚. *Mao shi zhushu*, 1.43. The *Song ben* text reads 校/枚 here, but this is clearly a copying error.
42. These two varieties of bamboo, *xiao* 篠 and *dang* 簜, are mentioned together in the "Tribute of Yu" chapter of the *Shangshu* 尚書. *Shangshu zhushu*, 6.82.
43. These white chrysanthemums, *baiju* 白菊, have occasioned a great deal of scholarly consternation, since it seems unlikely that the plant could be plastered up to make a wall; a number of variant characters have thus been suggested. The invocation of the Double Ninth Festival at the end of the poem, however, may perhaps suggest that chrysanthemums are indeed intended here. They may not, then, be plastered into the wall but may be planted in front of it.
44. "Fending off" derives from the *Shi jing*, "The People Are Heavily Burdened" 民勞, which also contains the phrase "evil sorts" from the next sentence: "Let us not indulge the wily and obsequious, / in order to restrain evil sorts. / And fend off robbers and bandits, / who act secretly and fear the light" 無縱詭隨，以謹無良，式遏寇虐，憯不畏明. *Mao shi zhushu* 17.630–31.
45. The "kind that harms horses" derives from a *Zhuangzi* parable wherein a herdboy tells the Yellow Emperor that governing the world is just like taking care of horses: "Just get rid of those things that harm horses" 亦去其害馬者而已矣. *Zhuangzi jishi*, 8.833.

	長夏無所為	Through the long summer there is nothing to do,
	客居課奴僕	lodging here, I set a task for my bondservants.
	清晨飯其腹	In the cool morning I fed their bellies;
4	持斧入白谷	then they took axes into White Valley.
	青冥曾巔後	After passing layered ridges into the dark blue sky,
	十里斬陰木	for ten leagues they chopped north-slope trees.
	人肩四根已	Each person shouldered four and then stopped,
8	亭午下山麓	and at noon they started down to the mountain's foot.
	尚聞丁丁聲	Even now I still hear sounds of chopping,[46]
	功課日各足	though each has fulfilled the task assigned him for the day.
	蒼皮成積委	The dark gray bark became a pile;
12	素節相照燭	their blemishless integrity shone on each other.
	藉汝跨小籬	I rely on you to go beyond my little fence;
	當仗苦虛竹	as for support, I must trouble hollow bamboo.[47]
	空荒咆熊羆	Bears roar in the deserted wilderness,
16	乳獸待人肉	and nursing beasts wait for human flesh.
	不示知禁情	If you do not show them the prohibitions they recognize,
	豈唯干戈哭	you will weep not only because of the war.
	城中賢府主	In the city the worthy governor
20	處貴如白屋	dwells in his high rank as if in a commoner's house.
	蕭蕭理體淨	He is strict, pure in the essentials of government,
	蜂蠆不敢毒	so that wasps and scorpions dare not sting.
	虎穴連里閭	But tiger lairs stretch right up to the villages,
24	隄防舊風俗	and defending against them is an old custom here.
	泊舟滄江岸	And in mooring my boat by the gray river's bank,
	久客慎所觸	long a traveler, I am cautious about what I might encounter.
	舍西崖嶠壯	West of my cottage the slope is high and steep,
28	雷雨蔚含蓄	thunder and rain have made dense cover there.
	牆宇資屢脩	Walls and roof need frequent repairs,
	衰年怯幽獨	and in my waning years I fear being alone.
	爾曹輕執熱	You all thought little of the persistent heat[48]
32	為我忍煩促	and on my behalf, endured vexation.
	秋光近青岑	Autumn light is approaching the green peaks:
	季月當泛菊	in fall's last month one should float chrysanthemums.[49]
	報之以微寒	I will repay you then in the light chill
36	共給酒一斛	by providing you all with a gallon of ale.

This is a difficult text, particularly the preface, with its affectation of an archaic imperial rhetoric modeled on the ancient *Classic of Documents*. This difficulty is worth keeping in mind when we consider the audiences Du Fu mentions here: his presumably illiterate servants and his young, likely undereducated son Zongwu, who is commissioned to

46. The phrase translated here as "chopping" comes from the *Shi jing* poem, "Felling Trees" 伐木: "We cut trees *ding-ding*; / the birds cry out *ying-ying*" 伐木丁丁，鳥鳴嚶嚶. *Mao shi zhushu*, 9.327.
47. Lines 9–14 are obscure and have occasioned numerous different interpretations.
48. "Persistent heat," *zhire* 執熱, is a phrase from the *Shi jing* poem, "Young Mulberry" 桑柔, but Du Fu frequently uses it in a sense different from its canonical interpretation in the *Mao-Zheng* edition of the Odes.
49. That is, on the Double Ninth Festival, the ninth day of the ninth month, when families and friends would climb to a high place, wear ailanthus, and float chrysanthemum petals in their ale.

read the poem out to these domestics in much the way that officials in the provinces declaimed imperial edicts to the local population.[50] The implication here is unmistakable: Du Fu is claiming for himself a kind of imperial centrality, as he orders the wilderness, assesses the contributions of his ministers, and disseminates Chinese civilization out to the barbarous southlands.[51] Yet this proffered vision of the poet-as-colonizer fails to account for the actual activity described in the poem, less the expansion of Chinese civilization than the poet himself following the local customs of Kuizhou. Equally importantly, the language's over-the-top archaism threatens to become unintelligible to those for whom was ostensibly written, rendering Du Fu's enactment of imperial prerogative a strange, mute farce. We can perhaps imagine how comical the scene must have been if Zongwu actually lined up the Du family domestics and struggled to read this document aloud to them.

Intelligibility is a problem as well with the other attempt the poem makes to connect its unpropitious matter back to elite culture: the poet's offer at the end of the poem to provide his hard-toiling slaves with a gallon of ale several months later. For Du Fu, the offer has a definite symbolic meaning, inviting his servants into the elite Chinese community that customarily congregated to drink chrysanthemum ale in celebration of the Double Ninth Festival. In effect, Du Fu is inviting them to become the equivalent for him of his long-separated family and friends, with whom he would normally expect to share a drink on that date. We can, however, doubt that these servants would have understood or particularly appreciated the gesture, especially since they probably did not know the poetic cliché that it enacts—one of the few clichés through which slaves could figure at all in Tang poetry—that, as Wang Wei 王維 (ca. 699–ca. 761) puts it, "In a distant land, friends and companions cut off, / the lonely traveler grows close with his servants" 他鄉絕儔侶，孤客親僮僕.[52] To them, the promise of a gallon of ale several months after the day they just spent toiling in the hot summer sun might have appeared rather meager.

Du Fu seems well aware of these problems, since the poem largely revolves around questions concerning the limitations of Chinese symbolic power. The archaizing preface, for example, is a winking attempt to cover up the poet's adaptation to the mores of an area he considers a cultural backwater, and his promise of fellowship and chrysanthemum ale attempts to mask the problems inherent in his position as an impoverished aristocrat and a merely nominal imperial officer, whose control over his slaves and servants was probably less easily assumed in Kuizhou than it had been in his youth. Du Fu's continued ability to keep and command slaves depended upon his connection to the empire, and thus most tangibly upon his patron in Kuizhou, Bai Maolin, whom the poem (perhaps with this problem in mind) praises here as being so virtuous that, within the area under his jurisdiction, even "wasps and scorpions dare not sting." Yet despite Bai's virtues, Du Fu seems less than fully certain of his safety, "sighing secretly"

---

50. Zongwu was probably around thirteen or fourteen at this time. Most of his life had been spent fleeing the calamities of the age; at most, he had had only about a year or so of relative stability around the age of five, when Du Fu was an official in the capital region, and then about five years of intermittent poverty and flight in Sichuan, when he might have devoted himself to the learning required of literati.

51. Du Fu also places himself in roughly the position of the emperor, vis-à-vis his "ministers," in "Xinxing Goes Far to Repair the Water-Tube" 信行遠修水筒. Owen, *The Poetry of Du Fu*, vol. 4, 170–73; Xiao Difei, *Du Fu quanji*, vol. 7, 13.3664–69.

52. Wang Wei, "Staying Over in Zhengzhou" 宿鄭州. *Quan Tang shi*, 125.1250. The general sentiment appears in several places in Tang verse.

about his fear that he lives among "evil sorts"—"the kind that harms horses," a phrase that can refer to tigers only through an ironic deflation of this traditional metaphor— and reinforcing his walls to protect against violent incursions. In this context, Du Fu's description of Bai as "living in high position as if it were a commoner's house" threatens to become ambiguous. The phrase's primary meaning is certainly its suggestion of Bai's humility and graciousness in his treatment of the poet. But given that Du Fu is working on reinforcing his own "commoner's house" here, it might perhaps suggest in an underhanded way that Bai too could become food for tigers—or fodder for the kind of local or ethnic uprising Du Fu had witnessed several times since the rebellion— whatever Chinese cultural virtues he might possess.

Tonally, then, this is one of Du Fu's most complex poems, alternately self-aggrandizing, self-mocking, self-pitying, generous, obtuse, confident in the beneficence of imperial patronage, and darkly foreboding about the possibility of revolt. Here we are far from the walled-off garden of the mid-Tang and from the comfortable or even transgressive humor of the private sphere—Du Fu is too aware of his dependence upon the empire, even in his physical distance from its center and his increasing recognition that imperial values may have little purchase on his Kuizhou existence. The poem's absurd imperial rhetoric, therefore, is not only a joke about the disconnect between the values Du Fu studied as a young man and the life he has come to live; it is also a recognition that his sons depend for their very safety upon the cultural learning their father has almost certainly had a hard time passing on to them throughout their lifetime of flight, poverty, and domestic labor.

催宗文樹雞柵 Urging Zongwen to Make Haste Setting Up a Chicken Coop[53]

	吾衰怯行邁	In my decline I fear long journeys,
	旅次展崩迫	so stopping a while, I relax from my rushing on.
	愈風傳烏雞	They say Silkie chickens are good for rheums,
4	秋卵方漫喫	but only in autumn can you indulge in eating their eggs.[54]
	自春生成者	Those that have been born since the spring, therefore,
	隨母向百翻	are about a hundred wings following their mothers.
	驅趁制不禁	We drove them off but couldn't keep them away,
8	喧呼山腰宅	and it was all racket at my mountainside house.
	課奴殺青竹	I thus gave my slave the task of drying green bamboo:
	終日憎赤幘	all day long we've hated their red turbans;[55]
	踏藉盤桉翻	Stomping about, the plates and table overturned,
12	塞蹊使之隔	we'll block their path and keep them away.
	牆東有隙地	East of the wall there is fallow land:
	可以樹高柵	there can we set up tall coops.
	避熱時來歸	At the moment, I've come home to escape the heat,
16	問兒所為跡	and ask my son how the work is going.

---

53. Owen, *The Poetry of Du Fu*, vol. 4, 172–77. Xiao Difei, *Du Fu quanji*, vol. 7, 13.3670–77.
54. This translation follows Zhao Cigong's note, to the effect that you should not eat the spring eggs because they will grow into chickens, the meat of which is good for one's health; you can eat the autumn eggs, though, because the chicks will not survive the winter. See Zhao Cigong, *Du shi*, 948.
55. The phrase "red turbans" derives from a Six Dynasties story, wherein a young scholar dreamed of seeing a man in a red turban, who turned out to be the human-like form of the rooster next door. See Gan Bao, *Sou shen ji*, 8.229–30.

織籠曹其內	Have a cage woven and put the flock inside,
令入不得擲	making them get in so they can't get away;
稀間可突過	If they can get through the openings,
20 觜爪還污席	they'll be back to soiling our mats with beaks and talons.
我寬螻蟻遭	We'll thus be spared disaster to ants and mole-crickets,
彼免狐貉厄	while they avoid calamity from foxes and raccoon dogs.
應宜各長幼	It would be right, moreover, if each, young and old,
24 自此均勍敵	from now on were equal in meeting opponents.[56]
籠柵念有脩	For the coop, think on its construction;
近身見損益	close at hand are examples of addition and subtraction.[57]
明明領處分	Clearly take the lead in giving orders,
28 一一當剖析	and every aspect you should analyze.
不昧風雨晨	We will henceforth not be in the dark on stormy mornings,[58]
亂離減憂慼	which should reduce our worries in this world in turmoil;
其流則凡鳥	And though their sort are but ordinary birds,
32 其氣心匪石	as for their temper, their minds are not stones.[59]
倚賴窮歲晏	Relying on them we can get through the end of the year;
撥煩去冰釋	dispelling bothers, which will disappear like ice melting.[60]
未似尸鄉翁	Yet I'm not yet quite like the old man of Shixiang,
36 拘留蓋阡陌	keeping them detained in the fields here.[61]

Like "Assessing the Cutting of Trees," this poem is quite obscure in parts, to the point that the seventeenth-century commentator Huang Sheng 黄生 calls it "the strangest poem in all of Du Fu."[62] The basic structure of the verse, however, is clarified by its similarity to the poems we have examined to this point. Again, Du Fu is creating a miniature empire down in his Kuizhou hermitage, trying to remediate the chaos and civil war that are plaguing his backyard. In his directions to Zongwen, who is to "take charge of" his

---

56. That is, the young should be put in a separate coop so they will not be picked on by the adults.
57. Commentators hear in this line an echo of the *Analects*: "The Shang dynasty used Xia ritual, and what they added and subtracted can be known; the Zhou used Shang ritual, and what they added or subtracted can be known; thus whatever dynasty follows the Zhou, even if it is one hundred generations away, can be known in advance" 殷因於夏禮，所損益，可知也；周因於殷禮，所損益，可知也；其或繼周者，雖百世可知也。 *Lunyu zhushu*, 2.19. The humorous point would be that Zongwen can look at neighbors' coops to design his own "chicken empire."
58. This line alludes to the *Shi jing* poem "Wind and Rain" 風雨: "Although the wind and rain be dark, / the roosters do therefore not stop crowing for dawn" 風雨如晦，雞鳴不已。 *Mao shi zhushu*, 4.179.
59. This line alludes again to the *Shi jing*, this time to "Cypress Boat" 柏舟: "My heart is not a stone, / it cannot be rolled away" 我心匪石，不可轉也。 *Mao shi zhushu*, 2.74. The phrase "ordinary birds," *fan niao* 凡鳥, can also be understood as a visual pun on its opposite: *feng* 鳳, "phoenix," the least ordinary of birds.
60. This line is obscure; var. 及/去, attested in the *Song ben* and chosen by Owen, makes for easier sense. It is also possible that Du Fu is saying, in a highly compressed way, that his "long journeys" of line 1 will continue when the ice melts next year: "dispelling bothers until we leave when the ice melts."
61. The "old man of Shixiang" was an immortal mentioned in the *Liexian zhuan* 列仙傳 who had several thousand chickens. He let them all roost at night in the trees and let them wander freely in the daytime. But since he had given each one a name, they would come when he called. Liu Xiang, *Liexian zhuan*, 1.30.
62. See Xiao Difei, *Du Fu quanji*, vol. 7, 13.3675. Note, however, that the version of this poem printed in the *Huang Sheng quanji* edition of Huang's "Du shi shuo" 杜詩説 lacks this comment. Huang Sheng, *Huang Sheng quanji*, 82–83. Other traditional commentators were divided on the merits of the poem. Wang Sishi, who was often critical of Du Fu's poetry on domestic topics, thought that "one who is concerned with accomplishing great things should not be so petty" 蓋成大事者不宜小察. Wang Sishi, *Du yi*, 7.249. Lu Yuanchang 盧元昌 (b. 1616), by contrast, says that the poem "manifests Du Fu's utmost benevolence and complete righteousness" 篇中亦見仁至義盡. Lu Yuanchang, *Du shi chan* 22.13.

minor officials—the family's servants and slaves—Du Fu envisions turning the destruc-
tive bug-eating predators of "Ballad of the Bound Chicken" ("Fu ji xing" 縛雞行) into
virtuous subjects, possessed of the constancy and diligence predicated of gentlemen
in the *Shi jing*.[63] Du Fu is thus preparing his son to take over from him the inheritance
of Chinese culture and its civilizing responsibility, which he can perhaps be seen as
inculcating in the boy by means of the poem's elaborate classical allusions.

By now, however, we recognize easily how absurd these allusions are, applied to
chickens, the reference to the *Shi jing* poem "Wind and Rain" ("Fengyu" 風雨) in line 29,
for example, performing a characteristically droll deflation of high-cultural language by
taking literally its use of chickens as a metaphor for higher virtues. Du Fu's attempts to
link coop construction with empire building seem, in fact, a bit too comic to take them
as anything much more than a learned joke—that is, up until the final couplet, which
performs the sort of reorienting twist we observed above in "The Garden Officer Sends
Vegetables." In this final couplet, Du Fu's self-deprecating comparison of his care of
chickens to that of the "old man of Shixiang"—who let his birds roam freely, confident
they would come when called—is interesting enough in itself, insofar as it suggests
that the construction of a "chicken empire," with its cages and enforced hierarchies, is
perhaps less optimal than the attainment of a state wherein such structures would be
unnecessary. More distressing to Zongwen, however, would have been the other way
in which his father does not match up to the old man of Shixiang: unlike the latter, Du
Fu is mortal. This twist is prepared in the first four lines of the poem, which discuss
both the rootlessness of his lodging here in Kuizhou and also his chronic illnesses, both
of which bear particularly threatening implications for Zongwen, who probably could
not expect continued patronage from imperial representatives once his father passed
away. If Du Fu's situation in Kuizhou was precarious, as we observed in "Assessing the
Cutting of Trees," that of his family was even more so, since little other than their patri-
arch's ability to produce elegant poetry for Bai Maolin's social occasions stood between
them and destitution in an area of the empire where they had no property and few
relatives. The poem's injunction that Zongwen think of his domestic chores in terms of
high-cultural precedents is thus simultaneously absurd and potentially quite serious.
These domestic tasks are necessary to preserve the family's lives now; the high-cultural
precedents will be necessary later, when Du Fu is gone.

Lacking any tangible property to pass on to his children, Du Fu's only significant
patrimony is the cultural capital encoded in his verse. And yet, he is intensely aware that
his precarious and impoverished situation makes his attempts to pass on this cultural
capital problematic. Elite Chinese fathers did not normally write poetry to their children
about the right way to build chicken coops; as is the case with cultural capital the world
over, they generally could assume that the milieus in which they lived and operated
did much of the training for them.[64] Du Fu, however, has only a limited opportunity in
Kuizhou to demonstrate high-cultural values through his own activity, and his children

---

63. Owen, *The Poetry of Du Fu*, vol. 5, 28–31; Xiao Difei, *Du Fu quanji*, vol. 8, 15.4350.
64. On this topic, see Du Fu's early poem, "Climbing the Wall-Tower at Yanzhou" 登兗州城樓, wherein Du
    Fu speaks of visiting his father at his official post in Yanzhou as "days of rushing through the yard."
    Owen, *The Poetry of Du Fu*, vol. 1, 4–5. Xiao Difei, *Du Fu quanji*, vol. 1, 1.8–9. The line alludes to a story of
    Confucius's relationship with his son, recorded in the *Lunyu*, with the moral that "the gentleman keeps
    his sons at a distance" 又聞君子之遠其子也. *Lunyu zhushu*, 16.150. Lacking an official post in Kuizhou, this
    was a cultural ideal to which he could hardly aspire in his own parenting.

probably have fewer resources, and more menial domestic responsibilities, than he did when he was a child. The decision to write to his children about these domestic matters is thus both a solution to the problem of the family's displacement from high-cultural society and inevitably a subversion of that solution.

Conclusion

Du Fu's sons were not the only heirs of his problematic legacy. Both the mid-Tang writers of private subjectivity and the millennium of commentators who have seen Du Fu as holding together worlds that in other poetry had come apart take something from his juxtapositions of high-cultural ideals to domestic affairs: the former picking up on his recognition of the incongruities between these two realms, the latter on his understanding of the depth to which empire reached down into realms of experience its rhetoric usually ignored. Yet the full complexity of his self-consciousness in these poems has not, I think, been generally recognized by either his poetic or critical heirs. In this respect, Du Fu's evident concern for his legacy in "Urging Zongwen" and other poems addressed to his sons seems to have been prescient. His engagement with the cultural tradition was both too hollowed out and too rich to be simply passed on.

In these poems, and in several other verses on domestic affairs that he wrote in Kuizhou, Du Fu's relationship to the empire has become inescapably ironic. As soon as he seeks to assert his continued connection with high-cultural values, he recognizes the absurdity of his overreach; and as soon as he recognizes the absurdity of his overreach, he acknowledges the subtler and often darker ways in which he remains dependent upon imperial hierarchies. A garden or a chicken coop can be only an ironic empire, but the ironies of laughing about the absurdity of these attempts to ennoble humble household economy rebound upon the insecurity of Du Fu's position in Kuizhou, leaving these poems endlessly shifting between tragedy and comedy. Du Fu can neither locate himself securely within the public world nor escape into a securely private sphere. And so he remains, for now, in an in-between space that mirrors the liminality of his position on the margins of the empire, both a slaveholder and an exile, on a journey ostensibly homeward that he in fact continually delayed.

Within Du Fu's corpus, these poems fit into a narrative of the poet's evolving thoughts about the empire over the course of his life. This narrative ends in 770, with his death from fever in Hunan, but it does not arrive at a final resolution of the complexities we have tracked here. If there is an inheritance we can value in these poems, then, beyond the enjoyment of their exquisite weirdness, it is most likely not to be found either in a final adherence to or rejection of the medieval Chinese empire's claims upon the individual. Instead, it will be found in Du Fu's ability to recognize, where his contemporaries generally did not, the gaps, absurdities, and injustices in ideologies to which he credited the relative peace and prosperity of his youth, upon which he remained dependent in his old age, and which were built into the elite, hegemonic art he had dedicated his life to practicing.

Section II

Poetry and Buddhism

5
Refuges and Refugees
How Du Fu Writes Buddhism

Paul Rouzer

In most survey histories of Chinese Buddhism, scholars will point out that the earliest mention of the faith in belletristic literature is the following couplet from Zhang Heng's 張衡 (78–139) "Western Metropolis Rhapsody" ("Xi jing fu" 西京賦). After evoking the beauty of dancing girls for twenty lines, the author adds:

展季桑門	Even Zhan Ji or a *śramana*—
誰能不營	no one—could not but be deluded.[1]

This little moment is cited as a reference for a straightforward empirical history of the faith in China. But no one points out some of the more interesting features of these lines. For one thing, there is the irony: the first mention of a Buddhist ascetic (*śramana*) in Chinese literature occurs in a genre often criticized for its descriptive excess and its evocation of sensual pleasures. Not only that, but it suggests that the beauty of native Chinese women could make a foreign holy man abandon the main quality that defines him: his self-control. This would not be a bad starting point for discussing the problematics of an ascetic imperative in literature and how Buddhist discourse may interact with certain Chinese *aesthetic* principles already present (in this case, the distrust of surface language and the representation of moral character in verse). These issues may create paradoxes in certain authors' works—in the poetry of Jia Dao 賈島 (779–843), for instance: an avowed Buddhist who nonetheless arouses suspicion for indulging in the superficial charm of couplet craft.

However, I would like to point out a more interesting aspect of these lines. We cannot know how much Zhang Heng knew about Buddhism; though there were Buddhist communities already present in China during his life (in Luoyang and Pengcheng, in particular), they received little attention in written records. The most likely scenario here is that Zhang Heng had heard vague legends concerning Buddhist holy men and had taken note of the foreign word *śramana* (here represented by the phonetic *sangmen* 桑門—later changed to *shamen* 沙門) as a bit of exotica, a flashy rhapsody-type gesture that would attest to the breadth of his learning. It is also linked here with a Chinese

1.   Xiao Tong, *Wen xuan*, 2.79. Translation from Knechtges, *Wen xuan*, vol. 1, 237.

example of self-restraint—Zhan Ji is better known as Liuxia Hui 柳下惠, a figure from the seventh century BCE. As David Knechtges describes him in his note to this line:

> The Mao commentary to *Mao shi* 200 (*Mao shi zhushu* 12.3.20b) and the *Kongzi jiayu* (2.21b-22a), most likely based on the Mao commentary, obliquely refer to the story of Liuxia Hui's allowing a homeless woman to sit on his lap all night without any aspersions being cast on his reputation.[2]

By linking a paragon of Confucian self-restraint with a Buddhist one, Zhang Heng covers the field, as it were—combining a figure from antiquity with a figure from far away. The girls are so lovely they can defeat exemplars of self-control from anywhere in time and space, as if a Victorian poet were to mention that a woman's beauty could have confounded Seneca on the one hand and an Indian holy man on the other.

This also introduces us to a fundamental issue involving literary references to the Buddhist faith throughout the medieval period. As knowledge of Buddhism spread among the Chinese elites and sutras were translated in increasingly accurate ways, a new vocabulary was introduced: Buddhist technical terms were rendered either as Chinese phonetic equivalents of Sanskrit originals (as with *śramaṇa*) or as "meaning" equivalents (for example, the use of *kong* 空 to translate *śūnyatā*, "emptiness"). Both methods have their problems: the former end up sounding exotic and un-Chinese, while the latter can easily result in the superficial assimilation of complex Buddhist ideas into a native Chinese discourse—particularly an emerging Daoist one. When one talks about the impact of this vocabulary on belletristic, non-Buddhist writing, curious problems result. If a writer uses the Sanskrit vocabulary, he often creates a sense of exoticism—or if the term has been completely assimilated into ordinary usage, it triggers an explicit Buddhist meaning that may seem at odds with the native literary traditions that the genre tends to express. If an author uses native vocabulary with Buddhist associations in a genre that is not normally religious, then his meaning may be unclear (or it creates the possibility of reading Buddhist meanings into a text where it was not intended). Perhaps the most noted example of this is the frequent use of *kong* in Wang Wei's 王維 (ca. 699–ca. 761) poems: it is unclear whether we are meant to see such references as a primary or even as a secondary reference to *śūnyatā*.

This is the central problem when writing about Buddhism and Chinese literature, if by Chinese literature we mean genres outside of technical Buddhist discourse (sutras, śāstras, gāthās, etc.). The Tang elite poetic tradition is a strong example of this. If, on the one hand, one discovers examples of explicit Buddhist language in elite poetry, one must remember that this may be introduced mainly for reasons of rhetorical effectiveness and not as a straightforward representation of the poet's preoccupation with religious concerns (which usually cannot be clearly reconstituted outside of the text). If, on the other hand, we argue that a Buddhist worldview is subtly influencing the aesthetics of a poem with no explicit Buddhist content, we may have difficulty proving it (I think here of writings by both Stephen Owen and Shan Chou that suggest that "mysterious closure" in Wang Wei is the result of an early High Tang fascination with nonexplicit endings as a reaction against the explicit emotional response characteristic of Early Tang verse).[3] Analyzing Buddhist effects and their impact on general writing is not an impossible task: Xiaofei Tian, for instance, has made an excellent argument for

---

2. Knechtges, *Wen xuan*, vol. 1, 236.
3. See Owen, *The Great Age*, 38–39, 57–58; and Chou, "Beginning with Images," 117–37, especially 119–21.

how Buddhist phenomenology comes to influence representation of physical surfaces in sixth-century verse.[4] But it is a difficult aspect to pin down. In modern scholarship, this difficulty is accentuated by two further factors: first, the general tendency in the Chinese reading tradition to ignore the Buddhist element in literature; and, second, the modern propensity to see Chan 禪 Buddhism as a sort of Chinese-friendly, intellectually sophisticated version of the faith that is free of "religious superstition" and thus compatible with elite aesthetic values (hence, the large number of works with titles like "Chan and Chinese literature" in academic writing). This latter tendency is particularly problematic, because it is rarely tied to any deep sensitivity to the historical factors that created the movement, factors that were still incipient and unclear through most of the Tang. Modern scholars, like the late John McRae, have spent decades pointing out how our modern view of Chan is a retroactive creation by later practitioners and that it does not start to take on familiar form until the late tenth century.[5] Thus, we cannot assume that when Wang Wei or Du Fu uses the word *chan* in a poem or alludes to the early patriarchs that he has this sort of full-grown vision of the movement in his head. Nor can we safely claim that one of their poems feels "channish" in this sense (either in its themes or in its images). Rather, there is a shared group of images and concepts already present in medieval Buddhist writing that entered later discourse, and those same images and concepts can be present in "secular" literature. Because they are expressed in vocabulary that can also express non-Buddhist ideas, we have to consider many different aspects before we can evaluate the impact of Buddhism in each individual case — and in many situations, such an evaluation must remain tentative. The social function of the poem can help in this respect: Who is the recipient of the poem (a monk associate or friend, for instance)? What are the circumstances for the poem's composition (most obviously, is it a "temple-visiting" poem)? Is Buddhist terminology employed more for rhetorical effect, or does it seem to have a bearing on what the poem is doing overall? And, even if we answer these questions positively, we should probably also keep in mind that the situational and social nature of Tang verse means we are seeing a performance of Buddhism in a single poem or occasion and not necessarily a representation of the author's daily concerns.

Before we turn to Du Fu, it might be instructive to note that the social and contextual presence of Buddhism in even such an obviously Buddhist poet as Wang Wei has been somewhat neglected. For most modern readers, Wang Wei is at his most "Buddhist" when he is writing as a seemingly lonely and isolated ascetic in search of greater truths (cf. for example frequently anthologized poems like "Visiting the Temple of Incense Amassed" ["Guo Xiangji si" 過香積寺]).[6] However, to gauge the role of Buddhism in Wang Wei's daily life and how that gets reflected in verse, one might turn to somewhat less well-known poems:

飯覆釜山僧	Feeding the Monks of Fufu Mountain
晚知清淨理	In old age I understand the principles of purity;
日與人群疏	daily I grow apart from the crowd.
將候遠山僧	I waited for these monks from the distant hills,
先期掃敝廬	sweeping my shabby hut before their appointed coming.

---

4. Tian, *Beacon Fire*, 233–59.
5. See especially McRae's *Seeing through Zen*.
6. Wang Wei, *Wang Youcheng ji*, 131–32.

果從雲峰裏	As expected, they come from their cloudy peak
顧我蓬蒿居	to visit me in my overgrown dwelling.
藉草飯松屑	Sitting on the grass, they dine on pine nuts;
焚香看道書	burning incense, they look through books on the Way.
燃燈晝欲盡	The lamps are lit as day draws to an end;
鳴磬夜方初	the temple chimes are struck at the beginning of the night.
一悟寂為樂	At once awakened to the joy of Stillness,
此生閑有餘	I have more than enough leisure for this life.
思歸何必深	A desire to retire—why must it be serious?
身世猶空虛	for both self and world are truly empty.[7]

The Buddhist laity are expected to provide food for the monastic community. Wang Wei uses that obligation as the topic of his poem but also combines this with some common conventions of the poetic tradition.

The poem begins as a typical Wang Wei verse celebrating his life as a recluse and does not hint at Buddhist content at all. This existence is then interrupted by a visit from outsiders. Ordinarily, these would be friends still living a secular existence; a situation would be introduced that contrasts public life with the joys of private retirement. However, Wang shifts the poem to a Buddhist context: he becomes a layman-patron, providing a modest vegetarian feast for some monks (the visiting outsiders). This allows him to reinterpret a Buddhist social obligation in ways that draw upon other traditions. Ordinarily, lay feasts would be celebrated in somewhat more luxurious terms—an evocation of the layman's generous act of donation to a community that has withdrawn from society in order to benefit all sentient beings. Here, however, Wang Wei symbolically offers an ascetic diet of pine nuts, the sort of food consumed by Daoist Transcendents (*xian* 仙). The Daoist associations are cultivated further by the situation: the poet himself purifies his surroundings in anticipation of their arrival, and they "descend" to him from the mountain peaks. However, once they arrive, they adopt the role of more traditional recluses. Wang Wei provides a space for them to worship but also a place to read. Note that the monks are not chanting sutras—they are looking through Books on the Way (which can ambiguously refer to all sorts of philosophies and faiths). These monks are not just monks but fellow recluses and friends, and their actions at Wang Wei's modest dwelling have a certain companionable nature to them. Wang Wei is attempting to resituate them within a discourse of non-Buddhist reclusion. Yet the ending reinforces a Buddhist message while also strongly asserting the poet's own role as a lay believer who is capable of profitable practice on his own. He has a moment of enlightenment ("At once awakened to the joy of Stillness"); and as a result, he illustrates his own personal transcendence of duality by recognizing that he can carry this awareness of emptiness into his everyday actions, whether they take place in the private or public realm. He has succeeded in combining elements of secular reclusion, Daoist transcendence, Buddhist lay obligations, and Mahayana philosophical nonduality all within one poem.

Even less popular but more attuned to contemporary Buddhist attitudes is a series of poems Wang wrote to a friend, a certain "Layman Hu" (Hu *jushi* 胡居士), when both Hu and the poet himself were suffering from illness.[8] In each of these difficult verses,

---

7. Wang Wei, *Wang Youcheng ji*, 39.
8. Wang Wei, *Wang Youcheng ji*, 30–33.

Wang Wei lectures the recipient with elaborate analyses of nonduality from a mainstream Mahayana viewpoint. Each is filled with doctrinal vocabulary:

一興微塵念	Once you give rise to thoughts of the trivial, dusty world,
橫有朝露身	you suddenly possess a body as fragile as the morning dew.
如是觀陰界	But if you look at the skandhas and the dhatus this way,[9]
何方置我人	nothing prevents you from creating Self and Other.
礙有固為主	Obstructed by Being, you definitely create the Subjective;
趣空寧捨賓	inclining towards Emptiness, how can you cast off the Objective?[10] (ll. 1–6)

This sample gives us a sense of how complex Wang Wei can make his Buddhist rhetoric; passages like this are hardly comprehensible to modern readers without considerable annotation. It is not a great surprise that these poems are not part of the Wang Wei canon, bordering as they do on versified philosophical discourse. But they do represent a world where the poet had friends who could understand and appreciate such verse easily. There may even be a certain humor derived from the context: since the poet is writing to a sick friend, he certainly would have had in mind the example of Vimalakīrti, the brilliant layman who feigned illness as a skillful means to lecture the Buddha's disciples on nonduality and the illusory nature of existence.

In other poems as well as in his prose, Wang Wei uses a Buddhist-inflected social occasion to combine Buddhist rhetoric and vocabulary with more distinctly Chinese elements. In "Stone Gate Monastery at Indigo Field Mountain" ("Langtian shan Shimen jingshe" 藍田山石門精舍), for example, he turns a temple-visiting poem into a rewrite of the Peach Blossom Spring narrative, thus deliberately confusing monks with an inaccessible utopian community and playing again on the association of Buddhist monks with Daoist Transcendents.[11]

These examples suggest that we cannot really estimate the impact of Buddhism on mainstream Chinese literature without careful attention to social context and to the play of allusion. This allows us to see Buddhism not as a previously alien philosophical system that impacts the aesthetics of the culture but rather as forms of practice and belief that gradually developed within daily life and became part of the shared language of the educated elite. In such a context, the nature of an individual's belief or the form it takes may not necessarily be inferred from Buddhist-inflected statements made in a text.[12] For Tang dynasty poets, we should note more the degree to which Buddhist activities formed a part of ordinary existence. To evaluate this praxis, we can, for example, note the relative emphasis that individual poets placed on it and how much of it appears in their writings in comparison to activities broadly associated with non-Buddhist traditions. In this sense we can thus think of Wang Wei with some justification as a Buddhist poet, because we can trace the network of friendships and associations that emerge in his literary works, as well as the ease with which he uses Buddhist terminology. Likewise, we can look carefully at the way Buddhist tropes and concepts emerge in

---

9. *Skandha* refers to the various forms of sensory perception and mental processes that lead to the illusory belief in the self. *Dhatu* here refers to various realms created by the interaction of the senses with sensory perceptions.
10. From Wang Wei, "Having Fallen Sick with Layman Hu, I Sent These Poems to Him and Also Showed Them to Some Fellow Students" 與胡居士皆病寄此詩兼示學人. Wang Wei, *Wang Youcheng ji*, 31.
11. Wang Wei, *Wang Youcheng ji*, 33–34.
12. The question of how to define "belief" in the Buddhist tradition (even what it means to be a Buddhist in the Tang) is a complex one and cannot be covered in detail here. See, for example, Lopez, "Belief."

poets who seem less likely to foreground Buddhism in their works—for them, aspects of practice and belief may constitute part of their daily experience without the faith becoming the dominant factor in their worldview.

And so we can turn finally to the issue of Du Fu and Buddhism—or, more accurately and more clumsily, "Du Fu's surviving poems and a collection of images, vocabulary, and concepts that may or may not be Buddhist, usually depending on the context in which they are used." To my mind, the most constructive approach is not to view Buddhist elements in Du Fu's poetry as an unfailingly clear guide to some sort of inner life, or commitment to the faith, but rather as part of a poet's toolbox, used to create an effective poem (though aspects of religious sincerity may still be an essential element). It is important in this respect to not fall victim to overly simple autobiographical readings. Though Du Fu's work itself became the prime and earliest example of how one might gain a complete autobiography of a poet through reading his works, we should note that his Buddhist-related poems are almost all occasional verse, often addressed to monk associates. Social interaction (including the requirements of etiquette or even simply the desire to bond with a good friend here) tends to work in creative tension with self-expression. The poems may still be autobiographical, but they are filtered through the relationship created between poet and recipient.

The level of Du Fu's engagement with Buddhism tends to vary widely from poem to poem. As might be expected, most common are temple-visiting poems that might make only passing reference to the religious nature of the sites he celebrates. It is not unusual in such cases to restrict Buddhist terminology or statement of faith to the opening and closing couplets. The opening poem in Du Fu's collection is a good example of this, a model he would follow repeatedly later:

遊龍門奉先寺 Visiting Fengxian Temple at Longmen

已從招提遊	I had already visited the temple
更宿招提境	and went on to stay over in the temple precincts.
陰壑生虛籟	Shadowy ravines produced piping from empty spaces,
月林散清影	the moonlit forests scattered their clear shadows.
天闕象緯逼	Constellations' woof pressed close on Heaven's towers,
雲臥衣裳冷	lying in the clouds, my clothes were cold.
欲覺聞晨鐘	About to be awakened, I heard the dawn bell
令人發深省	which brought out in me deep awareness.[13]

Mysterious and unearthly though the middle couplets are, it is unlikely that they contain coded messages for the specifically Buddhist reader. Occasionally, the visiting poem does engage with Buddhist content to a greater extent, as in this poem, written during his sojourn in Chengdu:

望牛頭寺　　Gazing at Oxhead Temple

牛頭見鶴林	I see a Crane Grove at Oxhead,
梯徑繞幽深	the stepped path circles into deep, secluded spots.
春色浮山外	Spring's colors float beyond the mountain,
天河宿殿陰	the Milky Way spends the night in the great hall's shadow.

---

13. Qiu Zhaoao, *Du shi xiangzhu*, 1. Owen, *The Poetry of Du Fu*, vol. 1, 2–3. I will use Owen's translations throughout the discussion that follows.

傳燈無白日	They transmit the lamp without regard for the daylight,
布地有黃金	spread out on the ground is yellow gold.
休作狂歌老	Cease to be a wildly singing old man,
迴看不住心	turn to look on the non-abiding mind.[14]

Specifically Buddhist content allows for some clever parallelism—the glittering white and yellow of the third couplet, for instance, evokes both the power of the lamp-trans-mission image (this is a lamp that is bright always, not just at night) and the reverence of laypeople who have gifted the monastery. But these are of a piece with the non-Buddhist images and are meant more as a display of poetic art (and are somewhat over-shadowed by the brilliance of the beautiful fourth line). The ending is perhaps more compelling than most conventional "I should give up this world and become a monk" endings in that it alludes specifically to Du Fu's vocation as a self-conscious poet. The mad singer as moral critic has a long pedigree in Chinese literature dating back to the figure of Jieyu in the *Analects*, and it strongly asserts Du Fu's role as a sort of antisocial participant in society. To suggest that he contemplated, even in an occasional verse, surrendering this role to one of quiet Buddhist contemplation is unusual and striking, though still perhaps a conventional gesture.

A completely different use of Buddhism can be seen in the late poem "Ballad of Two Temples, Marchmount Foothill and Daolin" ("Yuelushan Daolin ersi xing" 嶽麓山道林二寺行).[15] This is in some ways a glorious expansion of the Zhang Heng view of Buddhism, in which Du Fu displays his erudition, combining native Chinese kennings with obscure Buddhist allusion:

地靈步步雪山草	The place is numinous, at every step are plants of the Himalayas,
僧寶人人滄海珠	every one of these precious monks is a pearl of the dark sea.
塔劫宮牆壯麗敵	Their pagodas and compound walls are matched in glorious beauty,
香廚松道清涼俱	fragrant kitchens and paths through pines, together in pure coolness.
蓮花交響共命鳥	Among lotus blossoms cross echoes of the jīvajīvaka bird,
金牓雙迴三足烏	golden plaques in pairs bring back the three-footed crow. (ll. 7–12)

This is entertaining but still relatively superficial. Perhaps the most intriguing aspect is Du Fu's transference of Indian sacred geography to China—the sort of move in literary terms that finds its counterpart in the establishment of sacred residences for Avalokiteśvara and Mañjuśrī within Chinese borders. However, one may perceive that Du Fu is largely showing off to his Buddhist friends with lines like these by demon-strating his ability to incorporate fantastic Indian imagery within the scope of Chinese descriptive language.

A much more satisfying poetic encounter with the faith might be found in a cycle of four relatively early poems, written while Du Fu was still trapped in the capital during the early years of the rebellion: "Reverend Zan's Chambers in Great Cloud Temple" ("Dayun si Zangong fang sishou" 大雲寺贊公房四首).[16] I see this group of poems as belonging to a subgenre in Du Fu's oeuvre that might be called "refuge" poems—poems

---

14. Qiu Zhaoao, *Du shi xiangzhu*, 990. Owen, *The Poetry of Du Fu*, vol. 3, 208–11.
15. Qiu Zhaoao, *Du shi xiangzhu*, 1986–89. Owen, *The Poetry of Du Fu*, vol. 6, 96–97.
16. Qiu Zhaoao, *Du shi xiangzhu*, 333–38. Owen, *The Poetry of Du Fu*, vol. 1, 268–75.

that describe how he finds a temporary refuge with friends or with charitable strangers in times of unrest. At least two of his most famous poems can be said to belong to this group: "Pengya: A Ballad" ("Pengya xing" 彭衙行) and "Presented to the Recluse Wei" ("Zeng Wei ba chushi" 贈衛八處士).[17] Some of them were possibly composed as gifts to the people who assisted him.

The Reverend Zan sequence performs this same gesture against the context of a "temple-visiting" poem. But here Du Fu writes not simply as a Buddhist practitioner (or even curious outsider) who discovers peace and quiet in temple surroundings. Rather, he comes to find companionship and assistance with his monk friend, in spite of the pressures of life in the seemingly real world. Friendship then becomes a major theme in this group, and Reverend Zan is someone whose peculiar position as a member of the Buddhist clergy can supply the poet with additional comfort beyond that granted by an ordinary secular associate. One might see underlying this poem a standard Buddhist term, *gui yi* (皈依 or 歸依): the act of taking refuge in the three treasures of Buddha, dharma, and sangha. Du Fu thus merges two types of refuge into one. But, as we shall see, this combination of genres produces a complicated dynamic. Is Reverend Zan merely a friend, and is the temple simply the dwelling within which the duties and bonds of friendship are enacted? Or is Reverend Zan a spiritual mentor—even a bodhisattva? And, in that case, is the monastery a place of spiritual refuge as well, the numinous site where the poet can be refreshed spiritually as well as physically? These two roles create a tension in the poem—and while Du Fu suggests in his images and language that the Buddhist aspect of refuge is very much part of his experience, this aspect is undermined to a certain extent by a sort of dissonant voice that reasserts secular concerns.[18]

The four poems are highly sophisticated in the way they lay out the progress of Du Fu's visit. In the first, Du Fu is seen passing through one gate after another to arrive at the center of peace (and the place where his friend awaits him). In the second, Zan presents him with a gift of clothing, and the two bond over an act of aesthetic appreciation: they observe a painting of dragons by the noted Tang artist Wu Daozi 吳道子. The third portrays Du Fu's night at the temple. In the last verse he leaves and thanks his host for a temporary respite from his troubles.

The first poem carries out the beginning of this narrative effectively: it starts by noting the difference between inner and outer, thus marking Du Fu's entrance into the monastery; but it does so by suggesting a potential union of mental and physical states. Since the poet's mind already contains the Buddha nature, it already exists in a realm of purity.[19] His exterior self is less fortunate, as it encounters a soaking from the seasonal spring rain (even though this rain brings fertility, and, as we shall see, nourishing and purifying water becomes a recurring motif in the poems). Du Fu's first action, then, is to bring his physical form into that same realm of purity by entering the monastery proper—a world of calm order with its rules and schedules:

---

17. Qiu Zhaoao, *Du shi xiangzhu*, 413–17, 512–14. Owen, *The Poetry of Du Fu*, vol. 1, 348–53; vol. 2, 72–75.

18. In this sense, I see these poems as an inversion of what I believe the Cold Mountain poems are doing. In those, the ideal reader or *zhiyin* becomes the Buddhist believer who reads unchanging reality through the "skillful means" employed by the bodhisattva-poet. See Rouzer, *On Cold Mountain*, 57–65.

19. This was already a commonly accepted aspect of Buddha nature (*tathāgatagarbha*) doctrine: that the main problem for unenlightened believers is their inability to recognize that they are already enlightened, at least potentially.

I.

心在水精域	The mind lies within a realm of crystal,
衣霑春雨時	while my clothes are soaked by spring rain.
洞門盡徐步	I pace slowly through the series of gates,
深院果幽期	in the deep courtyard plans for seclusion are realized.
到扉開復閉	Every door I come to opens and closes again,
撞鐘齋及茲	the struck bell means that meal time is now.

Dongmen 洞門 in line 3 may be a particularly important term here, with its suggestion of hidden depths and mysteries (as in *dongtian* 洞天, the term for Daoist grotto heavens). "Plans for seclusion" (*youqi* 幽期) also has connotations beyond Buddhism in its portrayal of escape from the world and the adoption of a hermit life—though here its sense of "appointment" is also present: it refers to his imminent encounter with his friend Reverend Zan. By introducing hints of Daoist Transcendents, he reinforces the numinous power of the monastery grounds themselves. These lines bring up what will be the most important thematic trend in the poems: the fact that refuge and rest can only coexist uneasily with the numinous.

For the time being, though, material needs manifest themselves. The mention of mealtime allows the poet to make a witty allusion to spiritual nourishment—he is fed in both senses:

醍醐長發性	The ghee always brings forth the [Buddha] nature,
飲食過扶衰	with food and drink he goes overboard taking care of my frailty.

Spiritual concerns merge with material ones, and the language of Buddhism merges with the language of friendship; Zan enters as primary caretaker for the refugee.

As the poem moves into a passage of conventional parallel description, Du notes that birds have come to find refuge in the temple as well, perhaps wishing (like Du Fu) to get out of the rain. The monastery supplies a shelter for all sentient beings; clasping of arms creates an interwoven pattern reinforced by the grillwork on the doors:

把臂有多日	We have clasped arms for many a day,
開懷無愧辭	so we unburden our feelings with no polite phrases.
黃鸝度結構	Yellow orioles cross over the structures,
紫鴿下罘罳	purple doves descend to the door's grillwork.
愚意會所適	My mind here finds what suits me,
花邊行自遲	I naturally walk slowly beside the flowers.

Finally, in the last couplet we have Buddhist practitioner fully fused with literary friend, as the poet alludes to the world of intellectual interaction between cultivated monks and their lay companions in the Six Dynasties. The poet associates Reverend Zan with just such a literary monk, Tang Huixiu 湯惠休 (fl. mid-fifth century); and like such monks, he now participates in Du Fu's world of secular poetry composition. He even seems to be one of the poet's fans:

湯休起我病	This Tang Huixiu makes my illness better
微笑索題詩	and with a smile asks me for a poem.

However, Zan also knows that eliciting a poem from the poet will make him feel better by drawing him into an activity that he loves. In this case, he is administering the "dharma medicine" to Du Fu as a sort of skillful means—he is the sensitive bodhisattva who knows that what this suffering being needs is a good poem exchange. The equation of Buddhas and bodhisattvas as doctors is of course common in the sutra literature.

In the second poem, Du Fu begins by focusing on Zan's gift of clothes:

II.

細軟青絲履	Fine and soft, green thread slippers,
光明白氎巾	shining bright, white cotton kerchief.
深藏供老宿	Treasured deep away, to provide for aged monks,
取用及吾身	you take them out to use for my person.

Zan's generosity is illustrated here by a reversal of their position as monk and layperson the clothes he gives were originally "presented" (gong 供) to the monastery—this being the standard term used for lay gifts. One may also note that at this point Zan has presented the poet with the four standard forms of almsgiving that laypeople are meant to give monks: shelter (the monastery itself), food, medicine (through his "poem-prescription"), and clothing. The reversal allows for Du Fu to use Buddhist exchanges as a frame that accentuates the gratitude and sense of shame that he experiences in enjoying the cleric's charity. As a refugee, there is nothing that he himself can give (except perhaps his poems).

At this point, the poet evokes Six Dynasties friendship once more. Perhaps the two most eminent figures in the history of fourth-century Buddhism were Zhi Dun 支遁 (314–366) (here called by his courtesy name, Daolin) and Huiyuan 惠遠 (334–416). Both were essential in providing the intellectual framework that allowed for philosophical exchanges between monastics and traditional Chinese intellectuals. Of course, as is typical of this type of polite poetry, Du Fu links himself and the reverend in a similar relationship while denying (in typically polite fashion) that he is worthy of it:

自顧轉無趣	Considering myself, I feel ever more that I lack charm,
交情何尚新	how then does our friendship stay so fresh?
道林才不世	Daolin's talent is not of the common age,
惠遠德過人	Huiyuan's virtue surpasses others.

At the heart of this refuge—in the midst of gloomy weather and rain—Du Fu seems to feel safe in the calm of the monastery, and the two can appreciate Wu Daozi's painting. But there is also a note of the uncanny here that will continue into the third poem: while Wu Daozi's work is something to appreciate with a fellow connoisseur, this act of viewing does not completely disarm the sense of awe one has in encountering the painting, and the way in which it seems linked to the inhospitable weather outside of the sanctuary:

雨瀉暮簷竹	Rain streams from the bamboo by the twilight eaves,
風吹春井芹	the wind blows the celery by the spring well.
天陰對圖畫	In the sky's darkness we face the paintings
最覺潤龍鱗	I especially feel that the dragon's scales are moist.[20]

---

20. As Owen points out, "Dragons were responsible for rainstorms. The line suggests that the painted dragons had been doing their work bringing the rain in the preceding lines, and having returned to their walls, were still wet." Owen, The Poetry of Du Fu, vol. 1, 271.

The monastery originally provided shelter from the spring rain, but now at its mysterious center is the force that caused the rain to begin with. Since dragons are rain-bringers, we now can see the rain not just as something to escape but also as the product of the dragon in this role; meanwhile, Zan's generosity expands from the monastery to the world at large, providing a dharma-rain (as in the parable of the hundred herbs in the *Lotus Sutra*). Though this is positive (and perhaps reminds the poet that the rain is not a petty inconvenience that affects only him), once again it creates a tension between the homely repose Du Fu seeks and the more dynamic activity that seems to be emerging from the monastery's center. Friendship and conventional exchanges of poetry and clothes cannot quite overcome the unearthly and sacred nature of the poet's place of refuge and suggest that any sense of calm he experiences may be temporary.

If the poems are meant to represent the ideal of a temple visit, what would be the next stage? Under the best of circumstances, he should spend a night of refreshing rest and continue his narrative in the morning. His silence at this point would be a representation of inner peace and timelessness. Instead, we have an insomnia poem; he in fact does *not* free himself from the tyranny of time and the anxiety it produces. Rather, he acknowledges that his refuge and visit with his friend must end (and perhaps it is characteristic of Du Fu's character in general to always anticipate the problem to come and not to find peace in the moment). The monastery here is described in awe-inspiring terms; but though the effect is positive on the surface, there is an underlying sense of unease and disturbance, continued from the impressions of Wu Daozi's numinous dragons. Things are impermanent, ever shifting and looming:

III.

燈影照無睡	Lamplight shines on sleeplessness,
心清聞妙香	the mind is clear, I smell wondrous scents.
夜深殿突兀	Deep in the night the halls just high,
風動金銀鐸	the wind stirs the metal chimes.
天黑閉春院	The heavens are black, closing the spring courtyard,
地清棲暗芳	the place is pure, here unseen fragrances lodge.

This is a magical space, with its strange incense, its windblown chimes (caused by the wind following the passing dragon-rainstorm), and the buildings that loom (*tuwu* 突兀) outside his window. In the second poem, the heavens were dark and gloomy (*yin* 陰) from the rain, and now in the night they are black—even though this place is evidently pure, like the supposed "realm of crystal" that expresses the Buddha mind in the first line of the first poem. Instead of peace, he finds sublimity and transformation.

玉繩迥斷絕	The Chain of Jade breaks off afar,
鐵鳳森翱翔	the iron phoenix darkly soars.
梵放時出寺	Sanskrit chants sometimes come from the temple,
鐘殘仍殷床	the bell's reverberations still shake my couch.

This does not improve matters. Astrological and meteorological phenomena are shifting (constellation and weather vane, predicting upheavals in the world out there, where rebellion continues). The noisy rituals of the temple were soothing in the first poem but now contribute to his insomnia as they are chanted in an alien and magical Sanskrit. In the last couplet we see that this unease is a manifestation of his inner turmoil. Du Fu is not living in the peace of the moment but is constantly projecting himself into the anxieties of the unknowable future:

明朝在沃野	Tomorrow at dawn I will be in the fertile wilds,
苦見塵沙黃	pained to see the brown of dust and sand.

Finally, in the last poem the poet puts on a brave face as dawn breaks and he views the sunlit world from his window. There is a little vignette of an acolyte who amazes the poet with his intuitive skills (with hints of Zhuangzi's Butcher Ding perhaps—do we see Du Fu reading the intuitive skillfulness of practice here? Is the broom in fact a no-broom?)

IV.

童兒汲井華	A lad draws water from the well's sparkling,
慣捷瓶上手	the pitcher is in his nimble, practiced hand.
沾灑不濡地	He sprinkles it without soaking the ground,
掃除似無帚	he sweeps up as if he had used no broom.

The spring rain of the previous night has passed, bringing a beautiful blooming world:

明霞爛複閣	Bright auroras flash on the layered towers,
霽霧搴高牖	lifting fog draws up over the high window.
側塞被徑花	Flowers blanket the path, stuffing it full,
飄颻委墀柳	swaying in the breeze, willows dangle on the pavements.

The reader may be reminded here of the more famous later poem "Delighting in Rain on a Spring Night" ("Chunye xiyu" 春夜喜雨), which contains the lines "It enters the night unseen with the wind / and moistens things finely, without a sound" (隨風潛入夜，潤物細無聲) and "At daybreak look where it's wet and red— / the flowers will be heavy in Brocade City" (曉看紅濕處，花重錦官城).[21] We have a world of ordinary nature miraculous in a more conventional and less awe-inspiring way. And yet there are connections to the earlier themes. The acolyte draws from the well, continuing the function of water-bringer that the dragons had carried out the day before. And his sprinkling is meant to settle dust—the same dust of the secular world that Du Fu has escaped but to which he now knows he must return.

And, in fact, this beautiful landscape, nourished by the dragon-rains, *is* the "fertile wilds" into which he must depart. While he thanks Reverend Zan, he has to acknowledge that he has not taken true refuge in the Three Jewels—he has only come there to visit a friend. The numinous aspects of the Buddhist monastery (which he has viewed with ambivalence) are now dismissed, as the simple bonds of a traditional friendship are reasserted:

艱難世事迫	Hardship and trouble, the world's affairs press on me,
隱遁佳期後	the sweet time for withdrawal is postponed.
晤語契深心	Talking face to face suits the depths of the heart,
那能總鉗口	how can one always feel gagged?
奉辭還杖策	Taking my leave, again I take staff in hand,
暫別終回首	parted but a moment, I finally turn my head.

---

21. Qiu Zhaoao, *Du shi xiangzhu*, 798. Owen, *The Poetry of Du Fu*, vol. 3, 4–5.

His act of turning his head here is completely in keeping with the sorrow of leaving a friend. But it also evokes legends of uncanny meetings of monks with bodhisattvas—in particular, the tales in which monks encounter disguised manifestations of Mañjuśrī at Wutai. For example, this miracle tale found in Huixiang's 慧祥 account of Wutai from 677, in which a Buddhist lay devotee practices with a devout Buddhist community, only later to find that the whole community has mysteriously disappeared:

> Finally the day came when he asked to return home. The monks let him go without the slightest objection. He got back home safely, but after spending just a few nights there, he came running back to Wutai. The mountain slopes and valley were exactly as they were before, but there was no sight whatsoever of the monks and their compound. He searched about and made enquiries, but learned that the region had always been serene and uninhabited. The man suspects that the monks were saints of Wutai, and he has been heartsick about it ever since.[22]

If Du Fu is evoking this kind of narrative, the turning of his head may mean to imply the disappearance of the monastery altogether, an illusion conjured by bodhisattvas for his well-being but now no longer of use. He leaves his friend but also leaves sanctuary for good.

The last six lines are a sort of envoi to the entire cycle:

泱泱泥汙人	Spreading everywhere, mud mires me,
狺狺國多狗	many dogs back fiercely in the capital.
既未免羈絆	I am not yet able to avoid entanglements,
時來憩奔走	when the time comes, I will rest from this running.
近公如白雪	Being near you is like being near white snow—
執熱煩何有	what irritation do I feel taking hot things in hand?

Though the content alludes specifically to the rebellion, the final gesture of parting is more typical of poems in which the author bids farewell to a recluse: the claim that he would like to join his companion, but cannot do so quite yet. Yet the ending brings us back again to the images of purity/dust and the cleansing power of water yet once more. The poet is mired in mud but is soothed by the cooling snow of his friend's presence.

The "Buddhist" qualities of these four poems do not lie in what they can tell us of Du Fu's attitudes toward the faith. Nor do they show any signs of the sort of Buddhist influence that has attracted the attention of modern critics. There are no references to specific Chan concerns (in fact, all of the Buddhist allusions here are part of mainstream Mahayana belief). There are no nature images that subtly hint at the "emptiness" (*kong*) of things. Rather, the poems allow Du Fu to interweave certain Buddhist themes—refuge, monastic space, lay-clergy interaction, impermanence—with the more common Du Fu "seeking refuge / visiting a friend" poem and to a certain extent to reassert the latter at the expense of the former. The combination enriches the text and makes it more interesting; but we should keep in mind that what we are seeing is a vivid writing of merely one sacred moment.

Reverend Zan reappears in Du Fu's verse a few years later when the poet has moved to Qinzhou. The monk has now been deprived of his comfortable accommodations at Great Cloud Temple and has been exiled to this border district; deprived of his lofty position, he now no longer can serve as the poet's patron but interacts with him

---

22. *Gu qingliang zhuan*, 1098. Stevenson, "A Sacred Peak," 89.

as a fellow victim of political unrest. Du Fu wrote four poems to him at this time, all of which strike a very different tone from that of the earlier cycle.[23] The first is a regulated verse that briefly describes a visit:

宿贊公房	Spending the Night in the Chambers of Reverend Zan
杖錫何來此	How did you come here, supported by your tin scepter?—
秋風已颯然	already the autumn winds are howling.
雨荒深院菊	Rains lay waste to chrysanthemums deep in your garden,
霜倒半池蓮	the frost overturned the lotus over half your pool.
放逐寧違性	Though banished, how could you stray from your nature?
虛空不離禪	In emptiness you do not depart from Chan.
相逢成夜宿	Meeting you, I end up staying the night,
隴月向人圓	the moon facing us over Longtou is round.

Previously the poet could find a place of safety in the monk's lofty city temple. But now both are refugees, and Zan has nothing to offer him. Consequently, Du Fu's tone has changed from gratitude to empathy—he now sees Zan as someone whose predicament is the same as his own. He is no longer in control of a beneficent climate, manifested through his temple's all-powerful rain-dragons; instead, the climate oppresses him with rain, wind, and frost. In this new context, Du can identify him both as a monk *and* as a recluse, and also as someone who is threatened in both of these identities: the chrysanthemums indicate the secular retreat of a Tao Qian 陶潛 (365?–427) while the lotuses are Buddhist markers. Yet neither political exile nor the harsh weather can separate the monk from the essential aspects of his practice or keep him from recognizing the emptiness of his existence. Du Fu here is playing the role of consoling friend, reassuring Zan of his worthiness in spite of the crisis that has occurred in his career. This is the sort of tone Du might also use in communicating with a friend who failed in the examinations. Regardless, it is interesting to see how much of Zan's numinous power to console and refresh was rooted in the site in which he practiced; his magic was drawn from his home temple and its paintings, and now he is severed from it.

The other poems addressed to Zan have very little Buddhist content at all and chiefly concern Du Fu's anxiety over finding a suitable place to locate a modest residence in Qinzhou. Here, Zan's Buddhist identity is *completely* supplanted by his twin existences as suffering exile and as fellow recluse. Any significant reference to religious practice has been replaced by evocations of suffering and of nostalgia for the capital, the place that gave their lives meaning. Note this passage from the second of two poems, "Seeking a Place to Put a Thatched Cottage in West Branch Village, Staying Over in the Earthen Chamber of Reverend Zan":

躋攀倦日短	By climbing and clambering we had tired out the short day,
語樂寄夜永	the pleasures of chat we entrusted to the long night.
明燃林中薪	Brightly burning, kindling from the forest,
暗汲石底井	water drawn in darkness from a well below the rocks.

---

23. "Spending the Night in the Chambers of Reverend Zan" 宿贊公房 (Qiu Zhaoao, *Du shi xiangzhu*, 592–93; Owen, *The Poetry of Du Fu*, vol. 2, 150–53); "Seeking a Place to Put a Thatched Cottage in West Branch Village, Staying Over in the Earthen Chamber of Reverend Zan" 西枝村尋置草堂地夜宿贊公土室二首 (Qiu Zhaoao, *Du shi xiangzhu*, 594–97; Owen, *The Poetry of Du Fu*, vol. 2, 152–57); and "To Reverend Zan" 寄贊上人 (Qiu Zhaoao, *Du shi xiangzhu*, 597–99; Owen, *The Poetry of Du Fu*, vol. 2, 156–59).

大師京國舊	His Reverence is an old friend from the capital,
德業天機秉	by accumulated merit he holds to natural endowments.
從來支許遊	We used to roam, the likes of Zhi Dun and Xu Xun,
興趣江湖迴	our elation went far to the rivers and lakes. (ll. 5–12)

Fourth-century Buddhist-oriented literary figures (here, Zhi Dun and Xu Xun 許詢) are remembered more as symbols of past friendship and present regret. At this point, Du Fu's greatest hope is to build his own refuge close to that of his friend, so that they can share the pleasures of a free poverty with a certain amount of style ("panache," *fengliu* 風流)—as seen in the ending lines of "To Reverend Zan":

柴荊具茶茗	Though ramshackle, it [my house] will be provided with tea,
徑路通林丘	a path leads through to your wooded hill.
與子成二老	We'll become two old men together,
來往亦風流	even with some panache in our intercourse.

Comparing these later poems to the earlier "Great Cloud Temple" sequence, we can see quite clearly Du Fu's ability to adapt or ignore Buddhist materials to suit his occasional expressive needs. Not surprisingly, Buddhism recedes into the background the more easily that Reverend Zan can be assimilated into the Confucian narrative discourse with which Du is most comfortable: wrongful treatment, exile, virtuous reclusion. This calls for a different set of tropes and images.

If Du Fu rereads Zan as a suffering exile/recluse in these examples, a later poem shows him reinterpreting the entire Buddhist clergy in the same way. The twenty-eight-line "Mountain Temple" ("Shansi" 山寺), written during the Chengdu period, describes a monastery going to ruin and uses this to write a strikingly original protest poem that combines a lament for human suffering, foregrounding it at the expense of Buddhist themes.[24]

The poem begins with a vivid evocation of temple's decay:

野寺根石壁	Wilderness temple, rooted on a stone cliff,
諸龕遍崔嵬	many niches cover the looming slopes.
前佛不復辨	You can no longer distinguish the former Buddhas,
百身一莓苔	a hundred bodies, all covered in moss.
雖有古殿存	Although there is an ancient hall still standing,
世尊亦塵埃	the Revered One is in grime and dust.
如聞龍象泣	It is as if one can hear the dragons and elephants weep,
足令信者哀	enough to cause believers to lament.

Impermanence is of course a central concept in Buddhism, and that creates a sort of implicit irony in the situation: its art and architecture celebrate a faith that argues that such creative activity is ultimately empty and ephemeral. The cliff niches of the temple are filled with sculptures paid for by lay donations, but they are now so worn with age that their Buddhas and bodhisattvas have become indistinguishable from

---

24. Qiu Zhaoao, *Du shi xiangzhu*, 1059–61; Owen, *The Poetry of Du Fu*, vol. 3, 292–95. A note attached to the poem indicates the social origins of the verse: "Visited with Deputy Zhang, I got the rhyme *kai*." "Deputy" here is *liu hou*, short for *liu hou shi* 留後使, an officer who acted as liaison between military governors and the capital. Since the prefect of the poem (line 9—see below) is designated by the term *shijun* 使君 and probably refers to Zhang, it is likely that Du Fu wrote this poem after the events described as a compliment to him.

each other. Ever-destructive nature makes their identities irrelevant—and Du Fu also gestures slightly toward the "city in ruins" motif that had been part of the poetic tradition at least since Bao Zhao's 鮑照 (414?–466) "Rhapsody on the Weed-Covered City" (*Wu cheng fu* 蕪城賦). Yet the temple is also supposed to be the place that unites the numinous and the human, and its decline here is a genuine tragedy and not just the inevitable consequences of impermanence. Sentient beings, human and nonhuman, are grief stricken at the shabby state of the Buddha's statue. "It is as if one can hear the dragons and elephants weep, / enough to cause believers to lament." This is the same mysterious, numinous world evoked in the "Great Cloud Temple" poems, but now it is deprived of its universal power; like Reverend Zan in exile, the dragons are rendered impotent. It is also interesting that Du Fu does not designate the human world by an all-encompassing term but instead refers to "believers" (*xinzhe*) specifically—thus suggesting that the human mourners here are a subset of society at large and by no means all of the emperor's subjects.[25]

The local prefect now enters to put things right:

使君騎紫馬	The prefect was riding his purple horse,
捧擁從西來	surrounded by a throng he came from the west.
樹羽靜千里	His pennants, planted, made it calm for a thousand leagues,
臨江久徘徊	standing by the river he lingered long.
山僧衣藍縷	Mountain monks clothed in tattered rags
告訴棟樑摧	complained how beams and timbers were collapsing.
公為顧賓徒	Because of this, His Lordship looked around at his entourage,
咄嗟檀施開	with a pained sigh, began a donation.
吾知多羅樹	I know that the fan-palm tree
卻倚蓮華臺	will rest again by his platform of lotus.
諸天必歡喜	All the devas will surely rejoice,
鬼物無嫌猜	and spirit beings will have no complaints.
以茲撫士卒	By this deed he soothes the troops,
孰曰非周才	who says he is not a perfect talent?

If the first part subtly hints at a separation between believers and nonbelievers, the prefect's appearance increases this separation. In one sense, one might argue that he is a bodhisattva/layperson come to protect the faith; in Tang writing it is easy enough to find praise for court officials who are cast specifically in such a role. But Du Fu seems more comfortable seeing the prefect as a representative of nonsectarian authority, and *as such* he is the best resource the impoverished monks have for rectifying their situation. He responds not as a devout layperson but as someone aware that these conditions bespeak the suffering of the people in general (especially in times of rebellion): "Because of this, His Lordship looked around at his entourage, / with a pained sigh, began a donation." He turns to those who accompany him as if to ask for confirmation of his own sentiments: "Here now, we can't have this, can we?" He then plays the role of virtuous Confucian official—he provides an example by being the first lay donor to contribute to the repairs. The poet then goes into a rhapsodic description of the future restoration,

25. This does not necessarily mean that Du Fu does not rank himself among the *xinzhe*, but by using the category he does implicitly recognize the existence of those to whom the term does not apply. Incidentally, this is the only place in Du Fu's corpus where he uses *xinzhe*.

celebrated most by the gods and spirits whose positions again will be honored and respected. But then Du Fu comments, "By this deed he soothes the troops, / who says he is not a perfect talent?" This implies that the prefect is not pious himself but recognizes that his actions will go down well with his men and will improve morale. The Qing commentator Qiu Zhaoao goes even further and suggests that the couplet is mainly praising the flexibility of the prefect's virtues: "If he applies this mind-set on making offering to the Buddhas and applies it to soothing the soldiers—how is that not a talent that is set on saving all?"[26] For Qiu Zhaoao, it is not that the prefect is working for the restoration of the temple because he knows it will cheer his subordinates; rather, the prefect possesses a sort of universal compassion (but of a Confucian sort) that recognizes the benefit of treating both Buddha and troops well (in Qiu's interpretation, the couplet might be translated as "If he employs this sort of action in his treatment of the army, then who will say that he is not an all-encompassing talent?").[27] Regardless of the specifics of Du Fu's viewpoint on the prefect's actions, he is asserting the prefect's power to put things right and his role as the ultimate arbiter of justice. Both shabby monks and gods are dependent on him.

As if to continue this move toward more general ethical issues, Du Fu concludes with a broad meditation on suffering that compassionately brings the monks into its purview:

窮子失淨處　　The poor man loses this place of purity,
高人憂禍胎　　the lofty man worries about the womb of disaster.
歲晏風破肉　　The year is late, the wind tears the flesh,
荒林寒可迴　　to the wild forests the cold may return.
思量入道苦　　When I consider the sufferings of becoming a monk,
自哂同嬰孩　　I mock myself, as being like a child.

All will suffer from the coming cold, the monks not the least. But by placing the monks among those who suffer, Du subtly upends their significance as a social group in Tang society. Yes, they receive the charity of laypeople in the classic Buddhist social dynamic; but they do so that they can work for larger compassionate goals that should benefit all sentient beings. The donations of laypeople are to be given out of gratitude and humility, in recognition of the greater good monastics perform. For Du Fu, though, they are just another impoverished group suffering the chaos of the rebellion, a group whose position would improve if society were being run on harmonious political principles. Du Fu pities rather than respects them. In this sense, he decenters Buddhism with a competing form of universalism. If he wrote this poem in the presence of (and in praise of) the prefect himself, then he may have decided that Zhang too would find this orientation most appropriate.

With "Mountain Temple," we have a final example of Du Fu's poetic relationship with the Buddhist faith. The number of temple-visiting poems and other verses that make use of Mahayana terminology suggest that he was well informed in Buddhist doctrine, and the social role of the religion in his verse suggests that regardless of his

26. Qiu Zhaoao, *Du shi xiangzhu*, 1060. The original text reads, 若移此奉佛之心以撫恤軍士，豈非弘濟才乎？
27. The use of *zhou cai* ("perfect talent") here likely has specific application to public service. The Li Shan *Wen xuan* commentary to Wang Kangju's 王康琚 (fl. fourth century) poem "Against Calling Back the Recluse" 反招隱 specifically equates *zhou cai* with office holding, as opposed to the "narrow wisdom" (*pian zhi* 偏智) of the hermit. Xiao Tong, *Wen xuan*, 22.1031.

personal beliefs he accepted Buddhism's presence in society and culture. However, when he actually writes about Buddhist issues and ideas in his verse, one cannot help but notice the way in which he distances himself from accepting larger Buddhist claims about the importance of practice. For him, the old traditional literati concerns tend to win out—the desire for public service, concern for the well-being of the political order; and, when he feels unable to address these concerns, he turns, rather, to the life of a cultivated gentleman in retirement than to the tonsure or even to the solace of the devout lay practitioner.

6
Feeding the Phoenix

Du Fu's Qinzhou-Tonggu Series*

Xiaofei Tian

"Religious poetry" is an important topic of study across cultures, even though people do not always agree on what constitutes religious poetry, how one should define religious poetry, how religious is some religious poetry, or how poetic is much religious poetry. These vexing questions do not have a uniform, definitive answer and serve only to make one wonder how meaningful or useful the category of "religious poetry" ultimately is, either for the study of religion or of poetry. A more productive formulation is "poetry *and* religion," for it foregrounds the distinct identity of each concept and tradition, and enables us to focus on the various ways in which the two might intersect with each other in a given historical period.

In studying poetry and religion, China scholars usually look to two kinds of texts: those by religious practitioners such as ordained Buddhist monks and nuns or Daoist priests, and those by secular authors who describe their experiences of religious sites or events and their interactions with religious practitioners. The first kind of texts uses the outward social identity of the producer as a marker; the second, the subject and content of the product. These are sensible choices, whose relevance to the topic at hand is easy to demonstrate. But one is sometimes left to wonder how "religious" these texts really are and, in the case of overtly religious poems, such as versifications of religious dogma or moralistic teachings, how much literary value there is. Neither question is easy to answer in the abstract.

In this chapter I wish to draw attention to a third choice in our study of religion and poetry, namely, how a poetic text may be informed and inflected by the prevalent religious discourse and—for want of a better word—atmosphere. Buddhist and Daoist temples, itinerant monks and nuns, religious festivals and rituals for the dead and the living, visual arts, and performances of all kinds: an elite medieval Chinese man like Du Fu would have grown up surrounded by images, sounds, symbols, events, and personalities associated with Buddhism, Daoism, and any number of popular cults and beliefs in society. He would have most likely been familiar with some of the best-known Buddhist scriptures among medieval gentry and commoners alike, such as *The Lotus*

* An earlier, Chinese version of this chapter was printed in *Shanghai shifan daxue xuebao* 47, no. 1 (2018): 106–13.

Sutra and *The Vimalakīrti Sutra*. How would such multimedia information coming from the outside exert its influence on a poet, as it would almost certainly have, regardless of the poet's religious belief?

This is admittedly more difficult to explore than limiting one's analysis to poems by religious personages or poems with explicit religious subject matter. I nevertheless argue that there is merit in entertaining this position in our research, provided that there are obvious clues both in the internal properties of a text and in the external conditions that constitute a set of broadly defined paratexts. We also need to take the long view of social history and literary history. In the fifth and sixth centuries, for instance, the advocacy for Buddhism was a fierce ideological competition between the ruling houses of the Northern and Southern Dynasties, and the Buddhist faith was an extravagant public spectacle as well as a private matter of spirituality. This period witnessed a surge of poems on light and shadow, especially on the flames of a candle, a popular Buddhist metaphor for the fragility and brevity of human life, along with poems on the sensuous surfaces of the material world; many leading poets were also devout lay Buddhists and were engaged in writing about and lecturing on Buddhist scriptures. All this invites speculation that Buddhism not only brought novel terminology, imagery, and tonal considerations to classical Chinese poetry but also contributed to a more fundamental shift in the way the phenomenal world is viewed and articulated in poetry.[1]

What, then, about Du Fu? From the Song on, Du Fu has always been identified as a deeply Confucian poet, loyal to his ruler and devoted to the dynasty. In the past several decades, scholars have also begun studying his relationship with Buddhism, although such a reading constitutes a minority position in Du Fu studies, and most writings focus on his poems with explicit Buddhist content. In this chapter I would like to take "Du Fu and Buddhism" in a different direction by examining a famous set of travel poems from a Buddhist perspective. One of the set is a temple-visiting poem, thus having an explicitly Buddhist topic, and the last poem of the set exhibits a spirit of compassion clearly evocative of Buddhism. But instead of singling out a poem from the set and reading it in isolation, I propose reading the twelve poems as a carefully organized sequence that constitutes a coherent Buddhist narrative of transformation and enlightenment. By doing so we add a different dimension to the focus on Du Fu's poems with obvious Buddhist themes and references, entertain a new reading of a famous poetic sequence, and reflect on the larger question of how literature and religion intersect in a dynamic way, just as they do in any living reality, and not merely as two distinct discursive traditions in scholarly discussions.

In the early winter of 759, Du Fu and his family left Qinzhou for Tonggu (both in modern Gansu), hoping to find patronage and a stable life there. Twelve poems about this journey are grouped into a set by an original note added under the title of the first poem: "In the second year of the Qianyuan era, I left Qinzhou to go to Tonggu County and recorded the journey in twelve poems" 乾元二年自秦州赴同谷縣紀行十二首.[2] The set begins with "Setting off from Qinzhou" ("Fa Qinzhou" 發秦州) and ends with "Phoenix Terrace" ("Fenghuang tai" 鳳凰臺) at Tonggu County; each of the ten poems in between

---

1.   See Tian, *Beacon Fire*.
2.   The texts used in this chapter follow Wang Zhu's 王洙 (997–1057) *Song ben Du Gongbu ji*, 149–51. Also see Xiao Difei, *Du Fu quanji*, vol. 7, 13.1699–770. The translations are from Owen, *The Poetry of Du Fu*, vol. 2, 232–53.

describes one place on the way.[3] The poet's original note asks the reader to not read each poem as a stand-alone piece but to read the poems together as a whole. Such a reading brings out certain important motifs and images recurring through the series and offers a larger significance that each poem does not possess individually. Instead of representing individual places discretely, Du Fu creates a map of places that are connected to one another by the poet's itinerary.

Many scholars have observed the palpable influence of the great landscape poet Xie Lingyun 謝靈運 (385–433) in Du Fu's "Qinzhou-Tonggu-Chengdu" poems.[4] When Xie Lingyun was sent away from the capital Jiankang (modern Nanjing) to take up a provincial post at Yongjia (in modern Zhejiang) in 422, he wrote a number of poems recording his journey. The first of these poems is "Setting Off from the Capital to Go to the Commandery on the Sixteenth Day of the Seventh Month in the Third Year of the Yongchu Era" ("Yongchu sannian qiyue shiliuri zhi jun chu fa du" 永初三年七月十六日之郡初發都). Then he wrote "My Neighbors Saw Me Off at Fangshan" ("Linli xiangsong zhi Fangshan" 鄰里相送方山), "Passing through My Shining Villa" ("Guo Shining shu" 過始寧墅), "Fuchun Isle" ("Fuchun zhu" 富春渚), and "Seven League Rapids" ("Qili lai" 七里瀬). All these poems are included in the sixth-century literary anthology *Wen xuan* 文選, with which Du Fu was familiar. However, except for the fact that he wrote them all during his trip from Jiankang to Yongjia, there is no interconnection between Xie Lingyun's poems. In fact, a pattern detected in Xie Lingyun's nature poems—that is, in each poem the poet typically begins with melancholy or frustration but finds relief or achieves enlightenment at the end—precisely discourages a reader from reading the poems as a unified set, because the multiple enlightenments might undermine the validity of each single experience. In contrast, with the twelve Qinzhou-Tonggu poems harnessed into one set by the poet's note, Du Fu creates a coherent journey narrative, which culminates in a startling revelation in the last poem.

(1) 發秦州   Setting Off from Qinzhou

　　我衰更懶拙   In my waning years, I grow even more lazy and inept;
　　生事不自謀   I haven't thought out how to make a living.
　　無食問樂土   Having no food, I ask around for a happy land;
4　　無衣思南州   short of clothes, I long for southern prefectures.
　　漢源十月交   At the Han River's source in the tenth month,

---

3. The poet's "original note" 原注 is crucial in the establishment of the twelve poems as a series. Without the note it would have been unnatural to treat "Phoenix Terrace" as the final poem of a poetic set recording the poet's journey from Qinzhou to Tonggu, for Phoenix Terrace is a mountain to the southeast of Tonggu and would be out of the poet's way on his journey. See Yan Gengwang, *Tangdai jiaotong*, 836; also see Li Jizu, "Du Fu Longyoushi," 44–51. Indeed, a poem on another site at Tonggu, "Myriad Fathom Pool" 萬丈潭, which describes a deep pool with an invisible dragon in it, makes such a nice match with the "Phoenix Terrace" poem that some scholars have discussed the two poems together as a "pair." See, for instance, Huang Yizhen, "Lun 'Fenghuang tai,'" 83–128. However, in the early editions of Du Fu's collection, such as *Song ben* or the Guo Zhida 郭知達 (fl. twelfth century) edition, "Myriad Fathom Pool" is invariably placed *before* "Setting off from Qinzhou," with an original note appended under its title: "Composed at Tonggu County" 同谷縣作, as if the author wanted to make sure to convey the location and composition time of "Myriad Fathom Pool" and yet did not want the reader to confuse it with the "set of twelve Qinzhou-Tonggu poems." See *Song ben Du Gongbu ji*, 144; Guo Zhida, *Xinkan jiaoding*, juan 6. This is contrasted with the ordering of these poems in major Qing editions, which usually place "Myriad Fathom Pool" *after* "Phoenix Terrace" and the "Seven Songs Written While Residing in Tonggu County in the Qianyuan Reign" 乾元中寓居同谷縣作歌七首.

4. See, for instance, Su Yiru, "Du Fu zi Qin ru Shu," 203–36.

	天氣如涼秋	the weather is still like cool autumn.[5]
	草木未黃落	The plants and trees have not yellowed and shed,
8	況聞山水幽	I've further heard of the tranquility of its landscape.
	栗亭名更佳	The name of Chestnut Pavilion is even finer,[6]
	下有良田疇	below it there are good farming fields.
	充腸多薯蕷	There are plenty of yams to fill our bellies,
12	崖蜜亦易求	and cliff honey is easy to find.
	密竹復冬笋	Among the dense bamboos are also winter shoots,
	清池可方舟	and on clear pools one may link boats side by side.
	雖傷旅寓遠	Though pained about my far sojourn,
16	庶遂平生遊	I hope to realize the journey of a lifetime.
	此邦俯要衝	This land here [Qinzhou] looks down on a strategic thoroughfare,
	實恐人事稠	I really do fear the conflux of human affairs.
	應接非本性	Visiting and reciprocating is not in my nature,
20	登臨未銷憂	climbing for a view does not melt away cares.
	溪谷無異石	These stream valleys have no remarkable rocks,
	塞田始微收	and frontier fields produce only a meager harvest.
	豈復慰老夫	How can these comfort an old fellow any more? —
24	惆然難久留	disappointed, I cannot linger here long.
	日色隱孤戍	The sunlight was hidden behind a lone outpost,
	烏啼滿城頭	crows cried out, filling the tops of the city walls.
	中宵驅車去	At midnight I drove my wagon away
28	飲馬寒塘流	and watered my horses in the currents of cold ponds.
	磊落星月高	Scattered through the sky, the stars and moon were high,
	蒼茫雲霧浮	in the vast expanse clouds and fog drifted.
	大哉乾坤內	In this immensity between Heaven and Earth
32	吾道長悠悠	my way goes on long into the distance.

Physical journey and spiritual journey, the poet's way and the Way, are conflated in the last line and endow the journey with a symbolic significance. This poem becomes even more interesting if we read the poetic sequence first forward and then backward. For now let me just highlight some of the obvious points: the poet states he is leaving for Tonggu because Tonggu is in his mind a paradise on earth, with temperate weather and plenty of food that alleviate cold and hunger; more specifically, he envisions chestnuts, yams, honey, winter bamboo shoots, and clear pools. He sets off at midnight, and already his horses are getting plenty of water to drink, even though the subtext of "cold pond" is a third-century poem.[7]

(2) 赤谷   Red Valley

天寒霜雪繁	The weather is cold, frost and snow are heavy;
遊子有所之	and the traveler is going somewhere.
豈但歲月暮	Not only is the year drawing to a close,

---

5. Hanyuan, "the Han River's source," is the name of a county next to Tonggu. The tenth lunar month is the first month of winter.
6. Liting, "Chestnut Pavilion," is the name of a town at Tonggu.
7. See Chen Lin 陳琳 (d. 217), "Watering My Horse at the Pool by the Great Wall" 飲馬長城窟: "I water my horse at the pool by the Great Wall, / the water is cold and wounds my horse's bones" 飲馬長城窟, 水寒傷馬骨. Lu Qinli, *Xian Qin Han Wei*, 367.

4	重來未有期	I have no plans to come this way again.
	晨發赤谷亭	At dawn I set out from Red Valley station,
	險艱方自茲	it is hard going from this point on.
	亂石無改轍	Among jumbled rocks there is no changing course,
8	我車已載脂	my wagon has been well-oiled.
	山深苦多風	Deep in the mountains the wind is terribly strong,
	落日童稚飢	as the sun sets the children are hungry.
	悄然村墟迥	A hamlet lies remote in silence,
12	煙火何由追	how can we seek out its hearth fires?
	貧病轉零落	Sick and poor, I grow increasingly down-and-out,
	故鄉不可思	I cannot even think of home.
	常恐死道路	I always fear that I will die on the road
16	永為高人嗤	and forever be mocked by lofty men.

Before paradise can be reached, the poet has to go through hell: what he runs away from—cold and hunger—are chasing after him with a vindictive force. Being "short of clothes" is now made worse as "the weather is cold, frost and snow are heavy," and the categorical complaint about "having no food" returns, but, significantly, instead of his own hunger, he speaks of his children being hungry after traveling all day. As the sun is setting, it is going to get even colder after dark, yet a hot dinner and a lodging place is nowhere near. If grown-ups can bear the delay of a meal, little children cannot, making things doubly hard for the parents.[8] The "yellowing and shedding" (*huangluo* 黃落) of plants and trees back at Qinzhou are now being transferred to the poet himself with a noticeable echo of the "fall" (*luo* 落): "increasingly down-and-out" (*zhuan lingluo* 轉零落).

(3)	鐵堂峽	Iron Hall Gorge
	山風吹遊子	The mountain wind blows on the traveler,
	縹緲乘險絕	adrift, I mount the sheer steepness.
	硤形藏堂隍	The gorge hides the shape of a great hall,
4	壁色立積鐵	where the cliffs' colors stand as massed iron.
	徑摩穹蒼蟠	Our path winds, rubbing the gray vault,
	石與厚地裂	the rock and deep earth are rent asunder.
	修纖無垠竹	Tall and slender, boundless bamboo,
8	嵌空太始雪	sparkling tracery in primeval snows.
	威遲哀壑底	Wending our way along the base of this mournful gorge,
	徒旅慘不悅	the travelers are gloomy and cheerless.
	水寒長冰橫	The water is cold, long with ice athwart it,
12	我馬骨正折	my horse's bones are truly snapping.
	生涯抵弧矢	In my lifetime I've lived up to bows and arrows,[9]

8. A good note for this line would be another line from Du Fu's poem "A Hundred Cares Gather: A Ballad" 百憂集行 dated to 761, barely two years later, which ends with the couplet "My childish boys do not yet know the proper way to treat their father, / they shout angrily demanding food and weep east of the gate" 痴兒未知父子禮, 叫怒索飯啼門東. *Song ben Du Gongbu ji*, 157; Xiao Difei, *Du Fu quanji*, vol. 4, 8.2353; Owen, *The Poetry of Du Fu*, vol. 3, 52–53.

9. This contains a double entendre. *Hushi* 弧矢, "bow and arrow," is a term indicating warfare, but according to an ancient ritual, when a ruler's male heir is born, the archer must use a mulberry bow to shoot six arrows made of tumbleweed stems (桑弧蓬矢) toward heaven, earth, and the four directions to symbolize that a man's aims should widely encompass all the world. Du Fu is saying that his wandering life has

	盜賊殊未滅	and the rebels are hardly wiped out.
	飄蓬逾三年	Wind-tossed tumbleweed for more than three years,
16	回首肝肺熱	I turn my head, liver and lungs burning.

The poet is *lingluo* in the last poem, a phrase evoking withering and falling like autumn plants; this poem begins with being blown by wind up on high in lines 1–2 and then descends to the bottom of the gorge in line 9, and finally ends with the image of wind-tossed tumbleweed in line 15. Noticeably, the bamboos of Poem #1 appear again but clearly bear no "winter sprouts" because of the *primeval* snow—not even the frost and snow of the tenth month from Poem #2. Cold water also reappears but is not drinkable because of ice athwart it.

(4)	鹽井		Salt Well
	鹵中草木白		In the salt-lands plants and trees are white,
	青者官鹽煙		the green is the smoke from the official salt-works.
	官作既有程		Since there are set schedules in official work,
4	煮鹽煙在川		the smoke from boiling salt lies over the river.
	汲井歲榾榾		They toil yearlong, drawing from the wells,
	出車日連連		wagons go out daily, one after another.
	自公斗三百		From the officials they buy six kilos for three hundred cash,
8	轉致斛六千		then they sell sixty kilos for six thousand.[10]
	君子慎止足		A gentleman should take care to stop where there's enough,
	小人苦喧闐		whereas lesser men are terribly raucous.
	我何良歎嗟		But then why do I heave such sighs?—
12	物理固自然		this has always been the way things go.

The government kept a monopoly on salt, and salt tax would constitute half of the tax of the entire Tang empire by late 770s. In reading this poem it is perhaps useful to know that in the Tianbao reign (742–756) and Zhide reign (756–758) each *dou* (six kilos) was sold for ten cash only, but the price was raised to 110 cash per *dou* in the first year of the Qianyuan reign (the year before Du Fu wrote this poem).[11] We will not commit the fault of speculating on contemporary salt prices from Du Fu's poem, despite Du Fu's fame as a "poet historian"; instead, I wish to bring attention to the colors white and green. In the preceding poem, green bamboos are covered by white snow; in this poem, plants and trees, though not "yellowing and shedding" like in Qinzhou (#1), are turned white, dying, by brine, and the only green is of the smoke from boiling salt. The poet's romanticized fantasy about the winter bamboo shoots at Tonggu is gradually eroded by what he sees on the road. One is tempted to say that the desolate scene of environmental destruction is almost worthy of the depiction of a nineteenth-century factory in a Dickens novel; yet, underneath all the human greed, and despite the damage to plants and trees, salt *is* essential to human food and survival—and food and survival are what Du Fu looks for at Tonggu.

---

certainly met the prophecy of the "bow and arrows" intended for boys and that his wandering is caused by nothing but "bows and arrows."

10. That is, the salt merchants make twenty times profit. One *dou* was roughly six kilos and one *hu* was equivalent of ten *dou*.
11. *Xin Tang shu*, 54.1378.

(5)　寒硤　　　Cold Gorge

   　行邁日悄悄　It gets daily more quiet on our journey,
   　山谷勢多端　the forms of mountains and valleys are many.
   　雲門轉絕岸　A gate for clouds bends to a sheer slope,
4　積阻霾天寒　where a massed blockage buries heaven's cold.
   　寒硤不可度　We cannot cross through Cold Gorge,
   　我實衣裳單　our clothes are indeed too thin.
   　況當仲冬交　Even more at the juncture of mid-winter,
8　泝沿增波瀾　the swirling waters increase their waves.
   　野人尋煙語　Men of the wilds seek out our smoky fire to talk,
   　行子傍水餐　as the travelers dine beside the waters.
   　此生免荷殳　In this life I've avoided shouldering a falchion,
12　未敢辭路難　I dare not refuse the hardships of the road.

If the last poem speaks of an essential ingredient in human diet, this poem turns to the other element he looks for at Tonggu: a temperate climate to relieve him of the cold. Instead of warmth, the journey lasting from the tenth month into the eleventh month ("mid-winter" in line 7) takes him from "cold ponds" (#1) to Cold Gorge, where the poet stresses that their clothes are *indeed* too thin. The quietness of the wilderness — and of the travelers (too cold and too tired to speak) — is contrasted nicely with the men of the wilds seeking them out to talk. Smoke reappears and is again related to food, as they cook their meal over a campfire by the waters. The locals find the travelers by the smoke: a reversal of Poem #2, where the travelers cannot seek out hearth fires in the all-too-remote village and suffer from cold and hunger. Here, encouraged by the campfire, hot food, and human company, the poet grows optimistic at the end and tries to look at the bright side of his situation.

(6)　法鏡寺　　　The Temple of the Dharma Mirror

   　身危適他州　My body in peril, I go to another prefecture,
   　勉強終勞苦　all my efforts end up in bitter suffering.
   　神傷山行深　The spirit is wounded going so deep in the mountains,
4　愁破崖寺古　yet sadness dissolves before the ancient cliff temple.
   　嬋娟碧鮮淨　Winsome, the emerald freshness pure,[12]
   　蕭摵寒籜聚　crackling in wind, wintry bamboo sheaths cluster.
   　回回山根水　Waters at the mountain-foot twist and turn,
8　冉冉松上雨　trickling and glistening, rain on the pines.
   　泄雲蒙清晨　Oozing clouds hide the clear morning,
   　初日翳復吐　the rising sun is concealed and then breaks through.
   　朱甍半光炯　Its red roof-tiles are half in that sparkling light,
12　戶牖粲可數　doors and windows, gleaming, can be counted.
   　拄策忘前期　I lean on my staff, forget the stage ahead,
   　出蘿已亭午　as I emerge from the vines it's already noon.
   　冥冥子規叫　Dark and dim, a cuckoo's cries,
16　微徑不復取　that narrow path I shall not take again.

---

12. *Bixian* 碧鮮 is sometimes understood as emerald lichen, *bixian* 碧蘚. See Xiao Difei, *Du Fu quanji*, vol. 4, 7.1732.

This poem marks the midpoint of the series; it is a pause in the poet's journey, as the poet takes a detour to visit a Buddhist temple. Temple-visit poems had already had a long tradition before Du Fu. Examined against that background, this poem stands out as an odd specimen. A typical temple-visit poem usually ends with the poet's experience of enlightenment and transcendence on the temple grounds. This poem, in contrast, conjures up a dream-like atmosphere, a temporary forgetfulness of the journey still lying ahead, as if the experience were a mesmerizing spell cast over the poet's spirit. Overnight rain and early morning cloud even evoke the goddess of the Wu Mountain who promises the Chu king, in his erotic dream vision, to be his "morning cloud and evening rain." The luminous tiles and the glistening windows and doorways serve only to increase the feeling of daze, as the solid architectural form seems to dissolve into a shimmering light.[13] The time spent in the temple is marked by the poet's forgetfulness of his obligations in the mortal world (ll. 13–14). Since Buddhist temples almost always provide free meals and snacks for their visitors, the poet most likely has had nourishment during his enchanting visit. It is a welcome respite for both his "body in peril" and his "wounded spirit."

A cuckoo's cries, which are thought to sound like "better go home," are a wake-up call reminding the poet to get back to his journey. The bird call is as startling for the poet as for the reader, for cuckoo's (mating) cries are heard in only late spring and early summer, and we are informed in the last poem that the time is midwinter.[14] "Dark and dim" (*mingming* 冥冥) is likewise unexpected: many cuckoo species do call at night despite being diurnal; yet the time of the poem is now "high noon" (*tingwu*), and the preceding lines are full of sparkling light. There is a strong feeling of delusion and unreality about this line, and the poet's waking up from his spell is caused by something as illusory as the spell itself.

In many ways the temple visited by the poet in midjourney evokes the "phantom city," *huacheng* 化城, in Buddhist scriptures. In Chapter 7 of the popular *Lotus Sutra*, the Buddha tells the parable about a group of travelers seeking a great treasure. As the travelers are exhausted by their journey and desire to give up, their guide conjures up a phantom city for them to rest in, much to their delight. But, once the travelers have rested, the city vanishes. The Buddha explains that the phantom city is the expedient teachings of Buddhism to encourage people to stay on their path to seek ultimate enlightenment, which is represented by the great treasure.

Marked off as a liminal space by the "emerald freshness" of evergreens, the Buddhist temple deep in the mountains is just like the phantom city in offering rest to the weary traveler and subsequently disappearing into the concealing vines. In this poem we see bamboos again: they are washed afresh by overnight rain, their winter shoots having shed their sheaths about (ll. 5–6)—this is precisely what the poet wished to seek when he was back in Qinzhou. But he cannot stay at the temple, nor can he ever return to it. He must move on.

---

13. The interplay of light and shadow cast by the sun and through windows and doors evokes a couplet from a poem by Yu Xin 庾信 (513–581), one of Du Fu's favorite Southern Dynasties poets: "Dreaming of Entering the Hall" 夢入堂內: "Sunlight gleams, hairpin flames stir; / window casts shadow, mirror's flowers move" 日光釵燄動, 窗影鏡花搖. Yu Xin, *Yu Zishan jizhu*, 260.

14. Du Fu himself has a poem titled "Cuckoo" 杜鵑, dated to 766, which contains the couplet "The cuckoo would come at the end of spring, / and mournfully call out among them" 杜鵑暮春至, 哀哀叫其間. *Song ben Du Gongbu ji*, 172; Xiao Difei, *Du Fu quanji*, vol. 6, 12.3492; Owen, *The Poetry of Du Fu*, vol. 4, 100–101.

(7) 青陽峽　　　Greenlight Gorge

塞外苦厭山　　I am sick to death of mountains on the frontier,
南行道彌惡　　going south, the way gets steadily worse.
岡巒相經互　　Hills and ridges continue in all directions,
4　雲水氣參錯　　vapors of water and cloud mix together.
林迥峽角來　　The woods are remote, jagged gorge edges are in my face;
天窄壁面削　　the heavens are narrow, the cliff wall pared flat.
溪西五里石　　West of the creek, five leagues of rock,
8　奮怒向我落　　roused to rage, it seems falling toward us.
仰看日車側　　Looking up, the sun's coach is tilted,
俯恐坤軸弱　　looking down, I fear earth's axis will buckle.
魑魅嘯有風　　Goblins whistle when the wind blows,
12　霜霰浩漠漠　　frost and sleet spread everywhere.
昨憶踰隴阪　　I recall recently crossing Long's slopes,
高秋視吳嶽　　in high autumn I looked on Wu Mount.
東笑蓮華卑　　I laughed that Lotus Peak in the east was low,
16　北知崆峒薄　　and realized Kongtong in the north was meager.
超然侔壯觀　　Surpassing, it matched the grandest gaze,
已謂殷寥廓　　I thought it mighty in the empty immensity.
突兀猶趁人　　Up thrust, it still followed me,
20　及茲歎冥寞　　but reaching here, I sigh that it is lost in darkness.

After the Buddhist temple, a temporary refuge, the poet's journey became more perilous and arduous. The mountains seem to take on a demonic force at Greenlight Gorge, with raging rocks, pared cliff face, and screeching wind like whistling goblins. A paradigm developed in early medieval Chinese travel accounts of all sorts about going through hell to arrive at paradise,[15] and Du Fu is certainly describing Greenlight Gorge in hellish terms.

This is the longest poem after "Setting Off from Qinzhou" and indeed the longest before the final poem of the series. It noticeably contains the six directions (liuhe 六合): south, west, east, north (ll. 2, 7, 15, 16), as well as up and down (ll. 9–10). The poet indicates that his mountain-viewing experience has by this point reached a cosmos-encompassing fullness. Ironically, in "Setting Off from Qinzhou," the poet laments that climbing high at Qinzhou does not help relieve him of cares (as climbing high for a panoramic vista is supposed to do), and he also complains that Qinzhou's "stream valleys have no remarkable rocks." Now, however, he seems to have finally seen enough of "remarkable rocks."

(8) 龍門鎮　　　Dragongate Fort

細泉兼輕冰　　Thin streams combine with light ice,
沮洳棧道濕　　over the sodden ground the plankway is wet.
不辭辛苦行　　Yet I do not balk at this bitter journey,
4　迫此短景急　　hard-pressed by the shortness of the swift days.
石門雲雪隘　　A stone gateway, blocked by clouds and snow,
古鎮峰巒集　　an ancient fort where peaks and ridges gather.

---

15. See discussions in Tian, *Visionary Journeys*.

	旌竿暮惨澹	Its flagpole seems forlorn in the twilight,
8	風水白刃澀	where winds and waters are dull blades.
	胡馬屯成皋	When Hu horses camp at Chenggao,
	防虞此何及	what good is defending a place like this?
	嗟爾遠戍人	I sigh for you men in far outposts,
12	山寒夜中泣	the mountains cold, you weep in the night.

Chenggao was a strategic pass to the east of Luoyang. Earlier that year, Shi Siming's 史思明 (703–761) rebel army had taken Tang's eastern capital, Luoyang. A sense of uselessness and helplessness pervades the poem. Snow appears again, along with clouds forming a white blockade at the gateway, a weak barrier for any Hu army coming this way. Even wind and water, displaced weapons in this poem, are *se* 澀, dull and rusty; even those tough frontier solders weep at night.

Poem #1 mentions a darkening "lone outpost" (*gushu*), hinting at the hardship of military defense on the frontier (with echoes of Chen Lin's "Watering My Horse in a Pool by the Great Wall"). The motif is picked up in Poems #3 and #5, with references to warfare, soldiery, and the empire's trouble with rebels; now it resurfaces in this poem in a more full-blown description of a lone outpost. The poet's desire to escape cold and hunger at Qinzhou reverberates with the weeping of frontier soldiers suffering from cold—an old frontier *yuefu* motif actualized in a witnessed scene in real life.

(9)	石龕	Stone Niche
	熊羆咆我東	Bears roar to my east,
	虎豹號我西	tigers and leopards howl to my west;
	我後鬼長嘯	Demons give long shrieks behind me,
4	我前狖又啼	and before me baboons cry out.
	天寒昏無日	The weather is cold; murky, no sunlight,
	山遠道路迷	the mountains are far, the way is lost.
	驅車石龕下	I drove my wagon to below Stone Niche
8	仲冬見虹霓	and in mid-winter saw a rainbow.
	伐竹者誰子	Who is that fellow cutting bamboo,
	悲歌上雲梯	singing sadly as he climbs the ladders to clouds?
	爲官采美箭	He gathers good arrows for the officials,
12	五歲供梁齊	for five years they've supplied Liang and Qi.
	苦云直簳盡	But, sad to say, the straight shafts are gone,
	無以充提攜	and there's no way to fill up his baskets.
	奈何漁陽騎	Nothing can be done about Yuyang cavalry
16	颯颯驚烝黎	in a whoosh alarming the common folk.

As the poet moves on, he seems to descend further and further into disorientation. In Poem #7, "Greenlight Gorge," the road is "increasingly bad" (*dao mi e* 道彌惡); in this poem the way is altogether "lost" (*daolu mi* 道路迷). Like in Poem #7, this poem also describes the four directions—east, west, north (behind), and south (front); but if the mountains in Poem #7 have a certain sublimity, majesty, and realness to them, those qualities are completely missing here. The poet's seeming loss of grasp on reality is reflected in the fact this poem is the most "unreal" in the series, not in the sense that it describes a dreamlike experience in Dharma Mirror Temple but in the sense that it is a composite of two poetic types: the nightmarish landscape with howling beasts and screeching demons (ll. 1–6) is depicted in the allegorical mode of the *Chu ci*, and the bamboo-cutter character (ll. 9–14) is like one of the fictional personae (e.g., "the Soldier," "the Traveler," or the "Lonely Wife") typically featured in a *yuefu* poem rather than a fully individualized specific person.

The delirious nature of the poem is also manifested by the primarily aural imagery of the poem: the poet hears all kinds of disturbing sounds from all directions, complete with the bamboo-cutter's sad singing drifting down from the clouds and the whooshing rebel riders in the far northeast. The only thing "seen" in the poem is a rainbow (ll. 7–8); but since rainbows are supposed to hide themselves in the first month of winter, a rainbow spotted in the midwinter month has an aura of optical illusion (evoking the cuckoo's cries in Poem #6), and it is both an oddity and a bad omen.[16]

The bamboo-cutter's song complains of the depletion of bamboo due to prolonged warfare: bamboos are cut to make arrows, instruments of killing, not harvested as foodstuffs. The human destruction of the natural environment evokes Poem #4, "Salt Well," and here directly threatens the poet's fantasy about "the dense bamboos with winter sprouts." In the next poem, as he moves closer to his destination, he tries to come up with a more realistic wish for life in Tonggu.

(10) 積草嶺	Plantheap Ridge
連峰積長陰	Long shadows mass on a line of peaks,
白日遞隱見	the bright sun hides, then appears.
颸颸林響交	Gusting wind and pattering rain, forest sounds mingle,
4 慘慘石狀變	the somber shapes of the rock change.
山分積草嶺	The mountain divides at Plantheap Ridge,
路異明水縣	another road leads to Brightwater County.
旅泊吾道窮	Traveling and lodging, my road is at an end,
8 衰年歲時倦	in my decline, weary of the years.
卜居尚百里	It is still a hundred leagues to site my dwelling,
休駕投諸彥	I will halt my wagon and lodge with excellent gentlemen.
邑有佳主人	There is a fine host in the town,
12 情如已會面	I feel as if we had already met.
來書語絕妙	The words in the letter he sent were splendid,
遠客驚深眷	the far traveler is amazed at such deep regard.
食蕨不願餘	I wish for no more than to eat bracken ferns,
16 茅茨眼中見	and a reed-thatched hut to appear in my eyes.

This poem derives its meaning and interest almost solely from its contextualization in the poetic set. For one thing, the realization of the depletion of the local bamboo groves in the preceding poem and the exhaustion and poverty of the common folk becomes the context in which the poet expresses a much more modest desire for life at Tonggu than he has initially harbored. Instead of chestnuts, yams, cliff honey, and bamboo shoots, he now says that he wishes for "no more than to eat bracken ferns" when he arrives at Tonggu. For another, the poet inserts a mention of the "fine host" at Tonggu here, rather than in the last poem of the series or, for that matter, in the first

---

16. "The rainbow hides and is invisible" 虹藏不見 was a topic for poetic compositions in Tang *jinshi* examination. A Li Churen 李處仁 wrote a *fu* on the topic, whereas Xu Chang 徐敞, a *jinshi* in the Jianzhong era (780–783), wrote a *shi* poem. *Quan Tang wen*, 955.9516; *Quan Tang shi*, 319.3591.

poem, not just because the closer he gets to Tonggu, the more concerned he is about his reception there, but also because the poet can thus show the reader how disappointing that "host" eventually turns out to be. The complete silence about the local host in the last poem of the set is rendered very loud by his appearance in the "Plantheep Ridge."

(11) 泥功山	Mudwork Mountain
朝行青泥上	At dawn we walked upon green mud
暮在青泥中	and at dusk we were there in green mud.
泥濘非一時	The mud and muck, cumulating over time, are not of the moment;
4　版築勞人功	planks and pounding would have cost much human effort.
不畏道途永	I don't dread how far the journey is,
乃將汩沒同	only that we may all sink together.
白馬為鐵驪	My white horse becomes an iron-black steed,
8　小兒成老翁	my little boys turn into old men.
哀猿透卻墜	A mournful gibbon, leaping over, fell in,
死鹿力所窮	a dead deer there, its strength gave out.
寄語北來人	I send word to those coming from the north,
12　後來莫匆匆	don't be in too great a hurry coming here later.

The closer he is to the end of the journey, the more eager the poet becomes; yet he must endure one more test before arrival. In his monumental work, "Lament for the South" ("Ai Jiangnan fu" 哀江南賦), which mourns his fallen dynasty, the early medieval courtier poet Yu Xin describes the miserable journey of the southern captives taken to the north and the gloomy northern landscape: "Hungry, they pursued hibernating swallows; / in darkness they followed the darting fireflies. / In Qin the water is black, / the mud is green on the pass" 飢隨蜇燕，暗逐流螢。秦中水黑，關上泥青.[17] It turns out that Du Fu and his family must also trudge through endless green mud, even though he is going south, not north, here.

There is a black humor in this poem, as in lines 5–6 he wittily parodies Xie Lingyun's couplet: "I don't care that I am far away from people, / but only regret that no one shares this with me" 不惜去人遠，但恨莫與同.[18] Using the same syntactical structure and the same rhyme word, tong, Du Fu turns it around by saying that he doesn't care how far the road is but only worries that he and his family will all sink together. Whereas Xie Lingyun laments the absence of sharing his aesthetic experience of natural beauty, Du Fu wishes for not sharing when it comes to sinking into the mud. Indeed, Xie's poem begins with the couplet "As morning dawns, I set off from the sunny cliffs; / when the light falls, I rest in the northern shades of the peak" 朝旦發陽崖，景落憩陰峰. Its echo can be clearly heard in Du Fu's opening couplet ("At dawn / and at dusk") and makes Du Fu's poem a comic Xie Lingyun spoof.[19]

Another point of humorous contrast is between the "mud work" (nigong 泥功), the name of the mountain, and the "human work" (rengong 人功) in line 4. Just as the mud and muck have accumulated for a long time and are not of a day's work for the Creator, so would human beings spend a lot of effort to overcome the mud and muck

---

17. Yu Xin, Yu Zishan jizhu, 2.162.

18. "Going from South Mountain to North Mountain, I Crossed the Lake and Looked Far and Wide" 於南山往北山經湖中瞻眺. This is a piece anthologized in the famous Wen xuan. Lu Qinli, Xian Qin Han Wei, 1172.

19. It certainly also echoes an old ballad, "Yellow Ox Gorge," as pointed out by earlier commentators. See Xiao Difei, Du Fu quanji, vol. 7, 13.1756.

by building a plank path.[20] Indeed, even for travelers going through the mountain, it is not an easy thing to do, since animals much more nimble than human beings are trapped and even destroyed by the "mud work."

To take the name of the mountain literally recalls a similar move made by the poet in the first poem of the series, though it was a much happier act of imagination: in "Setting Off for Qinzhou," our poet is excited by the name of the Chestnut Pavilion, because he thinks it means the place has fine fields producing chestnuts as food. But now he knows his folly and wants to tell "those coming from the north" not to be in such a great hurry to come this way. For him, however, it is too late.

(12) 鳳凰臺		Phoenix Terrace
	亭亭鳳凰臺	Rising high, Phoenix Terrace,
	北對西康州	facing West Kangzhou to the north.[21]
	西伯今寂寞	The Earl of the West is now lost in silence,[22]
4	鳳聲亦悠悠	the phoenix too is far, far away.
	山峻路絕蹤	The mountain too steep, the road breaks off,
	石林氣高浮	a forest of stone with vapors floating on high.
	安得萬丈梯	How can I get a ladder of ten thousand yards
8	為君上上頭	and for you climb to the very top?
	恐有無母雛	I suspect there will be motherless chicks,[23]
	飢寒日啾啾	hungry and cold, that wail each day.
	我能剖心出	I can cut out my heart,
12	飲啄慰孤愁	they can drink and peck to console their lonely sorrow.
	心以當竹實	My heart can serve as the fruit of bamboo,
	炯然忘外求	gleaming, they need seek nothing more.
16	血以當醴泉	My blood can serve as a spring of sweet water,
	豈徒比清流	how can one compare it merely to any clear stream![24]
	所重王者瑞	What is important is a good omen for the king,
	敢辭微命休	dare I refuse to end my humble life?
	坐看彩翮長	Soon one will see their colored wings grow,
20	舉意八極周	with the intent to rise and circle the world's eight ends.
	自天銜瑞圖	In their beaks they will hold an auspicious diagram from Heaven,
	飛下十二樓	they will fly down to the twelve towers.
	圖以奉至尊	The diagram will be to present to His Majesty,
24	鳳以垂鴻猷	the phoenixes are to pass on the Great Enterprise.
	再光中興業	The legacy of the Restoration will cast new light,
	一洗蒼生憂	wash the cares of the common folk entirely away.

---

20. In "Swordgate" 劍門, Poem #10 in the Tonggu-Chengdu series, Du Fu talks about blaming the One in Charge (i.e., Heaven) for creating the mountain barriers.
21. West Kangzhou refers to Tonggu.
22. The Earl of the West refers to the Zhou dynasty's founding father, King Wen. A phoenix sang at Mount Qi during his reign, a good omen for his rule.
23. Although there is no indication of the plurality of the chicks, in phoenix lore a mother phoenix always has nine or ten chicks rather than only one. For instance, in an early *yuefu* song, "Longxi Ballad" 隴西行: "The phoenixes cry *jiujiu*, / one mother with nine chicks" 鳳凰鳴啾啾，一母將九雛. Lu Qinli, *Xian Qin Han Wei*, 267.
24. According to the "Autumn Flood" chapter in *Zhuangzi*, a phoenix "only rests on *wutong* trees, only eats bamboo fruits, and only drinks from sweet-water spring" 非梧桐不止，非練實不食，非醴泉不飲. *Zhuangzi jishi*, 6.605.

深衷正為此   My deepest feelings are exactly these,
28   群盜何淹留   how can the rebel hordes last on?

An original note appended to this poem states, "The mountain is steep, and I did not make it to its highpoint" 山峻，不至高頂. The note makes it clear that the poet never sees the Phoenix Terrace on the mountain top, a glaring contrast with how he has experienced the other sites of the trip. The poetic set culminates in a mental journey, with a site seen with the mind's eye.

Again, only contextualization in this poetic set brings out fully the incredible power of this poem. For the reader who has traveled alongside Du Fu on his gruesome journey through so many poems, this is decidedly a disturbing anticlimax. There is no earthly paradise at the end of the journey, not even any mention of Tonggu. Indeed, Phoenix Terrace is to the southwest of Tonggu. The poet has literally bypassed his original destination and instead focuses his vision on a mountain that, unlike in the preceding poems of the set, he did *not* climb.

On this mental journey everything is reversed from the beginning of his trip, and yet everything can be traced back to the origin. In "Setting Off from Qinzhou," the poet speaks of being driven by cold and hunger, and, in "Red Valley," his own children cry out from hunger at sunset. The human situation is all too familiar: all the way from Qinzhou to Tonggu, the children would ask their parents, "Are we there yet?" The parents would presumably comfort them by telling them about the wonderful Tonggu—and one can well imagine the depth of the children's disappointment, let alone the adults', when they realize Tonggu is not at all what they thought it to be. The poet, however, transforms his bitter disappointment into an act of supreme compassion: he envisions orphaned phoenix chicks on the mountaintop crying for food but having no parents to feed them, and, in a crazy moment, he offers himself as food for the chicks. The image of bamboo that keeps appearing throughout the series makes a powerful comeback: in a gory and baroque move, the poet invites the chicks to dine on his heart and blood, which he says will serve as bamboo fruits and sweet-water spring, the normal phoenix diet. At the beginning of the journey, it is the poet himself who seeks "winter bamboo shoots" and "clear pond" (#1) to nourish his body; now, he is willing to forfeit his body as a human sacrifice to nurture the phoenixes. Although wishing to climb "the ladders to clouds" like the bamboo-cutter in Poem #9, he does not intend to cut bamboos but wants to be their substitute—not becoming arrows to kill but becoming food to sustain life. Ultimately, he hopes his self-sacrifice will enable the divine birds to bring about the restoration of the dynasty and to "wash the cares of the common folk entirely away."

This transformation—from worries about oneself and one's own family, to a profound empathy for other people, and finally to concerns about the empire and the common folk—can be observed in Du Fu's other poems. The most famous example is perhaps "Song on How My Thatched Roof Was Ruined by the Autumn Wind" ("Maowu wei qiufeng suo po ge" 茅屋為秋風所破歌), in which he is kept awake all night by cold and leaks but turns his thoughts to the "poor scholars of all the world" (*tianxia hanshi* 天下寒士) and to the desire to build a great mansion of thousands of rooms for them. The "Phoenix Terrace" is nevertheless different: instead of human beings, specifically his fellow *shi* (scholars / members of the gentry), the poet expresses his compassion for birds, and the solution he suggests is to literally sacrifice his own life.

Many late imperial commentators were disturbed by the grisly imagery, passion, and extremity of the poem. They either begrudgingly give qualified praise or are downright critical.[25] In the age of neo-Confucianism, in the context of the predominant reading of Du Fu as a Confucian "sage" (shi sheng 詩聖), the poet's macabre fantasy of feeding his body to the birds strikes a discordant note in several ways. As stated unequivocally in the *Classic of Filial Piety*, one of the Confucian canon, "One's body, hair, and skin are received from one's parents, and one does not dare to do them harm: this is the beginning of filial piety" 身體髮膚，受之父母，不敢毀傷，孝之始也.[26] It is even more unthinkable to harm one's body for the sake of birds, divine birds notwithstanding. Confucius famously "inquired after people but not horses" after a stable was burned down; he also explicitly stated that he could not bring himself to "join the flock of birds and beasts" (i.e., leave human society behind and become a recluse).[27] A hierarchy between human beings and the other species is discernable in these quotations. The extreme gesture of self-destruction in graphic terms also constitutes an offense to the classical belief in emotional moderation and restraint in poetic expression.[28]

In the Buddhist discourse, however, there are many stories about self-mutilation and self-martyrdom, either as an offering to the Buddha or to save another sentient being from death. The great compassion that leads to self-sacrifice for the sake of other people is the very characteristic of a bodhisattva, as opposed to an ordinary Buddhist's efforts for self-cultivation and self-salvation. The best-known of such stories is the one about Prince Mahāsattva's 摩訶薩埵 compassion for starving tiger cubs. In the story the prince saw a mother tiger that was so hungry that it was about to eat its young and decided to offer himself to the mother tiger. Since the mother tiger was too weak to devour him, the prince used a dried stalk of bamboo to stab himself so that the tiger could drink his blood and become stronger and threw himself down from a cliff; the tiger subsequently fed on the blood and flesh of the prince. Later the prince was revealed as an incarnation of the Buddha himself.[29] This jātaka tale (often referred to as *Sachui taizi bensheng* 薩埵太子本生 in Chinese) is a favorite subject in medieval Chinese Buddhist visual arts, from the Dunhuang Caves to the Longmen Grottos.[30] It is particularly worth mentioning that

---

25. Zhang Jin 張溍 (1621–1678) refers to it as "permuted tune" *biandiao* 變調, saying that "if one looks at it by itself, it might well be excised [from the collection]" 以一首觀則若可刪. Qiao Yi 喬億 (fl. 1730s) admits reluctantly, "The intent is noble, so it does not matter if the words are wild and absurd" 意正不嫌辭誕. Guo Zengxin 郭曾炘 (1855–1928) opines, "This is after all not a good poem" 此詩畢竟不佳. Wang Shilu 王士祿 (1626–1673) comments tersely, almost grouchily, on this poem: "Just like Meng Jiao" 似孟郊. Meng Jiao (751–814) is noted for the impassioned anguish, harshness, and madness of his poetry. See Xiao Difei, *Du Fu quanji*, 7.1765–68.
26. *Xiaojing zhushu*, 1.11.
27. *Lunyu zhushu*, 10.90, 18.165. As Zheng Xuan 鄭玄 (127–200) glosses, "[Confucius] treasured human beings but treated animals as unimportant."
28. For instance, Confucius praised the first poem of the *Classic of Poetry* for being "joyful but not excessive, sorrowful but not acrimonious" 樂而不淫，哀而不傷. *Lunyu zhushu*, 3.30. "Gentleness and temperance" 溫柔敦厚 are considered the consequence of being instructed in the *Classic of Poetry*. *Liji zhushu*, 26.845.
29. This story appears in different forms in many popular sutras, such as *Liudu ji jing* 六度集經, translated by Kang Senghui 康僧會 (d. 280), *Xian yu jing* 賢愚經, translated by Huijue 慧覺 (fl. mid-fifth century), and the influential *Jin guangming jing* 金光明經, translated by Dharmakṣema (or Tan Wuchen 曇無讖, 385–433) and then again by the eminent Tang monk Yijing 義淨 (635–713). The version from *Jin guangming jing* is included in the seventh-century Buddhist encyclopedia *Fayuan zhulin* 法苑珠林. See Shi Daoshi 釋道世, *Fayuan zhulin jiaozhu*, 96.2756–762.
30. See Gao Haiyan, "Zhongguo Han chuan," 170–80; Wang Hanwei, "Mogao ku bihua," 42–45. For the story illustrated in the Binyang 賓陽 Cave at Longmen, see McNair, *Donors of Longmen*, 44–45.

the tale is prominently featured in early medieval mural paintings of the Mt. Maiji 麥積山 Grottos in Tianshui 天水, Gansu—the old Qinzhou where Du Fu had lived.[31] Indeed, one of Du Fu's Qinzhou poems, "Mountain Temple" ("Shansi" 山寺), is precisely about the Buddhist temple on Mt. Maiji.[32] One can be certain that the poet was familiar with the Mahāsattva jātaka narrative, and its extensive visual representations may well have left a deep impression during his sojourn in Qinzhou.

The phantom city in the *Lotus Sutra* that offers a temporary respite for the weary traveler is usually regarded a metaphor for teachings about self-cultivation and self-salvation, whereas the ultimate transcendence lies in striving for the liberation of all sentient beings from suffering, symbolized by the "great treasure" sought by the traveler. Although Du Fu's poetic set opens with echoes of Confucius, the last poem of the set provides a distinctly Buddhist resolution. The structure of the poetic set is established by the denouement, as the poet arrives not just at his destination but also at a spiritual enlightenment, in which the hardship of the journey finally finds meaning and coherence. The distinct travel poems become strung together in a Buddhist narrative of transformation and illumination.

After staying at Tonggu for less than a month, Du Fu was on the road again, this time to Chengdu. He wrote another set of poems for this journey. It is certainly no accident that the Tonggu-Chengdu set also contains twelve poems, making it a perfect match for the Qinzhou-Tonggu set. Each poem in the second set forms a counterpart, in one way or another, of the corresponding poem in the first. The architectonic structure of the two poetic sets, each of which constitutes the mirror image of the other, deserves further exploration, but here suffice to say that Buddhism is a key structuring device in the Qinzhou-Tonggu series. Poem #6 and Poem #12 both contain a distinctly Buddhist motif; read in context, they are the links that connect all twelve poems as a coherent story of change and redemption. The poet never finds his bamboo shoots and sweet-water spring at the destination of his journey, but he finds a new sense of purpose and a renewed sense of self.

Ultimately, I am not interested in adding to the discussion of questions such as "Was Du Fu primarily a Confucian or a Buddhist?" or "How much of Du Fu's thought is Confucian and how much Buddhist?" Rather, I hope to have demonstrated that Buddhism was a pervasive multimedia presence in medieval Chinese society and intersected with literature in a variety of ways. Its influence on a member of the literati cannot be understood solely as doctrinal assimilation or intellectual stimulation, and the manifestations of such influence in a poetic text exceed terms, allusions, and images. Accepting the complexity of social reality in a decompartmentalized manner contributes to a fresh reading of a set of famous "travel poems." Such a reading seeks to shed light on how a great poet uses the architectonic construction of a poetic sequence, a mimesis of his physical journey, to make sense of the world, and how he finds in the Buddhist teachings a perfect allegorical embodiment of his well-wrought experience.

31. Wei Wenbin and Gao Haiyan, "Gansu guancang," 63–73.
32. Xiao Difei, *Du Fu quanji*, vol. 3, 6.1517. Owen, *The Poetry of Du Fu*, vol. 2, 164–65.

Section III

Reception and Re-creation

7
Sources of Difficulty

Reading and Understanding Du Fu

Christopher M. B. Nugent

驥子好男兒	Jizi is a fine boy;
前年學語時	last year was when he learned to speak.
問知人客姓	He asked to know the names of our visitors,
誦得老夫詩	and was able to recite his old man's poems.

—Du Fu, "Expressing What Stirred Me" ("Qianxing" 遣興)[1]

In Old Du's poems every word has a source. If you read them carefully thirty or fifty times, searching for points where he has exercised his intent, then there is much that you will have gained.

老杜詩字字有出處，熟讀三五十遍，尋其用意處，則所得多矣。[2]

—Huang Tingjian 黃庭堅 (1045–1105)

In these two quotations, from Du Fu himself and from the Northern Song writer and critic Huang Tingjian, we find very different perspectives on the great poet's works. In Du Fu's poem a proud father boasts that his son, no more than three or four at the time, can already recite some of his poems. The emphasis here is on orality. Jizi, whose given name is Zongwu 宗武, can speak but is some years away from reading and writing. He has, no doubt, learned these poems from hearing his father recite them. Du Fu does not claim that his son understands his poems. To *song* (誦, "recite") is not necessarily to *tong* (通, "fully comprehend"), as centuries of schoolchildren and their teachers can attest. We can also assume—because we want to think well of Du Fu—that Du Fu has taught his son some simple quatrains and other *shi* poems, rather than his longer and more turgid *fu* 賦 (poetic expositions). Though in another poem about his son Du Fu claims that "poetry is our family business" 詩是吾家事,[3] in "Expressing What Stirred Me" it is not work—the result of painstaking effort—but an ability that comes as naturally as speaking.

---

1. Owen, *The Poetry of Du Fu*, vol. 1, 262–63. See also Xiao Difei, *Du Fu quanji*, vol. 2, 3.794. All quotations of Du Fu's works are from Owen and all translations follow Owen, sometimes with minor changes. Citations are also given to *Du Fu quanji*.
2. Hua Wenxuan, *Du Fu juan*, 128.
3. "Zongwu's Birthday" 宗武生日. Owen, *The Poetry of Du Fu*, vol. 4, 342–43; Xiao Difei, *Du Fu quanji*, vol. 5, 9.2647–50.

Huang Tingjian's claim instead focuses on Du Fu's works as written texts, under-standing of which comes only after great effort. Instead of speech (*yu* 語) we have char-acters (*zi* 字). Rather than recitation (誦), we have reading (*du* 讀). This is not to say that the oral/aural aspects were not still important for Huang—most of these terms are flexible enough to include both the oral and the written—but his emphasis is different, and the assumption is that the reader experiences Du Fu's works through a written text. Effort is more explicit as well: reading must be done repeatedly and with careful attention, as Du Fu is a poet whose oeuvre is fully and intentionally infused with the literary inheritance. His writings are the result of careful and deeply informed craft; only with careful and deeply informed reading can one grasp the true intent behind specific wordings.

This is an image of Du Fu as a difficult and challenging poet. Huang Tingjian ties this difficulty to what he sees as Du Fu's almost encyclopedic grasp of the literary and historical past. He specifically contrasts Du Fu (and, in this case, Han Yu 韓愈 [768–824]) with later readers in this respect:

> When Old Du composed poems and Tuizhi composed prose, there was not a single word that lacked a source. It is likely just that people in later days are less well read and thus say that Han and Du came up with these phrasings themselves.
> 老杜作詩，退之作文，無一字無來處。蓋後人讀書少，故謂韓杜自作此語耳。[4]

Du Fu's genius here is not due to his unprecedented use of particular words and phrases but rather the opposite: it is the precedent that matters.[5] To truly understand Du Fu, the reader must know what Du Fu knew; that, Huang Tingjian implies, takes hard work.

Huang Tingjian's reading of Du Fu is characteristic of an approach that quickly came to dominate the reception of the poet's works in the Song and has continued to do so in many quarters down to the present day.[6] For nearly a millennium, Du Fu, more than any other Chinese poet (and perhaps any other poet in human history, with the possible exception of Shakespeare), has been an object of study. The most recent anno-tated edition of his complete works, Xiao Difei's *Du Fu quanji jiaozhu*, runs to twelve volumes and well over 6,000 densely packed pages. If these annotations do not manage to trace every word to its source, it is not for lack of trying. The implication is that this apparatus is necessary to understand Du Fu in the way in which Huang Tingjian and his many successors have suggested we should: as the poet historian whose writings offer deep rewards only as the prize for arduous study.

In this chapter I approach Du Fu from a different angle. Instead of assuming that Du Fu had memorized the full literary inheritance and wrote nary a word for which he did not have every previous important usage in the front of his mind, I examine a sample set of Du Fu's works to determine, in broad terms, the extent to which they would have been comprehensible to a reader with a basic education in the period in which Du Fu wrote. This is a preliminary exploration of poetic difficulty, a notion that is itself difficult to pin down. When scholars in the modern West say that Du Fu is dif-ficult, part of what they mean is that he is difficult to translate in a way that conveys to a new audience why he is "China's greatest poet." This is a meaningful difficulty, and

---

4. Hua Wenxuan, *Du Fu juan*, 120–21.
5. See a discussion of a similar point in Chen Jue, *Making China's Greatest Poet*, 214–15.
6. For a discussion of the reaction against this mode of reading Du Fu in the Ming and Qing, see Ji Hao, "Poetics of Transparency," especially Chapters 1 and 2.

it explains why it is only with the publication of Stephen Owen's monumental achievement that China's greatest poet has been fully translated into English. But Du Fu was difficult to Huang Tingjian as well, for reasons that are different but overlapping.

The notion of a text being difficult or easy is always bound by context. Answers to the question "difficult for whom" do not always map easily onto judgments of literary sophistication: a teenager's text message may well be indecipherable to an accomplished middle-aged scholar of Milton but utterly transparent to another teenager. For my analysis here I will focus on two basic aspects of linguistic and poetic difficulty: vocabulary and allusions. The context in which I will address these forms of difficulty is based on our knowledge of the kinds of texts used in the early stages of literary training in the first half of the Tang. Our imagined reader will thus not be a Song scholar with a library of printed collections close at hand, and certainly not a modern scholar with heavily annotated editions and dozens of searchable electronic resources, but an average member of the medieval literary elite at an early stage of learning the vocabulary and references that would eventually allow him to meet the basic cultural demands of his social context.

I focus on a constrained sample: Du Fu's renowned series of poems written during his time in Kuizhou, "Stirred by Autumn" ("Qiuxing bashou" 秋興八首).[7] I do not claim that these works are somehow representative of Du Fu's larger output; they clearly are not (just as they are not the sort of works Du Fu would have recited to his three-year-old son), but they are characteristic of a certain late style. I have chosen them as a potentially revealing sample because of their widely accepted place as the height of poetic art in traditional China. As Owen has written, they "have a strong claim to be the greatest poems in the Chinese language."[8] This is itself a strong claim but one that finds ample agreement from centuries of readers and critics.[9] Equally important for my purposes here, the poems in this series are considered to be among Du Fu's most challenging, though it is not always made clear wherein this difficulty lies,[10] and have arguably accrued more commentary since the Song than any of his other works.[11] My goal here is neither to add to that commentary nor to reexamine the series on aesthetic or literary-historic grounds but instead to use these works as a test case to examine the notion of poetic difficulty. I approach these poems as information that can be quantified and analyzed as such. An analysis of this sort is only one lens through which to view these works. There is much that such a lens obscures, but it also has the potential to reveal new insights. Though this poetic series will be the focus of my argument, I will also briefly discuss some of Du Fu's *fu* works for comparative purposes, as *fu* are typically considered a more lexically and allusively challenging poetic form. My tentative conclusion is that, in the case of this particular set of Du Fu's works, perceived difficulty may ultimately prove to be a function more of particular reading practices and assumptions about Du Fu than of the content of the poetic works themselves.

---

7. Owen, *The Poetry of Du Fu*, vol. 4, 352–60. Xiao Difei, *Du Fu quanji*, vol. 7, 13.3798–41.
8. Owen, *The Great Age*, 265.
9. For a detailed discussion of the poems' merits, see the introductory section of Ye Jiaying, *Du Fu qiuxing*, 1–62.
10. Mei Tsu-lin and Kao Yu-kung have written convincingly of the innovative and carefully crafted phonetic patterns of the series. See Mei and Kao, "Tu Fu's 'Autumn Meditations.'"
11. Most of this commentary was gathered by Ye Jiaying in *Du Fu qiuxing bashou jishuo*.

Vocabulary Benchmarks

A poem is more than a succession of independent semantic units and their "diction-ary definitions," and no one would claim that understanding a poem is a matter of vocabulary alone. Analysis of vocabulary can, however, give us a sense of the minimum knowledge that would be necessary, if not necessarily sufficient, for understanding. A poem with a broad lexical range as indicated by a high percentage of more obscure words would likely present challenges that are a meaningful indication of difficulty to readers.

Our first task is to establish a baseline of literacy to use as a benchmark for evaluat-ing the difficulty of these poems on the lexical level. The question of what constitutes literacy has long been controversial, whether the context is the contemporary world or ancient ones.[12] Any definition of literacy is truly valid only for a particular context, with that context being a mix of social expectations, economic requirements, textual characteristics, and other factors. Aimée Dorr's basic definition of literacy as the "ability to read and write text, to encode and decode the symbol system of text, and to inter-pret meaning in textual representations" provides a serviceable starting point for our purposes here, though our interest is solely in reading, not writing.[13] Our real concern is not what constitutes literacy in Du Fu's day, but rather what set of written words we could expect readers to know at different stages in their education and the degree of overlap between these words and Du Fu's poetic vocabulary.

This question is not an easy one to answer with any certainty, as we know surpris-ingly little about the concrete aspects of early education in the medieval period. Most discussions of education in the Tang tend to focus on questions theoretical and moral, rather than methodological, and we lack anything approaching a systematic descrip-tion of specific pedagogical techniques. We do, however, have some sense of the materi-als that people preparing for the civil service examinations, or at least replicating that basic educational program, were likely to study. A work entitled *Miscellaneous Excerpts* (*Za chao* 雜抄), discovered at Dunhuang, includes among its diverse contents a list of titles following the question, "For the classics and histories, who compiled, composed, and annotated them" 經史何人修撰製注?[14] Actual classics and histories only make up a portion of the list, with the rest consisting of everything from the literary anthology *Wen xuan* 文選 to the rhyme book *Qie yun* 切韻. Zheng Acai believes the entry to be something akin to the modern "study outline" and argues that it was indeed intended as a list for students preparing for different portions of the civil service exam.[15] Whether or not this claim is accurate, the list does provide unique evidence for the kinds of works considered important for educational purposes. Among these are five works either clearly aimed at early learners or consistently named as works that were studied

---

12. For a good introduction to contemporary theoretical debates about literacy, see Street, *Literacy in Theory and Practice*. For a range of perspectives on ancient Greece and Rome, see Johnson and Parker, *Ancient Literacies*. Li and Branner's *Writing and Literacy in Early China* is the fullest set of approaches to issues of literacy for early China published in English. There remains little written for the medieval period in China.

13. Dorr, "What Constitutes Literacy," 136.

14. For full or near full texts of the work, see Pelliot manuscripts P.2721 and P.3649, accessed through gallica. bnf.fr. For discussions of the *Za chao* see Naba Toshisada, *Tōdai shakai*, 197–268, and Zheng Acai and Zhu Fengyu, *Dunhuang mengshu*, 165–93.

15. Zheng Acai and Zhu Fengyu, *Dunhuang mengshu*, 191.

by adolescents. These can give us an approximate sense of the vocabulary such a reader would be likely to master before moving on to more complex and difficult works, I here describe these five works briefly (as befits our use of them in this context).

The *Thousand Character Text* (*Qianzi wen* 千字文) was most likely composed in the early sixth century and is the best-known primer to survive from the medieval period. In continuous circulation and use as an early reading primer since its earliest days, it is arguably the most successful such work in history. Though there are many different stories of the work's origin, scholarly consensus attributes it to the Liang 梁 dynasty (502–557) official Zhou Xingsi 周興嗣 (d. 521), who was asked by Liang Emperor Wu 梁武帝 (r. 502–549) to arrange a set of 1,000 characters collected from rubbings of the famous calligrapher Wang Xizhi's 王羲之 (ca. 303–ca. 361) calligraphy into a coherent rhyming text.[16] The work famously consists of 1,000 nonrepeating characters put into parallel rhyming couplets of four-character lines. The few accounts we have of its use in the medieval period indicate that it quickly enjoyed wide circulation. Li Liang 李良 writes in his 746 presentation memorial for the later Tang primer, *Mengqiu* 蒙求 (*Child Seeks*), "In a recent era Zhou Xingsi composed the *Qianzi wen* and it has also spread through the realm" 近代周興嗣撰千字文，亦頒行天下.[17] Other writers depict its use as the basis of jokes and games in the period.[18] In terms of surviving textual evidence, there are more than 140 documents found at Dunhuang that include all or part of the *Qianzi wen*. There is thus ample reason to assume that it was broadly memorized and that its content was a part of most literate people's basic vocabulary from an early stage of their education.

Our second benchmark text, *Important Instructions for Beginners* (*Kaimeng yaoxun* 開蒙要訓) is far less well known but may actually be more representative of common primers from the period than the *Qianzi wen* is.[19] Like the latter, *Kaimeng yaoxun* consists of four-character lines organized into rhyming couplets, some of which are parallel while many others are not. There are 1,400 characters in all with scarcely any repetition. The extent and depth of vocabulary in the work is much greater than what is found in the *Qianzi wen*. *Kaimeng yaoxun* is generally organized by topics, which range from geography ("The Five Cardinal Peaks are named Song, Hua, Huo, Tai, and Heng" 五嶽嵩華, 霍泰恒名) to physical ailments ("leprosy, baldness, hives, numbness; ringworm, scabies, ulcer, carbuncle" 癩禿胗痹, 癬疥瘍疽). The work does not appear to have made it into the growing print culture of the Song and is completely absent from all surviving official and unofficial bibliographies in China. The two medieval period sources that mention it are the *Za chao*, which credits it to one Ma Renshou 馬仁壽, and Fujiwara Sukeyo's 藤原佐世 (847–897) catalog of Chinese books in Japan, *Nihonkoku genzaisho mokuroku* 日本國見在書目錄, which includes a listing for "*Kaimeng yaoxun* in

16. Judgments on the date of composition differ, but all fall in the first quarter of the sixth century, sometime between 507 and 521. See the discussion of dating in Zhang Xinpeng, *Dunhuang xieben*, 125 26. All Dunhuang copies of the *Qianzi wen* that included authorial information describe it as "set to rhyme" 次韻 by Zhou Xingsi. For a detailed discussion of the authorship attribution, see Zhang Nali, "'Dunhuang ben," 102–3.
17. *Quan Tang wen*, 19.10574.
18. See, for example, "Qianzi wen yu qi she" 千字文語乞社, in *Taiping guangji*, 252.1957; and "Huan mu bi ren" 患目鼻人, in *Taiping guangji*, 257.2007; and the discussion in Li Pengfei, *Tangdai feixieshi*, 45.
19. Zheng Acai and Zhu Fengyu, *Dunhuang mengshu*, 178–79. For additional discussion, see Naba Toshisada, *Tōdai shakai*, 235; and Wang Sanqing, *Dunhuang leishu*, 124–25.

one scroll, composed by Mr. Ma" 開蒙要訓一卷馬氏撰.[20] In part because it has survived only in Dunhuang, many scholars have treated *Kaimeng yaoxun* as a work intended for farming families and perhaps only popular regionally.[21] There is, however, no reason to associate the work exclusively with Dunhuang or with the "common people." It was likely composed and first circulated in the more central region, with its reach into both Dunhuang and Japan as evidence of extensive later circulation. The fact that it is included in the *Za chao's* list of works to study with the eventual goal of taking the exam shows that it was well known in the period as a basic educational work. This speculation is further supported by the forty full or partial copies of the work that have been found in Dunhuang, including versions with annotations (to which we will return below). By including it as a benchmark text, we get a more representative set of basic vocabulary than we would get from the *Qianzi wen* alone.[22]

The two other primer-type works I have included in the benchmark set are the Han period *Quick Mastery Text* (*Jijiu pian* 急就篇) and the *Classic of Filial Piety* (*Xiao jing* 孝經). Scholars have described the *Jijiu pian* as likely the most commonly used primer in the period from its composition in the first century BCE through the end of the Six Dynasties.[23] Its inclusion in the *Za chao*, likely a work of the first half of the eighth century, shows that it was still being used as an educational text well into the Tang period. Even more than the *Qianzi wen* and *Kaimeng yaoxun*, *Jijiu pian* is a list of important vocabulary. With 2,144 characters in all, it includes everything from common surnames to the names of body parts. There is significant overlap with the contents of *Kaimeng yaoxun* in particular, but *Jijiu pian* also fills in many gaps (*Kaimeng yaoxun*, for example, includes no names as such). The *Xiao jing*, which appears to have already existed by the beginning of the Han,[24] is the shortest of these four texts in terms of separate characters. Though its total length of 1,800 makes it longer than either the *Qianzi wen* or *Kaimeng yaoxun* overall, the *Xiao jing* includes a great deal of repetition and thus includes only 372 different characters.[25] The other three primers include little or no repetition. The real importance of the *Xiao jing* as a benchmark text is the fact that, to a greater degree than the other primers (and especially *Kaimeng yaoxun*), there are good indications that nearly every educated child learned it by heart early on.

The final complete text included in the benchmark set is also the only one not clearly composed for early learners—namely, the Confucian *Analects* (*Lunyu* 論語). While not a primer, it does seem to have been the first "adult" classic that every student learned and likely memorized. Biographical texts mention it repeatedly when discussing their subject's early education. To give just one example: Quan Deyu 權德輿 (759–818) notes

---

20. Yajima Genryō, Nihonkoku, 67.
21. See, for example, Zhang Xinpeng's suggestion that it is longer than the *Qianzi wen* because farming families would have less time to study and would have to cram in more vocabulary in that limited time (Zhang Xinpeng, *Dunhuang xieben*, 162).
22. As a work with no received text, *Kaimeng yaoxun* presents more challenges as a benchmark. The number of nonstandard characters, including many that cannot be reproduced in Unicode, is also substantial. I have taken the basic main text found in P.2578 and augmented it with Stein manuscript S.705. My goal is not to establish a "critical text" for *Kaimeng yaoxun* but rather to get a basic character set for early learners. For that purpose, I believe this approach is sufficient if not ideal.
23. Wilkinson, *Chinese History*, 295.
24. For discussion of dating, see Loewe, *Early Chinese Texts*, 142–46. For an English translation accompanied by commentary and the original Chinese text, see Rosemont and Ames, *The Chinese Classic of Family Reverence*.
25. Wilkinson, *Chinese History*, 296.

in an epitaph for his grandson, who died at age thirteen, that the boy had read the work as part of his studies.[26] At almost 16,000 character positions, the *Analects* is by far the longest text in the benchmark set. At the same time, these 16,000 character positions are filled by only 1,351 different characters, making the text quite similar to both *Kaimeng yaoxun* and the *Qianzi wen* for the purposes of serving as a benchmark.

Even with the full texts of these four works, there are still many common characters that are not covered. This is due in part to the fact that though these texts are indeed primers (most often described in Chinese scholarship as *mengshu* 蒙書), they are really best termed "intermediate" rather than truly "beginning" texts. That is, they are not intended for students at the earliest stages of their "literacy training." The *Qianzi wen*, for example, does not include such basic characters as *shan* 山 (mountain) or the characters for the numbers 1, 3, 6, 7, and 10. It also lacks both any sort of orthographically based structure that moves from simpler to more complex characters and a frequency-based progression. While *tiandi* 天地 (heaven and earth) are common terms found in a range of written materials, it is unlikely that young learners would quickly encounter opportunities to use *honghuang* 洪荒 (vast and desolate), which appears in the second line of the work. The same holds true for the other primers in our benchmark set. The *Kaimeng yaoxun* does not include most numbers or many other basic words. For example, it also lacks the word *shan*, though it does include the more advanced (that is, less common) "cardinal peak" *yue* 岳. The *Jijiu pian* does include *shan*, but it is also aimed more at an intermediate audience.

The texts for the most basic level of literacy training, if there even were established texts as opposed to just a range of variable practices, have not survived. The most likely reason is that such works were simply not valued enough to be reproduced and then later printed. The finds at Dunhuang do, however, provide us with some indications of what characters would have been considered more "basic" than those found in our four "intermediate primers." A version of *Kaimeng yaoxun* included in Dunhuang manuscript P.2578 includes, in addition to the full text of *Kaimeng yaoxun*, smaller interlinear characters that indicate the pronunciation of the main-text characters. For example, in one small section of the text we have the following main-text characters paired with pronunciation characters (here placed in parentheses): 霧 (武), 露 (路), 瞑 (明), 霞 (遐), 靂 (力), 震 (鎮), 嵩 (松), 雹 (郝), and 泰 (太).[27] All of these pairs seem to have been homophonous in the medieval period.[28] In all of these examples, the pronunciation characters are orthographically simpler than their main-text pairing, and that is almost always the case throughout the text. In many instances the pronunciation characters are the phonetic element of the more complicated characters, as is the case with 露 and its pronunciation character 路 here. In other cases there is no orthographic connection between the two characters, as we see with 霧 (武) and 靂 (力) above, and in the following examples: 舒 (書), 筆 (必), 穿 (川), and 冶 (也). In all, there are 442 instances of a character in the main text being paired with such pronunciation aids.

---

26. Quan Deyu, "Shang sun Jinma muzhiming" 殤孫進馬墓誌銘, in *Quan Tang wen*, 506.5152. I thank Anna M. Shields for bringing this piece to my attention.

27. For transcription of P.2578, including the pronunciation characters, see Zhang Xinpeng, *Dunhuang xieben*, 177–259.

28. For a full discussion of their phonology and medieval rhymes, see Zhang Xinpeng, *Dunhuang xieben*, 182–82nn9–18.

I have included this set of 442 characters as a benchmark not because we can assume most young learners would have used this particular text of *Kaimeng yaoxun*—we surely cannot assume that—but because they are the closest we can come to a set of characters that were likely to be commonly known. This is a speculative claim: beyond the fact that these characters indicate the pronunciation of the characters with which they are paired, we know very little about their role as paratextual additions. We do not, for example, know whether they are notes put in by a user of this particular manuscript or whether they are a feature of a particular textual lineage of *Kaimeng yaoxun*. Because each is orthographically simpler than the character with which it is paired and is, in most contexts, seemingly far more common, I do believe we are on firm ground in including them in our benchmark.

This set of five benchmark texts discussed above is far from exhaustive. One could rightfully argue that, for example, the full text of the *Classic of Documents* (*Shangshu* 尚書) or the *Classic of Poetry* (*Shi jing* 詩經) should be included as well, as they were often studied by learners at an early stage in their education. For our purposes here, however, a lower baseline is more appropriate. To claim that contemporaries who had memorized the Five Classics and spent years studying the *Wen xuan* would have the linguistic tools to understand Du Fu's work is to state the obvious. My goal here is to probe at the edges.

Lexical Difficulty

The most common critical approach to the "Stirred by Autumn" poems is to consider them as a set of regulated verse in the seven-character line composed by a particular historical figure in the second half of the eighth century.[29] This approach necessarily brings in a host of associations connected to genre, form, literary history, phonology, and other issues, all of which are indeed crucial to understanding and interpreting the poems. But there are other ways to approach these works as well. Thinking of them as a form of quantifiable information allows us to perform a type of analysis that may give a new perspective on how they would have been read and received by different audiences in different periods.

The raw numbers suggest that on the lexical level, at least, these poems are not particularly difficult.[30] The series has a total of 448 character positions filled by 340 distinct characters. Of these distinct characters, 286 also appear in the benchmark set, meaning

---

29. It is important to point out that my analysis here is based solely on written graphs and thus sidesteps complex questions of the distinction between aural and visual comprehension. There are clearly poems from the Tang that would have been difficult to fully understand, or were at least ambiguous, if only heard chanted. See Owen, "What Did Liuzhi Hear?" Even the apocryphal story of Bai Juji 白居易 (772–846) chanting his poems to an illiterate woman who lived down the lane so as to assure their aural comprehensibility implies that such comprehensibility was not a given. At the same time, focus on written texts provides possibilities for analysis that simply do not exist for oral practices. See Mei and Kao, "Tu Fu's 'Autumn Meditations,'" for an excellent example of the kind of phonetic analysis that is possible.

30. I have performed the statistical analysis of these poems and the *fu* discussed below by using the Literary Sieve program developed by Joshua Day and Sarah Schneewind with a grant from the University of California, San Diego. For a full description of the program, see http://ctext.org/tools/literacy-sieve. The version I have used is entitled The Sieve Online and was developed by Brent Ho. I accessed this through the MARKUS site developed as part of the project "Communication and Empire: Chinese Empires in Comparative Perspective" at https://dh.chinese-empires.eu/markus/beta/sieveOnline.html. For the benchmark texts, I have used the versions of the *Qianzi wen* and the *Xiao jing* included as part of The

the characters in those basic texts cover 84 percent of the full character set of "Stirred by Autumn." Because there is a fair amount of character repetition in the poems, the numbers are slightly different for total character positions. Of the 448 character positions, 391 (87 percent) are filled by characters from the benchmark set. The benchmarks, as noted, do not provide a perfect picture of the vocabulary a younger learner would likely know. To get a more accurate view of the ease or difficult of this vocabulary, we could tweak these totals a little. That is, there are a number of characters in "Stirred by Autumn" that, though not in the benchmark set, would most likely have been familiar to learners who had reached an intermediate stage of literacy. I would count among these the following: *kan* 看 (to look), *yu* 漁 (fisherman), *sen* 森 (thicket), *wo* 臥 (to lie down), *ou* 鷗 (gull), *hu* 湖 (lake), and *ku* 苦 (bitter). If these alone were added to the benchmark set, it would instead account for 86 percent of the distinct characters and 89 percent of the character positions. It is further worth noting that many of the remaining terms are far from obscure as well, whether the word for "parrot" (*yingwu* 鸚鵡) or for "companion" (*lü* 侶). We also find substantial variation between the separate poems. The final poem in the series has fourteen character positions with nonbenchmark characters (though these include *yingwu*, *lü*, and *ku*). In contrast, the only characters in the third poem in the series that do *not* appear in the benchmark set are *yu* 漁 and *ling* 陵 (mound), neither of which is obscure.

To put these numbers in context, we can compare them with another famous poetic set from approximately the same period, Wang Wei's 王維 (ca. 699–ca. 761) series of twenty quatrains written on locations at his estate and collectively entitled the *Wang River Collection* (*Wangchuan ji* 輞川集).[31] These poems make for an interesting comparison with "Stirred by Autumn": they include some of his best-known works but are not typically described as presenting notable difficulty on the lexical level; they also provide a similar sample size, with 400 total character positions. When we examine these poems against the benchmark texts, we get a result akin to that for Du Fu's series: of the 400 characters positions, 335 are filled with characters found in the benchmark set, for coverage of about 84 percent. As with "Stirred by Autumn," there are a number of characters that do not appear in the benchmark set but likely would be known to readers with even a minimal education (many of the characters are the same as those in "Stirred by Autumn"). These basic numbers indicate that the *Wangchuan ji* poems overall may have been slightly more lexically challenging than the "Stirred by Autumn" poems, though the numbers are close enough that the difference is not a meaningful one.

In purely lexical terms, it appears that the "Stirred by Autumn" poems would present few difficulties to a Tang reader at the intermediate stage of his education. The fact that the vocabulary used in these poems seems to be no more obscure than that employed by Wang Wei, a poet better known for his "simplicity of diction,"[32] implies that Du Fu's series would not strike a contemporary reader as particularly challenging. These are not works larded with obscure terms for unusual plants or rarely used duplicative binomes for the sound of wind through a particular type of tree but rather

---

Sieve. For the *Analects* and *Jijiu pian*, I have used the version available through ctext.org. I created the version of *Kaimeng yaoxun* and the pronunciation characters based on P.2578 as described above.

31. Wang Wei, *Wang Youcheng ji*, 241–50.
32. Owen, *The Great Age*, 36.

poems that mostly use a vocabulary available to learners who had mastered texts from the early stages of literary training.

An objection might be raised that this analysis simply tells us that what we would expect to be the case for *shi* poetry is indeed true: it has a limited lexical range. To explore the notion of lexical range and difficulty in Du Fu's poetry, the appropriate material is instead his *fu* compositions. Though less acclaimed, these are the writings he had used to display his learning and mastery of the more challenging aspects of the poetic art. On the face of it, this is a reasonable point; *fu* are, as a genre, associated with much greater lexical range and presented writers with the opportunity to flex poetic muscles less frequently used in *shi* compositions. Examination of Du Fu's limited *fu*, however, shows that they differ little from his *shi* on the level of lexical difficulty.

I base this conclusion on an analysis of three of Du Fu's *fu* against the same benchmarks used for "Stirred by Autumn," these being "Poetic Exposition on a Dawn Presentation at the Temple of Supreme Clarity" ("Zhao xian Taiqing gong fu" 朝獻太清宮賦), "Poetic Exposition for Performing the Feng Sacrifice on the Western Cardinal Peak" ("Feng Xi Yue fu" 封西嶽賦), and the "Poetic Exposition on the Eagle" ("Diao fu" 雕賦).[33] The coverage rates by the benchmark set for the total character positions are as follows: "A Dawn Presentation," 85 percent; "Performing the Feng Sacrifice," 86 percent; and "Eagle," 87 percent. These numbers are very much in line with those for "Stirred by Autumn," with the *fu* showing only slightly less coverage by the benchmark set. More strikingly, though all three of these *fu* were presented to the emperor, presumably with the intent of putting Du Fu's poetic abilities on full display, none appears to be more lexically challenging than the quatrains in Wang Wei's *Wang River Collection*.

I cannot claim that these numbers are definitive. A different benchmark set would likely produce a different result, as would an analysis of a different set of poems. At the same time, the numbers do seem to indicate that these poems, whether in the *shi* or *fu* style, would not have presented significant challenges on the purely lexical level even to those learners in the intermediate stage of their education.

Allusions

Lexical range indicates a basic level of difficulty in reading a poem. But when Huang Tingjian writes of Du Fu's poetry that "every word has a source," he is thinking of something different: words not as simple vocabulary items but rather as allusions to earlier writings, the knowledge of which would be crucial to understanding Du Fu's intent. While there was a reaction against this mode of reading Du Fu in the Ming and Qing periods, with many writers arguing that the only way to understand Du Fu is to ignore entirely the commentaries that purport to trace his sources and instead simply read aloud or even transcribe his poems repeatedly, the fact remains that Du Fu has long been regarded as a highly allusive poet. There are ample examples that support this notion, such as his lengthy *pailü* 排律, especially the "Eight Laments" ("Ba ai" 八哀) poems, about whose many allusions Eva Shan Chou has written in detail.[34] One of the oft-cited barriers to fully appreciating the "Stirred by Autumn" sequence is the

---

33. Owen, *The Poetry of Du Fu*, vol. 6, 242–62, 308–23, 328–41. Xiao Difei, *Du Fu quanji*, vol. 11, 21.6131–65, 21.6248–70, 21.6278–92.
34. Chou, "Allusion and Periphrasis."

background knowledge required to make sense of it, as the poems are deeply imbricated with the literary and historical past. Allusions thus make a second fruitful approach to assessing the degree of education that would be required to understand these works.

Allusions can be difficult to pin down. James Hightower has set out a tentative but useful list of seven sorts of allusions in the writings of Tao Qian 陶潛 (365?–427), ranging from those whose understanding is crucial to understanding the entire poem to those whose allusive quality is likely the figment of later commentators' imaginations.[35] In between these extremes is a range based on the importance and impact of a given allusion on the reading of the line in which it appears. Beginning in the Song, meticulous scholars have labored tirelessly to unearth any possible allusion Du Fu may have made in his poems; but, as Owen has noted in line with Hightower, there is "a great distance between the lexicographical citation of the earliest usage of a phrase and an allusion, which presumes that the reader will not only recognize the source as such, but must do so to fully understand the poem."[36] In many cases it is impossible to know for certain what textual context Du Fu had in mind when making an allusion. In possible quotations from earlier work, one can face a sorites paradox of allusion: What is the precise number of words at which a nonallusion becomes an allusion? There are some cases in which a single word would be sufficient and others in which a longer phrase, even it if appears in an earlier work, would not. Hightower writes, "I cannot supply accurate statistics for Tao Qian's use of allusion, neither the total number of allusions in his poems nor their distribution among the commoner Classical texts."[37] My goal here is likewise a modest one: to examine the references and allusions in the "Stirred by Autumn" poems to give a sense of what kind of literacy would be required in Du Fu's time to understand them. Again, this more limited scope will preclude any broader generalization about Du Fu's oeuvre but perhaps will result in more precision.

Others have undertaken more ambitious cataloguing of Du Fu's use of allusions, and some general speculations about the literacy level required to understand them might be ventured. A 2007 MA thesis by Lu Yuandun 路元敦 attempts to catalog and categorize every allusion Du Fu makes to the pieces anthologized in the *Wen xuan*.[38] He ultimately comes up with a total of 397 lines that he considers to be "influenced by the *Wen xuan*." His stated criterion is that an instance counts as "using an allusion" if "the expression has an intimate connection to the poet's expression of his sentiments."[39] Although one could quibble with many of Lu's specific choices, his work nonetheless provides a useful starting point from which to explore Du Fu's use of allusion. I have looked at each of the 397 lines he catalogs to see whether the original source he identifies from the *Wen xuan* is also found in the Tang period *leishu Record of Early Learning* (*Chuxue ji* 初學記). Why the *Chuxue ji* in particular? There were hundreds of similar works compiled in the medieval period, and a number of them survive in some form today. The *Chuxue ji* is an appealing example in part because it is long enough to contain excerpts from a very broad range and great number of works, from the classics to poems (including those from the early Tang), yet short enough that it could be memorized and was not used *only* for consultative purposes, as one would do with a dictionary.

35. Hightower, "Allusion."
36. Owen, *The Poetry of Du Fu*, vol. 1, lxxx.
37. Hightower, "Allusion," 5.
38. Lu Yuandun, "Lun Du Fu shi."
39. Lu Yuandun, "Lun Du Fu shi," 2.

Accounts of its composition make clear that it was intended to be read and learned, and sections such as the "parallel matters" (*shidui* 事對) in particular were structured to aid both learning and memorizing.[40]

Of the 397 instances of allusion made by Du Fu to work in the *Wen xuan* identified by Lu Yuandun, 167 (42 percent) are to works that are also included in the *Chuxue ji*. In many of these cases, however, only part of the work alluded to is in the *Chuxue ji*. If we count only instances in which the specific phrase or line to which Du Fu alludes appears in the *Chuxue ji*, we get a much smaller total of 70 instances (18 percent). To be sure, this does tell us that Du Fu did not depend on the *Chuxue ji* for his knowledge of the *Wen xuan*, though this is hardly surprising, as we know that he had read that compilation itself repeatedly and had even read it aloud with his son. Still, I would not say that we can make any larger statement about the obscurity of Du Fu's allusions overall from this limited sample. After all, the fact that these are allusions to the *Wen xuan*, one of the most widely and intensively read texts in the period, itself indicates that these allusions would likely be known to readers with a basic level of literary training.

Let us return to "Stirred by Autumn" and look more closely at some examples. The kinds of allusions that Lu Yuandun identifies—those that refer to specific works and typically to specific lines or expressions within those works (what David Lattimore calls "textual allusions")—are relatively few.[41] Moreover, catching the allusion is rarely necessary for a basic understanding of a given "Stirred by Autumn" line. For example, scholars have identified two possible allusions in the first line of the first poem: "Jade-white dew withers and harms forests of maple trees" 玉露凋傷楓樹林. The first is to an untitled poem by the Sui rebel Li Mi 李密 (582–618), which begins with "The metallic [autumn] wind shakes the early season [of autumn], / jade-white dew withers the declining groves" 金風蕩初節，玉露凋晚林.[42] Li Mi's poem is a melancholy meditation similar in theme to "Stirred by Autumn." Its autumnal setting and the author's association with dynastic collapse augment the mood of Du Fu's poem but do not lead to different readings of Du Fu's poem from those we would arrive at were we to disregard the potential allusion to Li Mi's lines entirely. This would fall under Hightower's fourth category of allusion: "The line makes perfect sense; the allusion, when identified, adds overtones that reinforce the literal meaning."[43] Lu Yuandun further reads "forests of maple trees" 楓樹林 as an allusion to Ruan Ji's 阮籍 (210–263) couplet, "So deep the Yangtze's waters, / on it[s banks] groves of maple" 湛湛長江水，上有楓樹林, which is itself an extended allusion to "Calling Back the Soul" ("Zhaohun" 招魂) from the *Chu ci*.[44] It does not seem clear that Du Fu is indeed making an allusion to the Ruan Ji piece (which is about spring rather than fall), and other commentators tend not to identify this as an allusion.

Most of the other textual allusions are of this sort. In the fourth poem the line "Mansions of counts and princes all have new masters" 王侯第宅皆新主 likely plays off a line in the third of the "Nineteen Old Poems" ("Gushi shijiushou" 古詩十九首):

40. *Shidui* are paired compounds found in every entry in the *Chuxue ji*. They provide ready-made parallel phrases along with the earlier texts to which they refer, serving as a highly condensed version of the knowledge on a given topic that the *Chuxue ji* entry contains.
41. Lattimore, "Allusion and T'ang Poetry," 409.
42. Cited in Xiao Difei, *Du Fu quanji jiaozhu*, vol. 7, 13.3791.
43. Hightower, "Allusion," 6.
44. Lu Yuandun, "Lun Du Fu shi," 29.

"The counts and princes have many mansions" 王侯多第宅. The allusion reinforces the sense of separation Du Fu feels from the capital he knew, and there is clear irony in the fact that his deeply melancholy poem borrows from an "Old Poem" that encourages the reader by suggesting "With a measure of wine we'll share our joy" 斗酒相娛樂 and ends with an admonition to keep sorrow at bay: "Feast to the limit, bring the heart joy / why be pressed down by worries?" 極宴娛心意，戚戚何所迫?[45] Yet these too fall into Hightower's fourth category: they add overtones but are not necessary for the line in question to be comprehensible.

One instance in which recognition of an allusion does more meaningfully change our understanding of Du Fu's lines is found in the last couplet of the third poem in the series: "The young men I once studied with are now most not of low degree / by Five Barrows their horses are plump and the mantles they wear are light" 同學少年多不賤，五陵衣馬自輕肥. This is a clear allusion to the *Analects* passage in which Zilu, when asked his aims, replies, "I would like to have chariots and horses and to wear light furs. I would share them with my friends and even if they ruined them, I would have no resentments" 願車馬衣輕裘，與朋友共，敝之而無憾.[46] In this case, while Du Fu's couplet makes sense in and of itself, the allusion potentially changes our reading, though the precise tenor of the allusion remains ambiguous. In one possible interpretation, Du Fu's regret about his own failures to have achieved success and fame and his resentment toward his former acquaintances become an even more cutting self-rebuke when compared with the generous sentiments of Zilu in the *Analects* passage. Approaching the allusion from another perspective would have Du Fu instead rebuking those friends for their own failures to live up to Zilu's example of sharing their good fortune. While they enjoy their luxurious life in the suburbs of Chang'an, Du Fu suffers far away, cut off and abandoned.

Most of the allusions found in these eight poems are, however, not of the sort of textual allusions Lu Yuandun identified. That is, they are usually not references to or intentional borrowings from earlier works for which the specific wording of the expressions or lines in those works matters. Instead, we find topical or informational allusions: they require knowledge of a topic, and the knowledge could come from a variety of sources. Unlike with the textual allusions discussed above, understanding these topical allusions, in most cases, is crucial to making sense of the line or poem in even a basic way, thus falling under Hightower's second category: "The allusion is the key to a line; one cannot understand the line without knowing the allusion."[47]

We see two examples in the second poem in the series, which includes the couplet "Listening to the gibbons I really shed tears at their third cry / accepting my mission I pointlessly follow the eighth-month raft" 聽猿實下三聲淚，奉使虛隨八月槎. Here we have two clear allusions, the first to, as Owen describes, "an old rhyme that a traveler in the gorges would shed tears when the gibbon cried out three times."[48] This is a well-known piece of long-standing lore. It appears in multiple forms in an entry on gibbons in the early Tang *leishu* Collection of Literature Arranged by Categories (*Yiwen leiju* 藝文類聚) and in an entry on similar animals in the *Chuxue ji* as well. Both works quote a poem by the sixth-century writer Xiao Quan 蕭銓, cited by the *Chuxue ji* as "Poem

45. Lu Qinli, *Xian Qin Han Wei*, 329.
46. *Lunyu zhushu*, 5.46.
47. Hightower, "Allusion," 6.
48. Owen, *The Poetry of Du Fu*, vol. 4, 353.

on the Night Calls of the Gibbon" ("Ye yuan ti shi" 夜猿啼詩 and by the *Yiwen leiju* as "Poem Composed to the Assigned Topic 'The Night Calls of the Gibbon'" ("Fude ye yuan ti shi" 賦得夜猿啼詩).[49] This latter title is further indication that the allusion was a common one. Its parallel in the second line of Du Fu's couplet refers to the story found in Zhang Hua's 張華 (232–300) *Bowu zhi* 博物志, in which a man who lived by the sea once boarded a raft that had passed him in the eighth month of each year and found himself riding the Milky Way and arriving in Heaven (though he does not disembark and ends up back in the human realm). The story shows up in various forms in multiple entries in the *Chuxue ji*. In the entry on the sea 海, for example, there is a *shidui* 事對 pair "Penetrate heaven; move the earth" (*tong tian*; *dong di* 通天動地) that quotes the entire *Bowu zhi* story.[50]

The poems in the "Stirred by Autumn" series differ substantially from one another in the extent to which they include these types of allusions. The fourth poem, for example, requires almost no understanding of specific historical or legendary events to make sense. The fifth poem, however, is at the opposite extreme: almost every line includes some sort of topical allusion:

蓬萊宮闕對南山	Palace towers of Penglai stand facing South Mountain,
承露金莖霄漢間	the metal stalk that catches the dew is high in the Milky Way.
西望瑤池降王母	Gazing west to Onyx Pool the Queen Mother is descending,
東來紫氣滿函關	from the east come purple vapors and fill Han Pass.
雲移雉尾開宮扇	Pheasant tails shift in clouds, palace fans open;
日繞龍鱗識聖顏	sunlight circles dragon scales, I see the Emperor's face.
一臥滄江驚歲晚	By the gray river I lay once and woke,
	alarmed that the year had grown late—
幾回青瑣點朝班	how often did I, by the gates' blue rings,
	take my humble place in dawn court's ranks?[51]

Most of these allusions result from the common trope of using the Han court and palaces as figures for those of the Tang, yet they still require more specialized knowledge of Han lore, from the dew-catching statue of an immortal erected by Han Emperor Wu 漢武帝 (r. 141–87 BCE) to the visit to the same made by the Queen Mother of the West. The purple vapors filling Han Pass, however, refer to Laozi's journey to the west (and immortality). As Laozi was a legendary ancestor of the Li family line, this image brings the poem back to the present dynasty. The remaining references are less complex: pheasant feathers on palace doors, the dragon scales as the patterns on the emperor's clothes, and the blue rings as a synecdoche for the palace gates. Understanding them is necessary to comprehend these lines in the poem, but they do not refer to specific legends or textual accounts.

In terms of a basic level of understanding, this fifth poem is arguably the most difficult of the series, in that it calls for knowledge of everything from the architecture of Han palaces to stories about Laozi. This perception of difficulty quickly disappears, however, when we acknowledge that all of these references would have been common knowledge to any contemporaneous reader of Du Fu's poem. And we can move beyond

49. *Chuxue ji*, 29.722. *Yiwen leiju*, 915.1652.
50. *Chuxue ji*, 6.116.
51. Owen, *The Poetry of Du Fu*, vol. 4, 356–57.

speculation to find solid evidence to back this assertion by looking at whether such topics are covered in the *Chuxue ji*. They are, in every case:

- Penglai and its towers appear in the mythological sense in dozens of entries, the first of which is the "General Account of Mountains" ("Zongzai shan" 總載山) where the *shidui* term "golden gate-tower" (*jinque* 金闕) is explained by a quote from the *Shi ji* 史記 about King Zhao of Yan dispatching men to seek the mythic mountain and its towers of gold and silver.[52] Du Fu's description of the towers facing South Mountain here make it clear that he is describing the Han palace instead of the mythological locale.

- Han emperor Wu's dew-gathering immortal is covered in many entries, with the term that begins the second line of the poem, *chenglu* 承露, specifically appearing in the first *shidui* item of the entry on "Dew" ("Lu" 露) in a description from (*Han Wudi gushi* 漢武帝故事) about the bronze immortal.[53] It also appears in a later *shidui* item "Han palace / Wei throne-hall" (*Han gong / Wei dian* 漢宮/魏殿) quoting the *Han shu* 漢書 on the same topic.[54] "Metal stalk" (*jinjing* 金莖) is found in the same section in a quotation from Ban Gu's 班固 (32–92) "Poetic Exposition on the Western Capital" ("Xidu fu" 西都賦).[55]

- The story of the Queen Mother of the West's visit to Han Emperor Wu appears in many entries, often citing the *Inner Biography of Han Emperor Wu* (*Han Wudi neizhuan* 漢武帝內傳) and giving the Onyx Pool as the site of the assignation.[56]

- The basic story of Laozi arriving at Han Pass to head west (with the gate keeper being alerted to the arrival of a sage by the gathering of purple vapors) appears in a *shidui* item "black ox / white deer" (*qing niu / bai lu* 青牛/白鹿) in the *Chuxue ji* entry "Chariots" ("Che" 車).[57]

- Pheasant feathers on palace doors are referenced in the descriptive section of the entry on doors (*shan* 扇), and pheasant tails are themselves a *shidui* item in the same entry.[58]

- Dragon scales are associated with the emperor in a *shidui* item in the entry "Emperors and Kings" ("Diwang" 帝王).[59]

- Blue rings are part of a *shidui* item in the entry "Gentleman Attendant at the Palace Gate" ("Huangmen shilang" 黃門侍郎).[60]

This pattern holds true for the majority of allusions of this sort that appear in the "Stirred by Autumn" poems. From the mention of Han dynasty figures Kuang Heng 匡衡 and of Liu Xiang 劉向 in the third poem to the statue of the Weaving Woman and the metal-scaled stone leviathan in the seventh, the information required to understand these references is almost all found in the *Chuxue ji* (and was likely in many other basic *leishu* as well). As Hightower warns, counting allusions is a tricky business, but it is worth venturing a guess for the limited set of these eight poems. By my count there are thirty-three examples of either textual or topical allusions in the series. Of these, twenty-seven appear in the *Chuxue ji* in ways that would likely ensure the reader would understand the references as used in Du Fu's poems. Some exceptions, such as the allusion

---

52. *Chuxue ji*, 5.91–92.
53. *Chuxue ji*, 2.33.
54. *Chuxue ji*, 2.34.
55. *Chuxue ji*, 2.34.
56. *Chuxue ji*, 4.77, 7.147.
57. *Chuxue ji*, 25.613.
58. *Chuxue ji*, 25.604.
59. *Chuxue ji*, 9.208.
60. *Chuxue ji*, 12.284.

to the "Nineteen Old Poems" and that to Zilu's words in the *Analects*, would have been known to any likely reader from other sources. In short, the difficulty in these poems clearly lies neither with the vocabulary Du Fu uses nor with the allusions he employs.

Allusions are an area in which the distinction between Du Fu's *shi* and *fu* is, as expected, more pronounced. To get a preliminary sense of the differences, I have examined the use of allusions in his "Feng Xi Yue fu." Though this work was likely meant to put Du Fu's poetic and rhetorical abilities on full display to the emperor, it is arguably no more lexically challenging than the "Stirred by Autumn" poems (or even Wang Wei's *Wangchuan ji*).[61] It is, however, overall far more allusive than those works.

The allusions Du Fu employs in "Feng Xi Yue fu," unlike those in the "Stirred by Autumn" poems, are primarily of the textual sort. That is, they are exact or near exact quotations from other works. Stringing together allusions of this type into a new work was referred to as *zhuiwen* 綴文 (literally, "stitching together writings"), a term that could also broadly indicate literary composition. As we have seen with "Stirred by Autumn," determining what counts as an allusion can be difficult, but our task is easier if we limit the category to clear and explicit textual allusions. For example, when Du Fu writes, "The ruler was going to ascend the Western Cardinal Peak to observe the circumambient wilderness" 上將陟西嶽覽八荒,[62] there can be little doubt that he is quoting a line from Yang Xiong's 揚雄 (53 BCE–18 CE) "Poetic Exposition on Hedong" ("Hedong fu" 河東賦): "He was going to the Western Cardinal Peak in order to observe the circumambient wilderness" 陟西岳以望八荒.[63] Similarly, Du Fu's use of the phrase "respectfully in accord with the gods of Heaven and Earth" 欽若神祇 is a clear reference to the use of a similar phrase in the same "Poetic Exposition on Hedong": "Respectfully in accord with the numinous luminaries" 欽若神明者.[64] At one point Du Fu simply repeats verbatim four lines from the *Classic of Poetry*: "'The worship was greatly glorious,' 'there was order, there was reverential demeanor,' 'The spirits arrive,' 'in their tens of thousands, in their millions'" 祀事孔明，有嚴有翼，神保是格，時萬時億. The first phrase appears in two *Shi jing* poems, "Thick Star-Thistle" ("Chu ci" 楚茨) and "Truly, Southern Hills" ("Xin nanshan" 信南山); the second phrase is from "Sixth Month" ("Liuyue" 六月); and the third and fourth are both from "Thick Star-Thistle."[65] All of these allusions are ones whose recognition is crucial for understanding Du Fu's *fu*. Indeed, as these are exact or near exact quotations, one could argue that recognizing the allusions would be the primary mode of reading the *fu*.

On the face of it, a poetic text so loaded with textual allusions might seem to present a higher level of difficulty than would the "Stirred by Autumn" poems. But, once again, a close examination of Du Fu's "stitching together" in "Feng Xi Yue fu" reveals that the range of his sources is quite limited and those sources are anything but obscure. By my count there are twenty-eight clear textual allusions in the work: seven are to Yang Xiong's "Poetic Exposition on Hedong," five are to the same writer's "Poetic Exposition on the Sweet Springs,"[66] four are to the *Shi jing* pieces just noted, and two are to Sima Xiangru's 司馬相如 (ca. 179–ca. 117) "Poetic Exposition on the Great Man" ("Daren fu"

---

61. Owen, *The Poetry of Du Fu*, vol. 4, 308–24.
62. Owen, *The Poetry of Du Fu*, vol. 4, 308–9.
63. *Han shu*, 87.3535.
64. *Han shu*, 87.3536.
65. *Shi jing zhushu*, 13.455, 13.462, 10.357, 13.456, 13.457.
66. For a discussion and translation of these two works, see Knechtges, *The Han Rhapsody*, 44–62.

大人賦). A smattering of other sources are alluded to no more than a single time each, and these include Ban Gu's "Poetic Exposition on the Western Capital" and "Poetic Exposition on the Eastern Capital" ("Dongdu fu" 東都賦), the *Han shu* biography of Jia Yi 賈誼 (ca. 200–168 BCE), and Emperor Xuanzong's own "Commemorative Inscription on Mt. Tai" ("Ji Taishan ming" 紀泰山銘). These are obvious candidates for allusions in a poetic exposition about the Feng and Shan sacrifices. Of the twenty-eight total textual allusions, twelve are to well-known poetic expositions by Yang Xiong on imperial sacrifices, and a total of sixteen are from the *Han shu* alone (along with two by Ban Gu, author of the *Han shu*). This is a narrow range that contains few, if any, truly unexpected choices. If Xuanzong was impressed by Du Fu's offering, it was not because the poet demonstrated unusually broad range in either his lexical choices or his textual sources.

This finding should not be surprising. Works composed to impress a very particular audience, in this case the emperor, would by necessity be confined in their allusive references. It would have been important to Du Fu to show that he had a command of the applicable literary and historical materials, but it was just as important that his audience easily recognize his allusions and their meanings. One would not wish to confuse the emperor and would certainly not want to make him feel inadequate in his own understanding of the literary inheritance. If Du Fu used these works to show off, he did so with considerable circumspection.

Conclusion

This preliminary investigation of some of Du Fu's works from the perspective of poetic difficulty indicates that the vocabulary and literary-historical knowledge necessary for a basic understanding of the language in these works does not exceed what would be found in the early stages of literary education in the Tang period. The "Stirred by Autumn" poems call for some general knowledge of historical lore with their topical allusions but rarely require knowledge of specific earlier texts. When such knowledge is called for, it is typically found in the most well-known sources, such as the *Wen xuan* or the *Analects*. The lore required for grasping the more frequent topical allusions that are crucial for understanding the poems is almost all found in such widely used *leishu* as the *Chuxue ji*. In the case of Du Fu's *fu*, the situation is more complicated but similar. In terms of lexical range, there is little difference from "Stirred by Autumn" (or Wang Wei's *Wangchuan ji*). The *fu* are, however, more allusive, employing extensive textual allusions, the understanding of which is crucial to grasp the works' meanings. At the same time, the corpus from which these allusions are drawn is a very confined one.

Returning to Huang Tingjian and those who have read Du Fu in a mode similar to what Huang suggests, it can be argued that difficulty is not only in the eye of the beholders but is quite possibly created by the very expectations these beholders have brought to the text. If one reads Du Fu with the belief that "every word has a source" and hunts down earlier uses of terms and phrases with the assumption that Du Fu must have used them with a particular meaning because of particular earlier uses, then any text that Du Fu produced will be difficult, even the poems that Zongwu could recite as a child. This tells us more about Du Fu's Song readers, who took his works and indeed much of Tang poetry as an object of scholarly study, than it does about Du Fu and his contemporary audience. It should be noted again that Huang Tingjian's mode of reading has not always been the dominant one; many Ming and Qing readers of Du Fu intentionally ignored the annotations and commentaries that traced every term and line back to an assumed origin, considering such practices as "the error of gathering facts" 摭實之病.[67]

This criticism acknowledges, perhaps unintentionally, the material reality of the period in which Du Fu composed and in which his original audience encountered his poems. While the emperor may have had an extensive library at his disposal, most of Du Fu's readers likely lacked such resources, as did Du Fu himself. More to the point, there is no reason to believe Du Fu had intended his poems to become the subject of scholarly analysis, in which the reader would hunt down all possible references and carefully document them. Du Fu wrote poetry to be read and heard, not studied. That is not to say that he meant his poems to be always transparent in their meaning, especially upon a single reading or hearing. He surely did not, as he famously portrayed himself as having read the *Wen xuan* and other earlier writings "to tatters" (*dupo* 讀破). This was an intensive and immersive engagement with texts, but it was not necessarily a scholastic one. To recognize an allusion, the reader would rely on his or her memory, not on extensive consultation of research materials (to say nothing of searchable databases).

Du Fu's "Stirred by Autumn" poems do make demands on their readers, but these demands are more complex than those of vocabulary and allusion alone. The language that Du Fu uses is, by and large, simple; the emotions and the meanings he expresses are not. This may account for much of the enduring appeal of these verses. Paradoxically, the simplicity of the language allows for a depth that could otherwise be lost in a sea of obscure words and allusions, had the poet taken that route. Instead, the reader here is not pulled out of poems by pedantic display but rather drawn in by a deceptive comprehensibility that begins to cloud as one experiences the full depth of what Du Fu is doing in these verses.

---

67. See discussion in Ji Hao, "Poetics of Transparency," 17–19. As Hao points out, the phrase was used by Song Luo 宋犖 (1634–1713) in the preface he wrote to Zhang Jin's 張溍 (1621–1678) commentary. See Zhang Jin, *Dushu Tang*, 161.

8
Ming-Qing Paintings Inscribed with Du Fu's Poetic Lines

Ronald Egan

The tradition of finding inspiration in Du Fu's poetic lines for a painting goes back to the eleventh century, so far as we know. Once it began, the tradition never ended, down to the present day. The premodern heyday of producing a painting keyed to a couplet or entire poem by Du Fu was the Ming-Qing period (1368–1911), which will be the focus of this chapter. My primary goal here is to examine the various approaches artists utilized as they rendered Du Fu's lines in painting. This is part of the rich history of the interaction between painting and poetry in Chinese cultural history, a field that is sometimes referred to as text-image studies. The artists' treatment of Du Fu's poetic lines may also be viewed as a distinctive part of the great poet's reception history, a part that is often overlooked. I will show that this visual treatment of Du Fu's lines manifests considerable range and creativity. The artists' reimagining of Du Fu's lines contributes to our understanding of the ways in which Du Fu could be read and his poetic achievement appropriated and redirected, in addition to constituting a subgenre in Ming-Qing painting history.

General Observations

Although we do not have a definitive tally of the number of paintings inspired by Du Fu's lines nor comparative tallies for those by other poets, it is clear that Du Fu's poetry was used as the source for what came to be known as "paintings of poetic thoughts (or lines)" (shiyi tu 詩意圖) more often than those by any other poet. We might suppose that this was a reflection of Du Fu's special status, which he certainly had achieved by late imperial times, as "the greatest poet." But consideration of the lines of his that got inscribed on paintings suggests that his fame was not the only reason painters were drawn to him.

We look first at a sampling of the couplets from Du Fu's poetry that Ming and Qing artists inscribed on their paintings:

藍水遠從千澗落	The Lan River comes from afar, falling from a thousand mountain streams,
玉山高並兩峰寒	jade Mountain's height matches the paired peaks in cold.[1]
孤城返照紅將斂	Sunlight cast back on the lonely wall, its red almost gathered in,
近寺浮煙翠且重	the drifting smoke from the temple nearby is azure and in layers.[2]
澗道餘寒歷冰雪	In lingering chill on the road by a torrent I passed through ice and snow,
石門斜日到林丘	with sinking sunlight on Sungate Mountain, I reached your wooded hill.[3]
請看石上藤蘿月	Just look there at the moon, in the wisteria on the rock,
已映洲前蘆荻花	it has already cast its light on sandbars on flowers of the reeds.[4]
含風翠壁孤雲細	The azure cliff catches the breeze, a lone cloud thin,
背日丹楓萬木稠	red maples, their backs to the sun, ten thousand trees dense.[5]
百年地關柴門迥	My whole life I've lived out of the way, my ramshackle gate remote,
五月江深草閣寒	in the fifth month the river runs deep and my thatched pavilion is cold.[6]
絕壁過雲開錦繡	Clouds passing the sheer cliff spread embroidery and brocade,
疏松夾水奏笙簧	sparse pines lining the waters play mouth organs.[7]
石泉流暗壁	Stony streams flow down cliffs unseen,
草露滴秋根	dew on plants drips on autumn roots.[8]
日出寒山外	The sun comes out beyond cold mountains,
江流宿霧中	the river flows on in the overnight fog [9]
返照入江翻石壁	Sunlight cast back enters the river, rolling the cliffs of stone,
歸雲擁樹失山村	returning clouds hug the trees, I lose sight of the mountain village.[10]

1. From "At Cui's Villa in Lantian on the Double Ninth" 九日藍田崔氏莊. Owen, *The Poetry of Du Fu*, vol. 2, 50–51. All references and translations, except where noted otherwise, are to Owen's complete English translation. The first seven couplets in this list are inscribed on paintings contained in Wang Shimin's "Du Fu's Poetic Thoughts Album," for which see below.
2. From "In the Evening Climbing to the Belltower of Si'an Temple, Sent to Pei Di" 暮登四安寺鐘樓寄裴十迪. Owen, *The Poetry of Du Fu*, vol. 2, 338–39. Wang Shimin's inscribed version of the second line has *si* 寺 instead of *shi* 市, and I have changed the translation accordingly.
3. From "On Zhang's Hermitage" no. 1 題張氏隱居二首第一. Owen, *The Poetry of Du Fu*, vol. 1, 4–5.
4. From "Stirred by Autumn" no. 2 秋興八首第二. Owen, *The Poetry of Du Fu*, vol. 4, 352–53.
5. From "The Officials' Pavilion at the Temple of Massed Incense in Fucheng County" 涪城縣香積寺官閣. Owen, *The Poetry of Du Fu*, vol. 3, 204–5.
6. From "In Mid-summer Lord Yan Goes Out of His Way to Visit My Thatched Cottage, Also Bringing Ale and Food" 嚴公仲夏枉駕草堂兼攜酒饌. Owen, *The Poetry of Du Fu*, vol. 3, 116–17.
7. From "The First Day of the Seventh Month, on Magistrate Zhong's Tower by the River" no. 1 七月一日題終明府水樓二首第一. Owen, *The Poetry of Du Fu*, vol. 5, 136–37.
8. From "Twilight" 日暮. Owen, *The Poetry of Du Fu*, vol. 5, 256–57. This couplet and the next are found in Shitao's *Du Fu's Poetic Thoughts* album, for which see below.
9. From "Traveler's Pavilion" 客亭. Owen, *The Poetry of Du Fu*, vol. 3, 148–49.
10. From "Sunlight Cast Back" 返照. Owen, *The Poetry of Du Fu*, vol. 4, 202–3.

As in this sampling, the great majority of such couplets are from seven-syllable-line "regulated verse." Aside from that, what other traits do they have in common? They are highly imagistic, being descriptive of natural scenery. More than that, they are imagistically complex. Often a single line features as many as three separate phenomena and presents some complicated way in which they relate to each other or interact. Spatial distance and placement are important (e.g., "The Lan River comes from afar, falling from a thousand mountain streams"). The lines are also full of color words. All of these are features of the lines that make them well suited to being painted. A perhaps less obvious trait most of the couplets share is that somehow time figures in them: "the river flows on in the overnight fog," meaning that the fog in the poetic scene is one that has lingered there since the night before. Or time is indirectly invoked by a reference to process: "I passed through ice and snow. . . . I reached your wooded hill." Even "its red [of sunset] almost gathered in" evokes time and duration, because the changing of sunset hues happens over time. Likewise, "I lose sight of the mountain village" also involves time, since the line implies that the village was visible previously but now no longer.

Spatial relations, color, the passage of time: all were features of the lines that caught the attention of the artists and suggested to them that these lines, which they knew from reading, might well be painted. The imagistic and spatial complexity of the lines would have stood both as an inspiration and a challenge to the artists. As painters they would have been challenged to see if they could actually construct a painting that contained all these elements and do so in a visually plausible manner. We will see below that they often rose to this challenge, ingeniously imagining just such a scene as Du Fu's lines evoke. The temporal element in the lines perhaps held a different kind of appeal for the painters. Unlike space and color, the passage of time is the one element that is notoriously difficult to suggest in a painting. By selecting couplets that evoke time, the painter added something that gave his painting a new dimension, thereby inviting a viewer to imagine the painted scene as one not frozen in time (as it meets the eye) but as one in which time exists, as it does in the real world.

As for the placement of these couplets in their original poem, they tend to be middle couplets, that is, couplets that were originally the second or third couplet (ll. 3–4 or 5–6) of the four-couplet regulated verse form. This is not an accident. It is exactly those lines that tend to be the most imagistic and least propositional. As such they were the portion of Du Fu's poems best suited to appropriation in a painting. Of course the artists did not necessarily think in such terms. Yet they were instinctively drawn to these lines because they are so painterly. It also bears mentioning that the lines the Ming-Qing artists chose for their paintings were rarely Du Fu's best-known lines, and usually they did not come from his most famous poems. The artists had their own criteria, determined by the use for the lines they had in mind, rather than by how well known the lines were.

I have been writing as if the artists chose the Du Fu couplets before they produced the painting on which the couplets were eventually inscribed. (In this chapter, I am looking only at couplets inscribed by the artists themselves, not inscriptions added by some later collector or admirer.) Of course it is also possible that Du Fu's lines were an afterthought, recalled only after the painting was already finished and added because it occurred to the artist that what he had painted, without having the lines in mind, made a good match with what Du Fu had written centuries before. This may have happened sometimes, but in general the order must have been the opposite: the artist first thought of the poetic lines and then set about to render them in painting. There are two reasons for this, one external to the paintings themselves and one internal. Many of the Ming-Qing paintings inscribed with Du Fu's poetic lines are found in albums of such works called *Du Fu's Poetic Thoughts* 杜甫詩意圖 (or some variant version of that title). If one is producing such an album, which typically contains eight or more paintings, some-times with the Du Fu couplet inscribed on the painting and sometimes with a painting and the matching Du Fu poem or couplet on facing double pages, one begins with the couplet and proceeds to "paint" it because that is the order such a project implies. For the artist to think of the couplet only after he completed the painting is something more likely to happen with a stand-alone painting than with a "poetic thoughts" painting album. The internal reason is that, as we will see below, the inscribed paintings are full of details that are very specific or even odd in a landscape painting and yet aptly match what Du Fu had written in those lines. When, for example, a painter depicts someone propelling a boat looking backward rather than forward (where he should be looking), it is more likely that the painter included such a detail because he is painting Du Fu's lines about someone on a boat "pointing behind" than that he only recalled Du Fu's lines after finishing the painting.

Two Seventeenth-Century Albums Compared

To get a sharper sense of the qualities and range of artists' use of Du Fu's lines in Ming-Qing times, we will examine two *Du Fu's Poetic Thoughts* albums by major painters, Wang Shimin 王時敏 (1592–1680) and Shitao 石濤 (1642–1707). We will see that although both men were drawn to Du Fu's poetry, the artistic uses to which they put his lines were very different.

We will first look at three leaves from Wang Shimin's album (which contains twelve paintings in all), held in the Beijing Palace Museum collection.[11] The first example presents a riverscape, with a few buildings on the far bank of the river, a dramatic cliff facing them across the water, with the river receding into mountains in the background (Figure 8.1). The painting is striking for its abundant use of color: many of the trees in the foreground and middle ground have red-tinged leaves, and the high cliff to the left is distinctly greenish. A band of white mist hovers in the air beneath the top of the cliff and the tops of the trees, its white stretching through and over the other elements, uniting them.

Here is the Du Fu poem from which the inscribed couplet, seen on the upper right of the painting, is taken:

涪城縣香積寺官閣	The Officials' Pavilion at the Temple of Massed Incense in Fucheng County[12]
寺下春江深不流	Below the temple the springtime River is so deep it does not flow,
山腰官閣迥添愁	an officials' pavilion at the mountain's middle high up adds to my melancholy.

---

11. The album is entitled *Duling shiyi tuce* 杜陵詩意圖冊, Beijing Palace Museum no. 故 00004873, 1–12. It was published as *Wang Shimin xie Du Fu shiyi tuce* 王時敏寫杜甫詩意圖冊.
12. Owen, *The Poetry of Du Fu*, vol. 3, 204–5.

含風翠壁孤煙細	The azure cliff catches the breeze, isolated mist thin,[13]
背日丹楓萬木稠	red maples, their backs to the sun, ten thousand trees dense.
小院迴廊春寂寂	In the small courtyard with winding porch, spring is lonely and still,
浴鳧飛鷺晚悠悠	bathing ducks and flying egrets in evening are at ease.
諸天合在藤蘿外	All the devas surely must lie beyond the rattan and vines,
昏黑應須到上頭	in the black of night I will surely reach the very top.

It is immediately clear that Wang Shimin is paying attention only to the couplet he inscribed. He has no interest in the poem as a whole and no sense of obligation to be faithful to its other aspects beyond those in the two lines he has selected. Thus the painting contains no temple halfway up a mountain, though that temple is mentioned in the poem's title and is the whereabouts of the poem's speaker. The only buildings visible in the painting appear to be ordinary homes and are, in any case, located along the riverbank.

What Wang Shimin is interested in is putting together in a plausible way the elements named in the second couplet (the red maples, the azure cliff, the thin mist, but not the breeze on the cliff, which would have been difficult to depict). These he weaves into a riverscape scene (the river having been mentioned in the poem's opening line). His use of the mist is particularly effective, since it effectively unites the whole scene and conspicuously stretches between the cliff and the red-leafed trees. The mist as he has drawn it is true to the word *xi* 細 in Du Fu's line; it is a thin band of mist. It is also interestingly *gu* 孤 (alone, isolated, apart), not quite in the way that a "lone cloud" would be but rather because it hovers by itself in the air, twisting around the other elements of the landscape, with nothing else (other formations of mist, clouds, etc.) either above or below it.

Another painting in Wang Shimin's album is inscribed with the closing couplet of the second of the eight poems in the well-known "Stirred by Autumn" ("Qiuxing bashou" 秋興八首) series (Figure 8.2):

請看石上藤蘿月	Just look there at the moon, in wisteria there on the rock,
已映洲前蘆荻花	it has already cast its light on sandbars by flowers of the reeds.[14]

The painting, again, has little to do with the other lines of Du Fu's poem. Wang Shimin is attempting only to provide a visual rendering of these two lines. This time it is not colors that he features but rather the spatial relationships of the several natural elements in the scene that Du Fu lists. The lines are packed with nouns that name plants and topographical features, but the lines also specify spatial relations between these things in a way that obviously interested our painter. Wang Shimin's solution to the challenge of sorting all this out is to put two persons in a boat, floating on the river, where we, the viewers of the painting, can readily imagine them taking in a view that includes all those things mentioned in the lines. Du Fu's opening phrase, "just look," implies a speaker who is in the act of looking at what follows and is also eager to share the sight with us. Du Fu's poem does not situate its speaker in a boat, so that element is Wang Shimin's ingenious addition. Is it possible that Wang Shimin got the idea for the boat from an earlier line in the same poem that refers to the speaker following an "eighth

---

13. Owen's text has *yun* 雲 in this line, but Wang Shimin inscribed the line with *yan* 煙 instead, and I have followed his version of the line and altered Owen's translation accordingly.
14. Owen, *The Poetry of Du Fu*, vol. 4, 352–53.

month raft" (*bayue cha* 八月槎)? Yes, it is possible, although that raft is a literary allusion to a well-known story of a man who unwittingly floats on a raft into the heavens (and meets the Weaving Maid and Oxherd stars) and could not be mistaken for a real boat in the setting of the poem.

It is no simple matter to arrange all the things named in Du Fu's two lines in a visually satisfying way. Wang Shimin puts the wisteria atop the rock in the foreground. Probably most readers of Du Fu's lines, if asked to specify how they imagine the two, would say that the moon should be directly above the wisteria, or even seen through the wisteria. But Wang Shimin still needs to accommodate in his painting all the other details mentioned in the following line. His painting gives, in fact, a surprisingly large amount of space to reeds growing on sandbars, which form such a pleasing contrast to the more commonplace image of the rock outcrop and its wisteria. Wang Shimin's painting deftly captures a feature of Du Fu's lines that many readers may have missed, as their minds move from one line to the next, if they visualize each in turn. That is the lovely contrast between the image of wisteria growing out of rock, with its qualities of hardness, angularity, and rigidity, and the supple, gentle, and yielding image of reed flowers on sandbars, illuminated by moonlight.

My last example from Wang Shimin's album is another riverscape that features a boat (Figure 8.3). It is inscribed with these lines, the second couplet of a poem Du Fu wrote as a farewell to Li Ba, his old friend, who had just visited the poet in Kuizhou and was leaving to take up a new appointment at the court:

石出倒聽楓葉下　Where rocks came out, from below you listened to the leaves of
　　　　　　　　　maples falling,
櫓搖背指菊花開　as the sweep moved back and forth you pointed behind to
　　　　　　　　　chrysanthemums in bloom.[15]

Wang Shimin had painted a vision of Kuizhou as a place of rounded serried mounds and peaks. But this time he gives more prominence to the human and narrative element in the scene, now depicting not just figures on a boat but figures actually doing something that accurately reflects what the lines say (Figure 8.4). In fact, the painting is remarkably true to the details of the two lines. There are rocks visible in the river, rocks that presumably would be submerged when the river flowed higher in other seasons. The bank from which Li Ba's boat is departing has maple trees with reddish leaves, and if we look closely at the trees on the extreme left, some of the leaves appear to be falling. Meanwhile, on the boat, both persons, the oarsman and the passenger, are clearly turning to look behind them at the bank they have just left, and the oarsman has his arm outstretched pointing backward. Now, when we follow the direction of his outstretched arm, we glimpse touches of yellow (and purple and red) on flowers growing out of the ground—those must be the painter's representation of the blooming chrysanthemums in Du Fu's line.

With the previous examples I have stressed how unrelated Wang Shimin's painting is to the rest of the poem from which he took the inscribed couplet. But, in this case, someone who sees Wang Shimin's painting may go back to the poem with a new appreciation of the richness of this couplet, although Wang may not have intended his

---

15. "Seeing Off Librarian Li (8) on His Way to Minister Du's Headquarters" 送李八秘書赴杜相公幕, Owen, *The Poetry of Du Fu*, vol. 5, 176–77.

painting to have this effect. Traditional Du Fu commentators do not have much to say about this couplet, aside from asserting that it stresses the hurriedness of librarian Li's departure (a questionable assertion). Mao Qiling 毛奇齡 (1623–1716) aptly points out that line 3 is concerned with vertical space (above and below) while line 4 concerns horizontal space (in front and behind, not to mention the sideways movement of the oar).[16] But these commentators do not say anything about the attractiveness of the scene the lines describe or their function in the poem. Wang Shimin's attention to them, his highlighting of them with his painting, may get us to think anew about them. The beauty of the autumn maple's red leaves and same season's late-blossoming chrysanthemum are well established in poetry and are associated with rural life, even reclusion. The odd detail about pointing backward to the chrysanthemums emphasizes the attraction that the rural scene has for the departing visitor (or should have, depending on who is doing the pointing, the visitor or the boatman—it is the boatman in the painting). The remainder of the poem emphasizes the sense of urgency Li Ba feels to respond to the opportunity he has been given to rejoin the court and how far he must travel to get there. But in this couplet Du Fu seems to intend gently to remind Li Ba of all that he is giving up by hurrying back to the capital. The backward glance to the chrysanthemum flowers, especially if it is indeed the boatman who wants to call his passenger's attention to what he is, in effect, now forsaking, is a vivid gesture toward such a caution. The poem's commentators have not picked up on this. But this couplet evidently held special meaning for Wang Shimin, the landscape artist, and so he gave it particular attention.

Shitao (Zhu Ruoji 朱若極) was born fifty years after Wang Shimin. They are both major seventeenth-century painters, but as artists they had radically different methods and priorities. We would expect Shitao's album of *Du Fu's Poetic Thoughts* to stand apart from Wang Shimin's album of the same name, and so it does.[17] Much of the disparity between the artistic styles of the two albums stems no doubt from the personal styles of the two painters. But, beyond that, it is also clear that Shitao's interest in and use of Du Fu's poetry differed from that of his older contemporary. Coming to Shitao's album from Wang Shimin's we get a sense of how varied was the interest that Du Fu's poetry held for readers of their century and how rich a source of artistic inspiration it was for those who worked in a visual rather than a literary form.

To begin with, in choosing couplets to inscribe on the paintings in his album, Shitao shows a preference for couplets with the five-syllable line rather than the seven-syllable line that Wang Shimin preferred. This preference has certain clear consequences: the five-syllable line is considerably less complex syntactically and semantically. It tends not to permit the two or three separate images or statements that we often find in the seven-syllable line, which frequently yield multiple possible readings depending on how we understand the relations between those components. As we have seen, those features of the longer line obviously fascinated Wang Shimin, and he exploited their complexity in his paintings.

Here, I will only discuss two features of the couplets that Shitao chooses to base his paintings on and what he does with them. Shitao is drawn to lines that use a particular word or words in unusual ways. Often this involves some manner of syntactical

16. Mao Qiling, quoted by Qiu Zhaoao, *Du shi xiangzhu*, 1681.
17. Shitao's album was published in Japan in 1968 as *Sekito To Ho shii satsu* 石濤杜甫詩意冊.

inversion or transformation. Shitao appears to be interested in these couplets and evidently sets himself the challenge of rendering these verbally unconventional formulations in visually exceptional ways. Here is one example (Figure 8.5):

春知催柳別　Spring knows to hurry the willows for parting,
江與放船清　the river gives clear waters for setting sail.[18]

These lines constitute the second couplet of a poem entitled "Moving My Dwelling to the Outskirts of Kuizhou" ("Yiju Kuizhou guo" 移居夔州郭). The mood of the poem is hopeful, as Du Fu looks forward to taking up residence in a place somewhat less mountainous than where he had been living. The first part of each line contains a conceit, asserting that the spring season "knows" to do something while the river "gives" a certain kind of water to the poet's boat. But what is more striking is the second half of each line. *Cui liu bie* 催柳別 "to hurry the willows for parting" is a compressed way of saying that the warm spring weather forces the "willows" (*liu* 柳) to bud and blossom so that their branches can be broken off and given to a departing friend, expressing the desire to "detain" (*liu* 留) him, as was the custom. *Fang chuan qing* 放船清 is equally odd in the sense of "clear/calm water [given to] a boat setting off." In his painting, Shitao makes the newly green willows prominent. He leaves an unpainted space for the river, and uses sails beyond another spit of land (just sails, not the boats they are attached to) to indicate that the horizontal empty space *is* a river, and a calm river at that. This way of using sails on unseen boats to intimate a river is a device that Shitao uses in several of his paintings. The painting may not be as novel or clever as the lines inscribed on it, yet it is subtle and evocative (no river is overtly depicted, still less a traveler or his well-wisher). We may think of this as Shitao's attempt to match the ingenuity of Du Fu's lines.

Another painting in the album has these lines inscribed (Figure 8.6):

高峰寒上日　High peaks coldly send up the sun,
疊嶺宿霾雲　layered ridges since last night are engulfed in cloud.[19]

These lines also feature words used unconventionally. It is, first of all, interestingly odd to say that peaks "send up" the sun. It is doubly odd to say they do so "coldly," with *han* positioned as an adverb. Of course, Shitao cannot paint mountain peaks "sending up" the sun, coldly or otherwise. But he does produce a painting with an exceptionally strong visual line rising diagonally from left to right, culminating with two mountain peaks that might well be imagined as capable to propelling something skyward from their upward thrust. Shitao refrains from painting a sun in the sky, leaving that to the viewer's imagination, which is probably an effective strategy.

The verb in the second line is *mai* 霾 ("to bury, engulf, cover over"). Du Fu often uses the word to denote how some liquid or gaseous substance (flood waters, fog, a sea, vapor) spreads over something solid, hiding it from view. The placement of *mai* in line 2 corresponds to the placement of the verb *shang* 上 in line 1, but the two verbs are grammatically different, *shang* being active and *mai* being used passively. Such a disparity is not unusual in lines that are supposed to be grammatically parallel, but it is an interesting variation. *Mai* is likewise modified by an adverb, in this case *su* 宿

---

18. "Moving My Dwelling to the Outskirts of Kuizhou" 移居夔州郭. Owen, *The Poetry of Du Fu*, vol. 4, 120–21.
19. From "Dawn View" 曉望. Owen, *The Poetry of Du Fu*, vol. 5, 256–57, with the translation modified.

Figure 8.1: Album leaf from Wang Shimin 王時敏, *Duling shiyi tuce* 杜陵詩意圖冊. Beijing Palace Museum, reproduced with permission.

請看石上藤蘿月
已映洲前蘆荻花

Figure 8.2: Album leaf from Wang Shimin, *Duling shiyi tuce*. Beijing Palace Museum, reproduced with permission.

Figure 8.3: Album leaf from Wang Shimin, *Duling shiyi tuce*. Beijing Palace Museum, reproduced with permission.

Figure 8.4: Detail of album leaf from Wang Shimin, *Duling shiyi tuce*. Beijing Palace Museum, reproduced with permission.

Figure 8.5: Album leaf from Shitao 石濤, *Du Fu shiyi tu* 杜甫詩意圖, published as *Sekito To Ho shii satsu* 石濤杜甫詩意冊, Tokyo, Sansaisha, 1968.

Figure 8.6: Album leaf from Shitao, *Du Fu shiyi tu* in *Sekito To Hu shii satsu*.

Figure 8.7: Album leaf from Shitao, *Du Fu shiyi tu* in *Sekito To Hu shii satsu.*

Figure 8.8: Detail from album leaf from Shitao, *Du Fu shiyi tu* in *Sekito To Hu shii satsu.*

Figure 8.9: Album leaf from Shitao, *Wilderness Colors* (*Ye se* 野色). Metropolitan Museum of Art, New York.

Figure 8.10: Album leaf from Shitao, *Wilderness Colors*. Metropolitan Museum of Art, New York.

Figure 8.11: Album leaf from Xie Shichen 謝時臣, *Duling shiyi tuce* 杜陵詩意圖冊. Beijing Palace Museum, reproduced with permission.

Figure 8.12: Album leaf from Xie Shichen, *Duling shiyi tuce*. Beijing Palace Museum, reproduced with permission.

("overnight, last night"). Shitao interprets the line to mean "since last night" and thus paints the clouds as still present in the scene, prominently stretching along the mountains, from lower left to upper right, winding around the peaks at midlevel. He paints the mountain peaks as poking through the transverse clouds. He has little choice but to do this. If he allowed the clouds to fully blanket the mountains, the viewer would have no way to be sure there are mountains there.

As we see in these two examples, Shitao has a flair for selecting Du Fu lines containing elements that cannot be painted. He does this more pointedly than Wang Shimin does. Wang Shimin tends to pick couplets in which most everything (if not actually everything) that is mentioned can be depicted in a painting and then proceed to do just that. But Shitao often selects couplets with a prominent component that defies depiction in a painting; for example, spring "hurrying" the willows to bud, the river "giving" smooth waters to the boat, mountain peaks "sending up" the sun, and peaks engulfed in clouds "since last night." By inscribing such lines on his paintings, Shitao adds a dimension to the scene that lies beyond the painted images, whether it be intentionality, fantasy, temporality, and so forth. It seems that Shitao, a remarkably creative artist, was aware that poetic lines could invest his work with meanings that would be difficult, if not impossible, to convey with painted images alone, and that he liked to experiment with adding such lines to his paintings. Doing so imparted additional layers of meaning to his work, making them truly composite works that brought the visual and literary together. There is a sense in which adding any poetic lines to a painting does this, especially if they are plucked from a poem written centuries earlier. But for the artist who wants to thus enrich his work, it would be natural to turn specifically to Du Fu, famed as his poetry is for verbal innovation and density of meaning.

The other conspicuous feature of Shitao's album is the preference the artist shows for paintings that feature a lone male figure appearing in the landscape. The man may be walking or sitting, but the key trait about him, seen in several paintings, is that he is alone and seems to be contemplating the scene around him, perhaps completely absorbed in it. Figure 8.7 is an example. The inscribed couplet is the third one in this Du Fu poem:

東屯北崦	North Mountain at East Camp[20]
盜賊浮生困	Rebels put this life adrift in hardship,
誅求異俗貧	unfamiliar folk here become poor from exactions.
空村惟見鳥	In an empty village I see only birds,
落日未逢人	as the sun sets I meet no one.
步壑風吹面	Pacing the ravine, the wind blows on my face,
看松露滴身	looking at pines, the dew drips on me.
遠山回白首	I turn my white-haired head to distant mountains—
戰地有黃塵	there is the yellow dust of a battlefield.

The painted image is an interesting transformation of the poetic lines, and this is true on two levels. First, looking only at the transcribed couplet, it is probably safe to say that, reading that couplet, few people would imagine the persona of the poet *sitting* on a cliff (Figure 8.8). Shitao has changed poetic lines about walking along a ravine to an image of a person sitting atop a bluff that overlooks a river, contemplating the scene. It is true

20. Owen, *The Poetry of Du Fu*, vol. 5, 276–77.

that Shitao has included a pine tree beside the person. But the original line calls to mind a pine forest with dense growth on which moisture collects and drips down. The lone pine depicted in Shitao's painting is a far cry from such a forest.

The second order of transformation is the general mood and tone of the painting compared with Du Fu's poem (the entire poem). We are already accustomed to the practice painters had of focusing on one couplet in a poem and rendering it according to their own vision, quite oblivious of the original poetic context. But in this painting it appears that Shitao quite overtly contradicts the sense and mood of the original poem. The painting evokes enjoyment of the river scene by the person who is perched on the rock, gazing out across the river. It is a quiet, attractive scene, infused with a certain whimsy and lightheartedness, which are hallmarks of Shitao's work. If we move from this scene back to Du Fu's original poem, the change is jarring. In the original the speaker is brooding over warfare and the dire consequences it has had on the local population; in the closing couplet he even imagines he can see dust from a battlefield not far away. There is nothing in the painting to suggest any such somberness, much less violence and suffering. Even the lines Shitao lifted from the original poem take on, once they are inscribed on this kind of scene, a genial and comforting aura, evoking the gentle way nature greets the visitor. In the original poem those same lines evoke a different feeling. As the commentator Qiu Zhaoao 仇兆鰲 (1638–1717) reads them, the lines about ravine wind and pine dew "describe the desolation of the autumnal scene."[21] Shitao has utterly transformed this mood that the lines evoke in their original context, apparently delighting in demonstrating that the poet's words can be paired with a very different scene.

Such a transformation is not unusual in Shitao's album. Another painting in the same album is inscribed with the couplet "Water of a stream, road in deserted mountains, / ramshackle gate, a village with old trees" 澗水空山道，柴門老樹村.[22] The painting presents an old man walking with a staff along a stream that is running down from mountains in the background. Beside the path is a wicker fence, with an open gate, leading to some dwellings behind, and next to the gate are a few rather scraggy-looking trees. The details seem a good match for the inscribed lines, except that the poem is entitled "Recalling My Baby Son" ("Yi youzi" 憶幼子), and that in it Du Fu, while captive in rebel-held Chang'an, is remembering his small son who is off living with the rest of Du Fu's family a hundred miles away in Fuzhou. The inscribed couplet presents Du Fu's memory of Fuzhou. If there is anyone featured in that imagined scene in Du Fu's mind, it should be the little boy, not an old man with a staff. Again, Shitao has envisioned the lines anew and in a way that does not match their original meaning.

Who, by the way, is this old man who keeps reappearing in Shitao's album? He is drawn similarly whenever he appears in paintings in this album. He wears a white robe, often carries a staff or walking stick, has a small rectangular cap tied on his head, and sports a beard. He is conspicuously alone, never socializing with others. Usually, in fact, there is no one else in the painting aside from this robed man. It is useful, at this point, to take a sidelong glance at a leaf in another Shitao album (Figure 8.9).

This album, known as *Ye se* 野色 (*Wilderness Colors*), is not specifically a Du Fu poetry album, but it too contains paintings inscribed with lines by Du Fu (as well as those by

21. Qiu Zhaoao, *Du shi xiangzhu*, 1771.
22. Owen, *The Poetry of Du Fu*, vol. 1, 260–61.

other poets).[23] The relevant leaf is a painting of a man standing under flowering trees with his gaze turned upward, and this man strongly resembles the lone man in the *Du Fu's Poetic Thoughts* album. The painting is inscribed with another Du Fu couplet: "I raise my face, avid to watch the birds, / I turn my head, mistakenly to answer someone" 仰面貪看鳥，回頭錯應人.[24] This time, Shitao has added a note in smaller calligraphy under the quoted lines: "I often take myself as a reincarnation of this old fellow. But I'm not sure if I have likewise 'skipped over the difficult words' or not" 多因此老後身，未識難字過也未. This note shows that in this instance Shitao was thinking of the lines in Du Fu's original poem that come immediately after the inscribed couplet, in which the poet speaks of skipping over the difficult words when he reads books and indulging in drinking wine as he does so. But for us the key phrase in the note is "this old fellow." It strongly suggests that Shitao is thinking of the man in his painting as Du Fu. It is not just a painting of *someone* standing under trees that Shitao inscribed with a couplet by Du Fu. It is Shitao's imaginative rendering of Du Fu as self-described in those two lines, being so eager to watch the birds in the trees that he fails to hear correctly something that is said to him by someone behind and proceeds to give a nonsense answer to whatever was said.

Does that mean that the lone man depicted in so many of the paintings in Shitao's *Du Fu's Poetic Thoughts* is also Du Fu? Perhaps it is preferable to leave some interpretive space in our answer to the question. It is tempting to say, at the least, that the lone figure in the album is Shitao's vision of Du Fu. In that vision Du Fu has become the iconic "poetry sage" who stands apart, moving serenely through the landscape as he describes it. This vision may partake of elements of Du Fu's stature and legacy that were widespread in Shitao's time, yet it also remains in a sense deeply Shitao's own. Few readers of Du Fu would single out the couplets that Shitao selects for inscription on his paintings. Collectively, Shitao's choices have the effect of presenting a Du Fu who is absorbed in nature (e.g., losing himself in watching the birds and blossoms overhead). Such a Du Fu surely has a lot in common with Shitao himself, who painted landscapes, birds, and flowers endlessly. In the end, we might decide it is impossible to draw a distinction between Du Fu as depicted in these paintings and Shitao's own ideals, so that it becomes just as plausible to say that the man featured in the paintings is largely Shitao's self-image. And this would be not just an image of nature lover but also an image of the artist, perhaps the archetype of the artist, who excels at capturing nature in his words (Du Fu) or with his brush (Shitao).

Another painting in Shitao's *Wilderness Colors*, inscribed with a couplet by Li Bai 李白 (701–762), makes an interesting comparison (Figure 8.10). This painting shows a distinctly different approach to the matching of a painting with earlier poetic lines. This is the entire poem, from which the inscribed couplet (the second couplet) is taken:

·

23. The album is held in the Metropolitan Museum collection, ID no. 19824, the Sackler Fund 1972 (1972.122a–l). All twelve leaves in the album are available on Artstor (www.artstor.org), listed as Shitao, "Wilderness Colors." The same album is sometimes elsewhere referred to as a *Shitao Landscape Album*. The title "wildness colors" comes from one of the leaves inscribed with lines that include the phrase *ye se* 野色.

24. Owen, *The Poetry of Du Fu*, vol. 3, 2–3.

與夏十二登岳陽樓   On Climbing Yueyang Tower with Xia the Twelfth[25]

樓觀岳陽盡   The entire Yueyang region can be viewed from this tower,
川迥洞庭開   the river leads distantly to Dongting Lake.
雁引愁心去   Wild geese fly off bearing my sorrowful heart,
山銜好月來   but the hills meanwhile discharge a beautiful moon.
雲間連下榻   Amid the clouds the banquet mats are set out,
天上接行杯   here in the heavens we pass the goblet of wine.
醉後涼風起   After drinking a refreshing breeze comes up
吹人舞袖回   that fills our dancing sleeves as we return home.

To begin with, the couplet Shitao chose for his painting *is* the most striking couplet of the poem that contains it, the most memorable one. More telling still, Shitao's rendering of the couplet in his painting clearly departs from the way he renders Du Fu lines. This painting by Shitao is very faithful to the particulars of the Li Bo poem. The migrating geese, the moon rising just over the distant hills, the river, Yueyang Tower—they are all represented in Shitao's painting. We can even clearly see two persons standing on the tower's balcony, looking out precisely toward the flying geese and the rising moon. These two persons must be Li Bai and his friend, Xia the Twelfth, named in the title of the poem. In this painting, Shitao does not show the preoccupation with the figure and presence of the inscribed poet that he typically shows when he composes paintings based on Du Fu lines. Shitao is also content to stick close to details of the Li Bai poem, presenting them almost prosaically in his painting. This painting shows little of the creative energy we find in his Du Fu paintings, which typically wrest the couplet away from its original import, turning it in a new direction. With such a redirection Shitao displays his special interest in Du Fu and his intent to recreate the protean poet in his own manner.

A Sixteenth-Century Album

It will be useful to conclude with a look at two other paintings inscribed with Du Fu couplets. These are part of a "poetic thoughts" album produced a century or more before the albums by Wang Shimin and Shitao. It is the work of the mid-Ming painter Xie Shichen 謝時臣 (1488–1547).[26] The Du Fu paintings it contains (it also includes paintings inspired by other Tang poets) show yet another approach to the task of depicting Du Fu's couplets in a visual medium. Consider the painting inscribed with this couplet (Figure 8.11):

棧懸斜避石   The suspended plank walkway curves to avoid the rock,
橋斷復尋溪   bridge broken, I look for another crossing over the creek.[27]

---

25. *Quan Tang shi*, 180.1838.
26. The album is entitled *Duling shiyi tuce* 杜陵詩意圖冊 and is held in the Beijing Palace Museum collection, no. 新 100457. It is published in Xie Shichen, *Gugong bowuyuan cangpin daxi* 故宮博物院藏品大系, vol. 8. The two paintings discussed below are on pages 38 and 36 of that volume.
27. From "From Langzhou Taking My Wife and Children Back to Shu: Traveling in the Mountains" 自閬州領妻子卻赴蜀山行三首第二. Owen, *The Poetry of Du Fu*, vol. 3, 340–41. I have replaced *que* 卻 in line 2 with the variant *fu* 復 because that is what Xie Shichen has inscribed on his painting, and I have altered the translation accordingly.

The poem the couplet is taken from describes a journey on foot that Du Fu took with his family, moving through the mountains from Langzhou (in the Eastern Circuit of Sichuan) back to another residence in Chengdu (in the Western Circuit). The painting presents Du Fu by himself, as if his family were not with him. Aside from that, however, the painting does a remarkably faithful job at representing the details in the two inscribed lines. The suspended plank walkway, curving (*xie* 斜) around a rock jutting out from a cliff, is featured in the foreground, as is the bridge over the stream, broken in the middle so that it cannot be used. To capture the second line, Xie Shichen has ingeniously shown Du Fu speaking with another man, who is presumably a local familiar with the area (if not a servant, since this man is carrying something, who has scouted out a way ahead). This man is motioning off to the side, pointing behind him as he speaks to Du Fu. We surmise that he is telling Du Fu about another way across the creek, which he can find by circling around behind the cliff, bringing him to the creek again further downstream, where it can be crossed, perhaps via a bridge in good repair or perhaps a natural crossing spot. This is the main interest of the painting, the way the painter has represented both the elements of the scene designated in the two lines and the clever way he has dealt with the issue, broached in the second line, of our poet needing to find another way to get across the water. Xie Shichen accomplishes this by introducing a key element that is *not* in the poem's couplet, the second man who is informing Du Fu about a solution to his problem. This treatment of the couplet stands apart from Wang Shimin's focus on colors and complex spatial relations, and it also remains much closer to the scene and situation of the original poem than Shitao evidently feels obliged to do in his Du Fu album. Xie Shichen's painting is heavily descriptive and, most of all, narrative in a way that the other Du Fu albums are not. Xie treats the lines he quotes like a story, a sequence of events unfolding in time, and he is so committed to making that story sound plausible that he invents a new character who literally points a way to a successful conclusion to the problem of getting Du Fu across that stream.

Another painting in Xie Shichen's album (Figure 8.12) illustrates an early poem by Du Fu that describes a summer outing he took by boat to a scenic spot along a canal in Chang'an. Du Fu was accompanying a group of "noble gentlemen" on this outing and was probably among the lower-ranking of those in attendance. The couplet from the poem that Xie Shichen chose for his painting describes the enjoyments of the destination that day once the group arrives:

竹深留客處　　The bamboo is deep, with places that detain the guests,
荷淨納涼時　　lotus washing clean, the moment we enjoy the cool.[28]

True to these lines, the painting is organized around two distinct spaces and sections. In the foreground a man sits on a deck that extends out over the canal or lake. Lotus plants cover the surface of the water close to him. The man holds a fan, but he has put it down, not using it to fan himself, presumably because the air where he sits over the water is already cool. This section illustrates the second line of the couplet. The second section of the painting occupies the background and consists of a bamboo grove, within which two other men sit on the ground, chatting. This section illustrates the first line of the couplet. Xie Shichen has added a man walking along a bridge that leads to the bamboo grove, structurally connecting the water scene in front with the bamboo grove behind.

---

28. Owen, *The Poetry of Du Fu*, vol. 1, 126–27.

This painting too is fundamentally descriptive and finds a visually convincing way of depicting the two distinct aspects of the scene and types of enjoyment denoted in Du Fu's lines. Although the narrative element is not so pronounced in this painting as in the broken bridge painting, it also evokes a clear sense of temporality: in this case it is not the temporality of events unfolding but rather that of time passing while the figures depicted do *not* move about. That is the point: that the enjoyments of this scene are such that the persons in it simply want to stay put idly, as the hours slip by.

Another feature of Xie Shichen's album is that as "faithful" as his paintings appear to be to the couplets inscribed on them, there are aspects of the larger poems that are conspicuously absent from what he shows us. We have already noted the omission of Du Fu's family from the traveling scene in the first painting discussed. In the second painting the omission is even more conspicuous (and telling). The poem title is this: "Taking Singing Girls to Enjoy the Cool at Yard Eight Canal in the Company of Various Noble Gentlemen: On the Verge of Evening It Rained" ("Pei zhu guigongzi Zhangbagou xieji naliang wanji yuyu" 陪諸貴公子丈八溝攜妓納涼晚際遇雨). Moreover, the singing girls are present not only in the title: they are mentioned prominently in the two poems Du Fu wrote on this occasion, paired with the gentlemen in one couplet in the first poem and the subject of an entire couplet in the second. But this feminine presence, which Du Fu freely allows in his poems, is completely elided in the Ming album leaf. Xie Shichen transforms the scene Du Fu describes into one that would be more compatible with images of his day of "elegant gatherings" (*yahui* 雅會) of literati, without the company of the female entertainers. Xie Shichen also completely ignores the rainstorm featured in Du Fu's second of the two poems, which abruptly reduces the party to a dreary and soggy trip home. So we see that Xie Shichen is capable of being both very true to his poetic inspiration and very untrue simultaneously. And yet his transformation of the poem is of a different kind than what we have noticed in Shitao's album. Shitao does not simply suppress something he considers incompatible with contemporary standards of good taste; rather, he likes to completely recast Du Fu's lines according to his own idiosyncratic vision.

* * *

The seventeenth century is widely recognized as a particularly important and innovative period in Chinese painting. We should hardly be surprised if it turns out, as suggested by the examples discussed here, that seventeenth-century artists took the visual re-creation of Du Fu's lines to new levels of creative adaptation, moving away from the more narrative approach exemplified in Xie Shichen's album. But there are other earlier painters not examined here, and their treatment of Du Fu's lines might complicate the chronological contrast sketched here. This chapter is, after all, little more than a preliminary inquiry into a promising subfield of Ming-Qing painting and its relationship to the literary tradition. It should be clear enough, even from this initial survey, that Du Fu's poetry was a subject of intense interest among later artists and also served as a catalyst for their creative energies. Naturally, the later artists' adaptation of earlier poetry was not limited to Du Fu, but Du Fu retained a special claim upon their attention, his lines providing them with material particularly amenable to visual experiment and re-creation.

9
Six Modernist Poets in Search of Du Fu

David Der-wei Wang

Luigi Pirandello's (1867–1936) *Six Characters in Search of an Author* (1921) is a landmark of high modernism in European theater. The play opens with six strangers showing up to a drama company's rehearsal of a play. These strangers claim that they are the characters of a play waiting to be finished and demand that the director stage their story. Over the course of the play, they critique the actors' and the director's interpretations, and reveal and even act out the plots that purportedly form the real basis for the play within the play. As a result, the play becomes a sequence of quarrels between the characters and the actors and production crew, and among the characters themselves, culminating in an anarchy in and about the theater.

Six Characters in Search of an Author touches on many of the central concerns of modernism as a global movement, such as the boundaries of mimesis, the feasibility of form and formality, the criteria of canon, and above all the legitimacy of authorial subjectivity. At the center of Pirandello's play, as its title suggests, is the search for the missing author. The "author" is the most important "character" in the entire the play; his absence, or more paradoxically, his haunting omnipresence, brings about both the crisis and the carnivalesque potential of the production. Pirandello's inquiry into the dissipation *and* enchantment of the author—and by association, the embodiment of authoritative subjectivity, the paradigm, and the origin of a tradition of authorship—in the modern age had a lasting impact on Western literary discourse, including Harold Bloom's *The Anxiety of Influence* (1973) and Roland Barthes's *The Death of the Author* (*La mort de l'auteur*, 1967).

When one brings the concepts of the absence (or even the death) of the author to bear on the dynamics of Chinese modernism, however, one confronts a different set of questions, the most pressing of which are whether the "author" occupies a position of the same significance in the Chinese literary tradition as in its Western counterpart, and whether the invocation of this "author" necessarily gives rise to "authorial and intentional fallacies" or "the anxiety of influence" in the Chinese context. Above all, has the "author" truly been eclipsed in modern Chinese discourse? One case that throws all of these questions into relief is Chinese modernist poets' reception and appropriation of

Du Fu, the "poet sage" (*shi sheng* 詩聖) and the arch-practitioner of the canon of "poetry as history" (*shi shi* 詩史).

This chapter argues that, for all the iconoclastic impulses of modern Chinese literature, Du Fu continued to enjoy being an icon and a ground for cultural and even political contestation throughout the twentieth century, inspiring and challenging poets of various styles, generations, and ideologies. Feng Zhi 馮至 (1905–1993), whom Lu Xun 魯迅 (1881–1936) famously identified as the "best modern Chinese lyricist,"[1] modeled himself after Du Fu as early as the mid-1920s while Wen Renping 溫任平 (b. 1944), a renowned sinophone poet based in Malaysia, critiqued the politics of Penang by assuming the posture of Du Fu as recently as March 2016.[2] Whereas the Taiwanese American poet Yang Mu 楊牧 (b. 1940) cites Du Fu as the inspiration for the conceptual and stylistic metamorphosis of his poetry in the 1970s,[3] the Singaporean poet Liang Wern Fook 梁文福 (b. 1964) reminisces in the new millennium about the days when he coped with the drudgery of military training by mentally reciting Du's poems.[4] Moreover, Du Fu has been cited so frequently for cultural, political, and commercial purposes in contemporary China that, to make fun of the trend, there appeared a popular internet meme titled none other than "Du Fu henmang" 杜甫很忙 (Du Fu is busy) in 2012.[5]

The fact that Du Fu is the "author" worshiped by multiple modern Chinese poets during the past century prods us to reconsider the motivations of Chinese literary modernity. Conventional wisdom has it that Chinese modernism arose as part of the May Fourth literary reform, a movement purportedly predicated on radical antitraditionalism. Moreover, modernist Chinese poetry is often considered a genre modeled on Western forms. As the conventional view would have it, modernist Chinese poetry is a far cry from classical Chinese poetry in both form and content. Therefore, the way in which Chinese modernists have continually treated Du Fu as a source of inspiration—or more, finding in him a kindred spirit, or *zhiyin* 知音—is a highly intriguing phenomenon. Their "search" for the ancient "sage of poetry" not only points to a unique dialogical relationship between the moderns and a premodern "author" but also offers an important clue to the genealogy of Chinese literary modernity.

Accordingly, inspired by Pirandello's dramatic scenario, this chapter introduces six modernist Chinese and sinophone poets in search of Du Fu—Huang Canran 黃燦然 (b. 1963), Xi Chuan 西川 (b. 1963), Wai-lim Yip 葉維廉 (b. 1937), Xiao Kaiyu 蕭開愚

---

1. Lu Xun, preface to *Xiandai Zhongguo wenxue daxi*, 4.
2. Lim Guan Eng, then the chief minister of Penang in Malaysia, was criticized by the media for purchasing a luxury condo for half its market price in March 2016, a scandal that compelled Wen Renping to compose "Untitled" 無題, which reads, "Lim Guan Eng walked toward Du Fu's thatched cottage / On stone steps soaked wet by the spring rain after a humid summer / His escorts hurried to cover the path with wood planks / The Master's feet must not get wet / Otherwise his clean reputation of incorruptibility would be stained" 林冠英向杜甫草堂走去 / 石階被溽暑後的春雨沾濕 / 隨扈慌不迭忙, 用木板舖路 / 主子的雙足不能濕 / 濕了有損廉潔清譽. The poem is published on Wen Renming's Facebook page at https://zh-cn.facebook.com/permalink.php?story_fbid=972052262832686&id=972044979500081.
3. Yang Mu, "Paying Tribute to Du Fu in Autumn" 秋祭杜甫 (1974). See Zhang Songjian's discussion in "One Poet, Four Faces," 179–203. I thank Professor Zhang for helping with the collection of poetry related to Du Fu in sinophone Malaysia and Singapore and for the insights of his essay.
4. Liang Wern Fook, "Taking the 2.4 k Run with Du Fu" 與杜甫共跑 2.4. Published in *Lianhe zaobao* 聯合早報, July 13, 2003.
5. See http://knowyourmeme.com/photos/278875-du-fu-is-busy. On March 26, 2012, the Chinese news blog *Ministry of Tofu* published an article titled "'Du Fu Is Busy'—Netizens Have Fun with Photo-Shopping Portrait of Ancient Chinese Poet," which quickly drew national attention and gave rise to a trend of "redrawing" the poet's sanctioned portraits in multiple contemporary media.

(b. 1960), Luo Fu 洛夫 (1928–2018), and Luo Qing 羅青 (b. 1948)—along with their aspirations and conjurations, appropriations and revisions. For the sake of comparison, I will also discuss Feng Zhi, whose poems on Du Fu have received ample attention.[6] In the name of Du Fu, these poets form an imagined community within the republic of poetry. Subsequently in this chapter, I will divide these poets according to two interrelated themes. While the first group—Huang Canran, Xi Chuan, and Wai-lim Yip—composes poems to emulate Du Fu, the second—Xiao Kaiyu, Luo Fu, and Luo Qing—writes in such a way as to "simulate" the master. In both cases I examine how these modern poets stage imaginary dialogues with the "sage of poetry" and probe issues such as canonicity and its subversion, iconography and the "anxiety of influence." Above all, the chapter seeks to understand their engagement with Du Fu's legacy in light of various historical circumstances, thus reviving the concept of "poetry as history."

Emulating Du Fu: Huang Canran, Xi Chuan, Wai-lim Yip

Modern Chinese poets' engagement with Du Fu is best represented by Feng Zhi's lifelong "search" for the "sage of poetry." In December 1938, Feng Zhi and his family arrived in Kunming, Yunnan, after a long journey fleeing the Japanese invasion. Before the outbreak of the Second Sino-Japanese War the year before, Feng had already enjoyed a reputation as both "the best lyricist of modern China" and a first-rate scholar of Goethe, Rilke, and German literature in general. Feng Zhi had long found his kindred spirit in Du Fu. In the epigraph of his collection *Bei you* 北游 (*Northern Journey*, 1929), Feng Zhi quotes Du Fu's line "I stand alone in a vast expanse chanting a poem to myself" 獨立蒼茫自詠詩.[7] But it was the hardship of the journey he took westward to the hinterland that made him truly understand the pathos Du Fu harbored during the An Lushan Rebellion. In 1941, Feng wrote the following quatrain:

攜妻抱女流離日	Now as a refugee, taking my wife along and carrying my daughter,
始信少陵字字真	I begin to believe the truth of Du Fu's every word;
未解詩中盡血淚	Unable to understand the blood and tears filling every poem,
十年伴作太平人	for ten years I pretended to be a person living in a peaceful world.[8]

Written in the form of a seven-character-line quatrain, the poem is a far cry from the modern form for which Feng Zhi was known. It testifies to his determination to emulate the Tang poet's engagement with poetry *as* history.

Notwithstanding its antitraditional claims, modern Chinese literature did not do away with the *shi shi* discourse but rather intensified it, as evinced by Feng Zhi's poetry and poetics. The devastation and hardship of wartime life compelled Feng Zhi to contemplate a series of questions: the cycle of life and death, the necessity of change, and the burden of making choices and commitments in life. Rilke and Goethe loom around his works, but it is Du Fu who inspired Feng Zhi when he was pondering the role that a poet plays during a historical catastrophe. The result is a collection of twenty-seven

---

6. See Zhang Songjian's essay, "One Poet, Four Faces."
7. From Du Fu's "Song of Leyou Park" 樂遊園歌. Translation is Stephen Owen's. Owen, *The Poetry of Du Fu*, vol. 1, 68–69.
8. Feng Zhi, "For the Inauguration of *Caotang*" 祝《草堂》創刊, in *Feng Zhi quanji*, vol. 4, 226. I thank Dylan Suher for helping translate this and other poems in the chapter.

sonnets titled *Shisihang shi* 十四行詩 (*Sonnets*, 1942), arguably the best of Feng's oeuvre. In this collection, Feng Zhi explicitly praises the poet of poets:

> You endure starvation in a deserted village,
> Thought about the dead filling up the trenches,
> But you sang the elegies incessantly
> For the fall of human magnificence.
>
> Warriors die, were wounded on battlefields,
> Meteors fall at sky's end,
> Ten thousand horses disappeared with the floating clouds
> And your life was the sacrifice for them.
>
> Your poverty shone,
> The tattered robes of a saint,
> A single thread from it
>
> An inexhaustible spiritual force in this world,
> All caps and canopies before your brilliance
> Are only reflections of pitiful images.[9]

> 你在荒村裏忍受饑腸，
> 你常常想到死填溝壑，
> 你却不斷地唱著哀歌
> 為了人間壯美的淪亡：
>
> 戰場上健兒的死傷，
> 天邊有明星的隕落，
> 萬匹馬隨著浮雲消没……
> 你一生是他們的祭享。
>
> 你的貧窮在閃爍發光
> 像一件聖者的爛衣裳，
> 就是一絲一縷在人間
>
> 也有無窮的神的力量。
> 一切冠蓋在它的光前
> 只照出來可憐的形象。

The poem was composed in 1941, a difficult time for Chinese people trapped in the war. By celebrating Du Fu, Feng Zhi clearly means to parallel the fate of wartime Chinese poets with that of the master, who suffered through the chaos of the An Lushan Rebellion and pondered what poetry means when civilization falls apart. He foregrounds in the sonnet Du Fu's interaction with things both trivial and magnificent, and contemplates the natural cycle of birth and death vis-à-vis cosmic eternity. The only subject he does not confront directly is the war. But war and everything associated with it—exodus, meltdown of human relationships, cultural destruction, and, above all, death—constitute the background against which his poem comes into existence. Feng Zhi has little intention of promoting patriotism, however. The communal relationship he envisages is more immense and idealistic than the bond between fellow citizens.

---

9. Cheung's translation with slight modification, *Feng Chih*, 83.

It is a relationship between people who acknowledge both individual sufficiency and collective plenitude, both existential solitude and essential solidarity with all the beings in the world.

Such an attempt to consecrate Du Fu would become a rhetorical trope in subsequent years, a trope used by poets such as Yang Mu, Yu Guangzhong 余光中 (1928–2017), Da Huang 大荒 (1930–2003), Luo Fu, Wai-lim Yip, Chen Yi-chih 陳義芝 (b. 1954), Xi Chuan, and Huang Canran. Here we focus on Huang Canran, Xi Chuan, and Wai-lim Yip. As if speaking to Du Fu through Feng Zhi, the Hong Kong poet Huang Canran writes "Du Fu," also in the sonnet form:

> How humble he is, in comparison with his poetry.
> The record of his life is as threadbare as his life itself,
> Only leaving us a tattered image,
> One that saddens the innocent, and strengthens the miserable.
>
> Heaven wanted him to be noble, so it made him ordinary;
> His days were like white rice: each grain is difficult.
> The soul of Chinese language was looking for an appropriate vessel,
> And found a safe and stable home in this exile.
>
> History, compared with him, is just an interlude;
> War, if it knew of him, would itself declare a ceasefire.
> Even pain must find its utmost depths in his body.
>
> Heaven gave him an inconspicuous mortal coil,
> Bedecked him with landscape and scenes of life, loss and love,
> And let him live an epoch in one human life.[10]

> 他多麼渺小，相對於他的詩歌；
> 他的生平捉襟見肘，像他的生活。
> 只給我們留下一個襤褸的形象，
> 叫無憂者發愁，叫痛苦者堅強。
>
> 上天要他高尚，所以讓他平凡；
> 他的日子像白米，每粒都是艱難。
> 漢語的靈魂要尋找適當的載體，
> 這個流亡者正是它安穩的家園。
>
> 歷史跟他相比，只是一段插曲；
> 戰爭若知道他，定會停止干戈。
> 痛苦，也要在他身上尋找深度。
>
> 上天賦予他不起眼的軀殼，
> 裝着山川，風物，喪亂和愛，
> 讓他一個人活出一個時代。

Huang Canran envisions a Du Fu who lives out the sorrow of an epoch and yet thrives on the virtue of endurance and his own humanist vision. It is a vision that resonates with that of Feng Zhi, who conjures up Du Fu as a model of surviving through all adversity. Huang considers it a poet's moral imperative to unveil the obscure façade of

---

10. "Du Fu," in Huang Canran, *Wode linghun*, 50.

the status quo and in doing so points to a vision of communication not only between human beings but also between human beings and the world beyond: "Heaven gave him an inconspicuous mortal coil / Bedecked him with landscape and scenes of life, loss and love, / And let him live an epoch in one human life."

In a similar vein, Xi Chuan describes the magnanimity of Du Fu's compassion and his spirit of fortitude in life and in poetry. His poem starts with a reflection on Du Fu's capacity to endure and identify with the downtrodden and then zeroes in on a specific historical moment, "this night," when Xi Chuan himself comes to terms with the desolate landscape engulfing his own existence. As Xi Chuan suggests, his changed vision of his own existence hinges on the transformative power of Du Fu's poetry:

> Your deep benevolence and great compassion contain
> So much sunshine and rain; so much sorrow
> Was turned into poetry in the end
> Numerous autumns point to this night
> At long last I came to fall in love with the fading
> Streets and pine groves in front of my eyes[11]

> 你的深仁大愛容納下了
> 那麼多的太陽和雨水；那麼多的悲苦
> 被你最终轉化為歌吟
> 無數個秋天指向今夜
> 我終於愛上了眼前褪色的
> 街道和松林

Unlike Huang Canran, who makes Du Fu into an Olympian figure, Xi Chuan seeks a closer relationship to the Tang poet, even adding personal touches so as to better understand his magic power. He declares that Du Fu has "a voice" 一種声音 that captures his attention, a voice "majestic, solid, and calm" 磅礴, 结實又沉穩 just like the "belated blossoming of the gorgeous peony in Chang'an" 有如茁壯的牡丹遲開於長安. And he concludes that Du Fu is "the lone soul / Of a dark and gloomy time" 在一個晦暗的時代 / 你是唯一的靈魂.

Xi Chuan thus implies an allegorical reading for his poem: one wonders whether "this night" Xi Chuan inhabits is also a "dark and gloomy" time. If so, is Xi Chuan yearning for an epiphanic outburst of poetry just like the "belated blossoming of peony of Chang'an" 1,200 years before? Nevertheless, just as he appears to affirm his spiritual tie with his idol, Xi Chuan suddenly takes a contemplative stance, a stance removed from his earlier, cordial tone, and he ends his poem with a sober, ironic note:

> Hundreds and thousands of mansions eclipse the horizon
> You built them so as to better commemorate
> Those men and women on the journey in the midst of wandering
> And it is futile to come to their rescue, you know these better than all of us:
> The so-called future is nothing but the past
> So-called hope is nothing but fate[12]

---

11. From "Du Fu," in Xi Chuan, *Yinmi de huihe*, 101.
12. Xi Chuan, *Yinmi de huihe*, 102.

千萬間廣厦遮住了地平線
是你建造了它們，以便懷念那些
流浪途中的婦女和男人
而拯救是徒勞，你比我們更清楚
所謂未來，不過是往昔
所謂希望，不過是命運

Here one can distinguish between Xi Chuan's and Huang Canran's strategies for fashioning the authorial image of Du Fu. Huang Canran adores the Du Fu who seeks recourse to poetic vision in order to negotiate historical contingency; by way of contrast, Xi Chuan is less confident of the outcome of the eternal struggle between historical tumult and poetic redemption. He renders instead a negative dialectic, so to speak, at the end of his poem: he finds spiritual solidarity with Du Fu because the master knows only too well the gratuitousness of any poetic attempt to salvage the destitution of reality.

The veteran sinophone poet Wai-lim Yip has been known for his modernist poems since the early 1960s, and he has written a series of poems connected to Du Fu over the years. What distinguishes Yip from the two poets above is that he tends to dehistoricize Du Fu, calling attention instead to the overarching aesthetic configuration the poet has perfected. In "On a Spring Day, Recalling Du Fu" ("Chunri huai Du Fu" 春日懷杜甫), Yip begins:

1
Beyond the end of sight
A boundless garden
Called home
In the hollow of the bosom
Continuously expands
2
The skeleton of
Wind
The footprint of
Water
Creates minute by minute
3
Air holds together
Darkness holds together
Waves hold together
Earth holds together
From the ancient times[13]

1
看不見周邊
龐大無朋的一個園
叫做家
在心胸的內裏
不斷的擴展

---

13. Yip, *Ye Weilian wushinian*, 462–63.

2
風的
骨骼
水的
履迹
每一分鐘都在製造著
3
氣凝聚
黑暗凝聚
波浪凝聚
泥土凝聚
從遠古開始

Unlike Huang Canran's or Xi Chuan's poem, Yip's stanzas do not reference Du Fu's biography; instead "Du Fu" comes across more as an evocative figure that triggers a chain of associations, a poetic function reminiscent of the function of *xing* 興 (poetic evocation) in traditional poetic discourse. What Yip tries to call forth is a kind of sentiment crystalized by imagining Du Fu, the primordial "author" of Chinese poetry. This "author," as Yip would have it, is one endowed with the "skeleton of wind" and the "footprint of water," capable of creating something out of nothing. Thus, instead of a poet incessantly immersed in the historical condition as suggested by Huang Canran's and Xi Chuan's poems, Du Fu under Yip's pen personifies the pure form of poetry as such. Yip's poem gives one the impression that Du Fu appears as ethereal as a phantom and as symbolic as a gesture:

Arriving from nowhere
Departing for nowhere
Fast and slow
Are all relative
Just like
The thin divide between tragedy and comedy

來而無由
去而無止
快與慢
都是相對的
正如
悲劇喜劇紙一隔

The way in which Yip "aestheticizes" Du Fu may have to do with his unique approach to classical as well as modern Chinese poetry. An established critic, Yip has envisioned Chinese poetic creation as a process of symbolic fusion of subjectivity and the world, a process amounting to a transcendental leap that generates "secret echoes and complementary correspondences" (*mixiang pangtong* 密響旁通).[14] Hence, in the case of Du Fu,

---

14. Yip, *Diffusion of Distances*, Chapter 5.

A gesture
And that is enough
Word lives
Word dies
I understand all
One hand gesture
Is enough[15]

一種姿式
便够了
文字生
文字死
我全明白
一種手勢
便够了

But, as critics have pointed out, Yip's theory is more indebted to Western Imagism than classical Chinese poetics.[16] That is, he seeks to inscribe, or even prescribe, in poetry the encounter between the poet and the world by means of the configuration of images. Poetic language and imagery, accordingly, are treated as the media that allow the epiphanic linkage between the animate and the inanimate, the subject and the object.

Yip's view of Du Fu and poetry is contested by Stephen Owen. In a comparison of Chinese and Western poetics, Owen notes that the "*poiêma*, the literary 'thing made,' becomes tertiary and disturbing in the Platonic scheme of things. The counterpart of 'making' . . . in most Chinese literary thought is 'manifestation': everything that is inner—the nature of a person or the principles which inform the world—has an innate tendency to become outward and manifest."[17] Accordingly, in his comparative study of Wordsworth and Du Fu, Owen notes that, whereas the former's "Composed upon Westminster Bridge, September 3, 1802," is premised upon metaphor and fictonality, Du Fu's "Writing of My Feelings Traveling by Night" ("Lüye shuhuai" 旅夜書懷) suggests a manifested association: "The process of [poetic] manifestation must begin in the external world, which has priority without primacy. As a latent pattern follows its innate disposition to become manifest, passing from the world to mind to literature, a theory of sympathetic resonance is involved."[18] Du Fu is recognized as the arch-practitioner of "poetry as history." This term refers not merely to the poet's historiographical and mimetic capacity but also to his vision, which makes his poetic mind resonate with the turbulence of history and the cosmos. Whereas Yip's Du Fu abstracts poetry from history through the use of imagistic configuration, Owen's Du Fu evokes poetry in resonance with history, producing a mutual manifestation.

---

15. Yip, *Ye Weilian wushinian*, 472.
16. Zhang Wanmin, "Bianzhe you bujian."
17. Owen, *Readings in Chinese Literary Thought*, 21.
18. Owen, *Traditional Chinese Poetry and Poetics*, 21. Also, James Liu describes, "a poet does not take an experience as the 'content' of his point and pour it in to a 'form;' he is prompted by some experience, be it an emotion, a thought, or an event, to write and while he is searching for the right words, the right pattern of sounds and sequence of images, the original experience is transformed into something new—the poem." Liu, *The Art of Chinese Poetry*, 96.

Simulating Du Fu: Luo Fu, Xiao Kaiyu, Luo Qing

Feng Zhi continued to work on Du Fu in the postwar years as he underwent a drastic ideological metamorphosis: he was drawn to Communism and became a supporter of the revolution. By the time he published *A Biography of Du Fu* (*Du Fu zhuan* 杜甫傳) in 1952, he had developed a new agenda of poetry as history. In Feng's portrait, Du Fu came across as the "people's artist" of the Tang dynasty, sympathizing with the misery of the people and anticipating the Chinese proletarian revolution.[19] In the same year, Feng dedicated a poem to Mao Zedong 毛澤東 (1893–1976), "My Thanks" ("Wode ganxie" 我的感謝):

> You make the mountains and rivers
> Look so beautiful, lucid
> You make everyone regain their youth
> You make me, an intellectual,
> Have a conscience again.
> . . .
> You give birth to us anew
> You are our benefactor forever.[20]

> 你讓祖國的山川
> 變得這樣美麗、清新，
> 你讓人人都恢復了青春，
> 你讓我，一個知識分子，
> 又有了良心。
> ……
> 你是我們再生的父母，
> 你是我們永久的恩人。

Given the ideological strictures placed on all Chinese intellectuals during that period, we cannot help asking whether Du Fu's calls for individual sobriety helped Feng discern any flaws in Mao's utopia, or whether Du Fu's historical pathos, as suggested by the famous cycles of "Three Officers" ("San li" 三吏) and "Three Partings" ("San bie" 三別),[21] ever disturbed him when he composed the following lines at the height of the Great Famine (1959–1961):

> In our nation,
> This is common sense:
> Tillers of the land do not starve; weavers of cloth do not freeze;
> The people are happier and healthier year after year.[22]

> 在我們的國家裡，
> 有一個道理本來很平常：
> 種田的不挨餓，織布的不受凍，
> 人民一年比一年更幸福，更健康。

---

19. See Zhang Hui's criticism in Zhang Hui, *Zhongguo shishi chuantong*, Chapter 6.
20. Feng Zhi, *Feng Zhi quanji*, vol. 2, 50–52.
21. That is, "The Officer of Xin'an" 新安吏, "The Officer at Tong Pass" 潼關吏, and "The Officer at Stone Moat" 石壕吏; "Newlyweds Parted" 新婚別, "Parted When Getting Old" 垂老別, and "Parted without a Family" 無家別. Owen, *The Poetry of Du Fu*, vol. 2, 82–97.
22. From Feng Zhi, "Zai women de guojia li" 在我們的國家裏. *Feng Zhi quanji*, vol. 2, 312.

I am not suggesting Feng Zhi's worship of Mao in poems such as "My Thanks" and "In Our Nation" was disingenuous. Quite the contrary, I argue that after the Liberation in 1949, at least for a while, poets such as Feng Zhi felt compelled to express their "thanks" *because of* their conviction that the new regime reinvigorated the paradigm of "poetry as history"—in a celebratory mode. In historical hindsight, however, a poem such as "My Thanks" or "In Our Nation" indicates more the "exegetical bonding"—the technology of self- and mutual examination through discursive exercises—sanctioned by the party than the inculcating subtlety of poetry as history. As a result, Feng's effort to make himself a socialist Du Fu ends with an embarrassing parody of the "sage of poetry" as well as himself as "the best lyrical poet" in the Republican era.[23]

Feng Zhi's failed attempt to become a modern Du Fu prods one to rethink the eternal dialectic between authorial intention and poetic persona. At a time when "poetry as history" was made, or tamed, in such a way as to echo nothing but Maoist propaganda, select poets in diaspora ventured to reinterpret the canon by giving it a dramatic twist. In a sharp contrast with the poetics of emulation demonstrated by Feng Zhi and his followers, they created a poetics of simulation. By simulation, I refer not only to the deliberately mimetic, or even mimicking, rhetoric with which these poets try to revitalize Du Fu (as evinced by the group of poets discussed in the first section in terms of "emulation") but also to the bold endeavor of trying to dramatize the Tang poet or his poems under varied circumstances. The result is the surprising discovery of how *relevant* Du Fu's historical concerns can still be in the contemporary era. Take, for instance, Luo Fu's "Reading Du Fu on a Bus" ("Cheshang du Du Fu" 車上讀杜甫):[24]

"Beyond Swordgate the news suddenly comes that we've recaptured Jibei."

Staggering,
The bus passes the Chang'an West Road, beholding
Smoke and dust flee like An Lushan's panicked, defeated troops.
In those days, on his way back to the capital from Sichuan, Emperor Xuanzong
happened to cast a look backward
Only to fall into speechless sorrow
Over a silk scarf blown away by the wind at Mawei.
And now suddenly hearing the news of triumph, you must be thinking of going
home too.
May I share the same boat with you on the homecoming tour?

劍外忽傳收薊北

搖搖晃晃中
車過長安西路乍見
煙塵四竄猶如安祿山敗軍之倉皇
當年玄宗自蜀返京的途中偶然回首
竟自不免為馬嵬坡下
被風吹起的一條綢巾而惻惻無言
而今驟聞捷訊想必你也有了歸意
我能搭你的便船還鄉嗎

---

23. I am referring to David Apter and Anthony Saich's argument in *Revolutionary Discourse*, 263.
24. Luo Fu, *Yinwei feng de yuangu*, 296.

Luo Fu belongs to the generation of émigré mainlanders who fled to Taiwan after the 1949 National Divide. After graduating from the naval academy in 1953, he spent the next two decades in the navy while becoming better known as a surrealist poet. Luo Fu has written a series of poems about Du Fu, of which "Reading Du Fu on a Bus" is the most popular. The poem comes across as a deliberate "staging" of Du Fu's ""Hearing That the Imperial Army Has Retaken He'nan and Hebei" ("Wen guanjun shou He'nan Hebei" 聞官軍收河南河北) in the modern context of Taipei, Taiwan. Each of the eight stanzas of Luo Fu's poem is subheaded by one line of Du Fu's famous poem.[25] Thus, the reader can hardly miss the parallel between the poetic persona, presumably an émigré mainlander stranded in Taiwan like Luo Fu himself, and Du Fu in exodus during An Lushan's rebellion. Just as the Tang poet rejoiced to learn of the surrender of the last rebel generals and aspired to return home, Luo Fu appears to be relishing, or daydreaming of, a homecoming trip upon hearing a piece of "good news" about the Nationalist return to mainland China—most likely, the end of martial law in 1987, which allowed thousands of émigré mainlanders to visit their old homes. But the parallel is ironic from the outset because of the fact that the modern poet is traveling on a city bus in Taipei and there is no news whatsoever about the fall of the Communist regime.

The key irony of Luo Fu's poem lies in his use of the stops along this Taipei bus line to invoke Chinese national geography as well as Du Fu's poetry. Readers familiar with the city planning of Taipei after 1949 would know that all the major streets of the city were named after the major cities and places from the Mainland that were under the control of the Nationalist regime before 1949. The mapping of Taipei is therefore a phantom cartography of Republican China (and even its premodern, dynastic incarnations) and, by association, an invocation of the imperial sovereignty of premodern China. As the bus takes the poet-passenger from, say, Chang'an East Road to Hangzhou South Road, metaphorically he is traveling from Chang'an, the capital of the Tang in Northern China to Hangzhou, the capital of the Southern Song in the South. Nevertheless, whereas the city of Taipei can serve as cartographical encapsulation of China, the poet-passenger cannot but contemplate the fact that the national divide has taken place and any geographical recapitulation of the past can only accentuate the sense of diaspora and loss of the present.

Luo Fu concludes his poem as follows:

"Then on down to Xiangyang, where I'll head to Luoyang."

Entering Shu, leaving from Sichuan,
From Chang'an "Viewed in Spring,"
Traveling all the way to Kuizhou "Stirred by Autumn,"
You have now finally made it Luoyang, a city full of peony blossoms.
But I get off the bus halfway, on Hangzhou South Road,
Stumble into the hazy red dust.
However I try, I cannot see the foggy, rainy West Lake,
Where is my canal town south of the Yangzi River?[26]

---

25. See Owen, *The Poetry of Du Fu*, vol. 3, 186–87.
26. Luo Fu, *Yinwei feng de yuangu*, 301.

便下襄陽向洛陽

入蜀，出川
由春望的長安
一路跋涉到秋興的夔州
現在你終於又回到滿城牡丹的洛陽
而我却半途在杭州南路下車
一頭撞進了迷漫的紅塵
極目不見何處是煙雨西湖
何處是我的江南水鄉

One cannot miss the dramatic tension created by Luo Fu throughout the poem. When he likens a plebeian bus ride to a medieval emperor's flight from the capital, he strikes the dark note of the unbearable lightness of being a wandering Chinese in Taipei. At the same time, Luo Fu foregrounds the poet-passenger's infirm posture, suggesting that he may be too old to take a homecoming trip even if he wanted to. Du Fu was at least able to plan a homecoming trip after the An Lushan Rebellion; by way of contrast, his modern counterpart is seen getting off the bus (of life?) and stumbling into the middle of nowhere in Taipei. In the end, it is the poet-passenger's imaginary voyage to the world of Du Fu's poetry, one made up of such masterpieces as "View in Spring" and "Stirred by Autumn," that brings a tentative redemption for the reality of his unavoidable loss.

Shi shi or "poetry as history" has become a canonical term of Chinese poetics since the eighth century, thanks to Du Fu's works that chronicled the fates of individuals vis-à-vis a dynastic cataclysm. The Tang literatus Meng Qi 孟棨 (875 *jinshi*) famously commented, "When a poetic incantation is occasioned by an event, it is precisely where deep feelings concentrate" 觸事興詠，尤所鍾情.[27] Meng Qi considers both the circumstantial and emotive functions of *qing*, thus articulating the reciprocal relationship between historical experience and poetic mind. Meng Qi's engagement with "poetry as history" points to one element of poetic manifestation that has been important since ancient times: "The process of [poetic] manifestation must begin in the external world, which has priority without primacy. As a latent pattern follows its innate disposition to become manifest, passing from the world to mind to literature, a theory of sympathetic resonance is involved."[28] As Owen puts it, Du Fu's poetry is not supposed to be treated as "a fiction: it is a unique factual account of an experience in historical time, a human consciousness encountering, interpreting, and responding to the world."[29] It points to the "authentic and spontaneous revelation of the self."[30]

Through the dramatic form of simulation, Luo Fu and like-minded poets appear to push Owen's observation one step further. They recognize the lyrical core of Du Fu's poetics but seek to act out its existential dimension in theatrical terms. Instead of paying

---

27. See Zhang Hui, *Zhongguo shishi chuantong*. Leonard Chan has also pointed out in an unpublished paper that in the Tang dynasty a Lu Huai 盧懷 (or Lu Gui 盧瓌) authored *Accounts of Lyrical Expressions* 抒情集. The work is no longer extant except for some fragments, but judging by its title, it is a collection of narratives and poems in relation to memorable events. As is the case of Meng Qi's *The Original Events about Poems* 本事詩, *Shuqing ji* is a collection stressing affection as expressed by the poetic inculcation of historical experiences.
28. Owen, *Traditional Chinese Poetry and Poetics*, 21.
29. Owen, *Traditional Chinese Poetry and Poetics*, 15.
30. Owen, "The Self's Perfect Mirror," 74, 93.

homage to the master in a conventional manner, Luo Fu stages in his poem an unlikely event in which the themes, figures, and events of Du Fu's poetry and life are reenacted. Thus, as a "figure," Du Fu appears to trigger a new cluster of associations about the intertwined relations between the lyrical and the historical, everyday routine and epic cataclysm.

With "Reading Du Fu on a Bus," the stage is set, so to speak, for contemporary poets' continued dramatized dialogue with Du Fu. In "Du Fu," for instance, the Hong Kong poet Liu Waitong 廖偉棠 (b. 1975) depicts Du Fu as a worn-down modern-day businessman facing pressure from all sides. The "sage of poetry" who lived 1,300 years ago is seen as stepping down from his saintly pedestal to become a white-collar professional struggling to make a living in a postcolonial society. "He is a victim not of imperial violence but of market logic."[31] Hidden beneath Liu's playful, anachronistic style, however, is a contemplation of the frailty *and* tenacity of the poetic subject vis-à-vis adversity and the cyclical doom that characterizes the human condition. In a similar manner, the Singaporean poet Liang Wern Fook depicts a Du Fu's "coming home" to nowhere but the Singaporean subway, as the government was campaigning for "poeticizing" through advertisement there. As the premodern lament of dynastic vicissitudes is invoked to promote a postmodern project of city planning, "poetry and history" cannot sound more poignant.

In Xiao Kaiyu's long narrative poem, "Paying Tribute to Du Fu" ("Xiang Du Fu zhijing" 向杜甫致敬, 1996), the act of "simulating Du Fu" is undertaken with greater sincerity and empathy.[32] The poem contains ten sections, each featuring a social or political issue in contemporary China of great concern to the poet. While Du Fu is never invoked in the poem, as he is in Xi Chuan's or Huang Canran's poem, Xiao Kaiyu means to dramatize the question, How would Du Fu have responded were he made to live, and write poetry, in contemporary China?

Xiao Kaiyu starts his poem with the following lines, and the reader can sense immediately the poet's political concerns.

This is another China.
For what reason is it existing?
No one can answer, and there is no need
To answer in echoes.
This is another China.

Same as before, three generations live under one roof;
A diminished private life
Is equal to a performance; the young generation
Is molded by the measured cruelty
To doze off, to show mother
And father gratitude and at the same time
Learns the skill of amusing oneself, but just as the textbook
Repeats the teacher's shouts;

31. See Zhang Songjian's discussion. "The modern 'Tu Fu' resulting from Liu Waitong's adaptation is a humiliated and wounded person who vents his ridiculous animosity and frustration by ranting. Thus, the divine aura around the traditional 'Tu Fu' fades away, revealing a person who is decadent, vulgar, shabby and insane." Zhang Songjian, "One Poet, Four Faces," 195, 196.
32. Xiao Kaiyu, *Cishi cidi*, 149–96.

Ah, just like that, the human and the ox
Drive the plow through the fields.
Life is but endurance.
This is another China.[33]

這是另一個中國。
為了什麼而存在？
沒有人回答，也不
再用回聲回答。
這是另一個中國。

一樣，祖孫三代同居一室。
減少的私生活
等於表演；下一代
由尺度的殘忍塑造出來，
假寐是向母親
和父親感恩的同時
學習取樂的本領，但是如同課本
重複老師的一串吆喝；
啊，一樣，人與牛
在田裡拉着犁鏵耕耙。
生活猶如忍耐：
這是另一个中國。

In the following sections, as if mimicking T. S. Eliot's "Waste Land," Xiao Kaiyu features a series of personae from whose perspectives contemporary Chinese malaise surfaces for examination. A runaway schoolkid, a patient waging his final battle with his disease and with the hospital, an explorer losing his life on the road, a secretary right before her attempted suicide, and a retired soldier defeated by capitalism take turns expressing their confusion, anxiety, despair, melancholy, and sense of irony as they are faced with a society that promises no hope. The gallery of characters constitutes a *tableau vivant* of Chinese lives at their most raw and rustic. Against the master narrative of the sublime mandated by the state, Xiao means to offer a counternarrative, a montage of vignettes and snapshots of Chinese lives as they truly are.

Thus in Section 2, Xiao Kaiyu introduces a kid who plays truant:

The fact reveals that this afternoon
Lazy sunshine lends itself to daydreaming;
Carelessly think of someone
And a few others who are familiar but seemingly remote.
He tempts a kid
To compromise with the whip, a ten-minute talk
Plus a few meaningful gazes will liberate
His wild nature, ah wild nature, he runs away for the summer camp,
His computer stores bread
And an obscure, inscrutable will.[34]

---

33. Xiao Kaiyu, *Cishi cidi*, 149.
34. Xiao Kaiyu, *Cishi cidi*, 156–57.

事實表明這個下午
陽光懶洋洋地宜於遐想；
不經意地想起某個人，
與一些人密切但彷彿無關。
他誘使一個孩子
和鞭子妥協，十分鐘交談
加上幾個眼神就解放了
他的野性，啊野性，他逃出夏令營。
電腦裏存有麵包，
和一段晦澀難懂的遺囑。

In Section 7, Xiao describes a prostitute on an overseas trip, creating a persona strongly suggestive of a Baudelairean figure:

The boarding announcement in Japanese declares I am dead,
Now the dead opens her mouth to speak Shanghainese. My accent,
My high-pitched voice got me in trouble long time ago on the park bench
And in the hallway, and once was used to tease the model soprano. I . . .
    understand
The turbid glance that breaks away from the bondage of night
And the swallow's beak forced open by the willow twig, I understand you,
Bringing the tone of city people to the countryside, and shrinking the presentable
    look
On display in the shop window onto a wood case,
In the midst of a dessert of lies,
You hungrily take the measure of the swollen bellies
Of the starving masses.[35]

登機前口語宣布我死亡，
現在死者開口說上海話。我的口音，
我的高腔很早就在公園長椅
和門廳裏闖禍，也曾經用於
挑逗樣板女高音。我……了解
掙脫黑夜的捆綁的混濁的眼色
和柳條撬開的燕子的嘴巴，我了解你，
把城裡人的語氣帶進田野，把你
在櫥窗裡的顯赫樣子縮在
木箱上，從謊言的甜食
你飢餓地打量過身體腫胖的
飢餓的人群。

Maghiel van Crevel has noticed that "in content [Xiao Kaiyu's] poetic creed has much in common with classical Chinese poetry—from which it differs in the form of his poems, which is mostly free verse. However, Xiao's work may have its roots in a recognizable world, but no more than classical Chinese poetry is it a simple reflection of that world."[36] Indeed, although his work is an exposé of contemporary life, there is

35. Xiao Kaiyu, *Cishi cidi*, 179–80.
36. Van Crevel, "Xiao Kaiyu."

something classical in Xiao Kaiyu's vision, something that he is willing to link with Du Fu's humanistic compassion. But, as Xiao Kaiyu points out, for contemporary poets, the problem with the campaign to pay tribute to Du Fu "lies in not only self-righteously monopolizing Du Fu but also imposing the political correctness of themes derived from Du Fu on contemporary poetry in general. . . . On the other hand, contemporary poetry has become more and more isolated and removed from reality, such that one may need the political force of a social criticism that can lift up poetry and connect it to some point of action in life."[37]

Xiao Kaiyu believes the "action of life" lies in not only observing but also inhabiting the Chinese world with poetic imagination and compassion. Here Du Fu surfaces as a model because of his capacity to feel the pains and needs of society and to generate the social criticism and lyrical vision that can "lift poetry and hook it up with some point of action in life." Through a sequence of dramatized subjects, Xiao Kaiyu seeks the fusion of his feeling with not a "scene" but an "event" of the world, a fusion that will allow him to intensify the sense of urgency of his poetry. And he surprises us by even identifying himself—and by extension, Du Fu—with the personae being described. In the final section of his poem, Xiao reveals that, for him, paying respect to Du Fu means paying respect to the runaway kid, the prostitute, the insulted, and the injured, among others.

> Why they rather than I,
> Why they rather than a glamorous man,
> A woman secretary standing on the top floor of a skyscraper,
> Why is it a prostitute traveling on an airplane,
> Why there is no thought but memory, but delusion,
> No successful dialogue, just guesswork.[38]

> 為什麼是他們，不是我自己，
> 為什麼是他們，不是一個光芒四射的人，
> 是一個女秘書站在高樓的頂層，
> 為什麼是一個妓女，在飛行，
> 為什麼沒有思考，只有回憶，只有錯覺，
> 沒有成功的對話，只有揣測。

Then he declares:

> When I walk through streets and alleys
> Walking to a family, I am a doctor.
> I am a member of the family waiting for the doctor
> Entranced by the smell of medicine and a low fever. I am the youth
> Who signed the contract with you and then dashed off.
> I am the young hostess, who opens her mouth to the office head.
> I am the driver going anywhere you ask.
> I am the janitor and the cleaning woman. I am the sickening sweat
> Blown away by the electric fan, I am pleasure
> That grabs men and women firmly, I am not sadness

---

37. Quoted in Qin Xiaoyu, *Yu ti*, 106.
38. Xiao Kaiyu, *Cishi cidi*, 192.

Masquerading to serve literati and elegant gentlemen.[39]

當我穿過大街和小巷
走向某個家庭，我就是醫生。
我就是那些等待醫生的家庭中
着迷於藥味的低燒成員。我就是和你
簽下合同，白衣一閃的青年。
我就是小姐，嘴巴向科長開放。
我就是司機，目的地由你們吩咐。
我就是清潔工和掃帚。我就是電吹風
吹散的噁心的汗味，我就是喜悅
牢牢抓住的男人和女人，而不是悲哀
假意伺候的文人雅士。

By inhabiting all human encounters through a first-person voice, Xiao Kaiyu lets his voice oscillate between the lyrical and the theatrical, the individual and the social. In the end, the opening lines of the poem resound with us: "This is another China. / For what reason is it existing?" Through engaging with Du Fu's pathos theatrically, Xiao demonstrates what C. T. Hsia once called the "obsession with China."[40]

I am at the at lowest level of the elevator
All open to nothingness.[41]

我在底層的電梯口
而一切向虛無開放。

Finally, the modern canon of Du Fu underwent a "deconstructive turn" in fin-de-siècle Taiwan. In "On How Du Fu Was Influenced by Luo Qing" ("Lun Du Fu ruhe shou Luo Qing yingxiang" 論杜甫如何受羅青影響, 1994), Luo Qing invites his reader to join in a postmodernist reappraisal of Du Fu.[42] A veteran Taiwanese poet known for his modernist and postmodernist poetry, as well as his painting and literary criticism, Luo Qing seeks to critique the relationships between postmodernity and history by envisioning the dilemmas Du Fu would face in contemporary society. His poem opens with a playful statement:

Please don't laugh your head off
Pleases don't shout out abuse
Please don't think that I purposely
Wrote an academic paper into a poem
Nobody would believe Goddess Chang'e
Learned from the astronauts how to take a spacewalk
But that she must have observed in Dunhuang Caves
The fairies' ribbon dance is a fact beyond dispute

請不要捧腹大笑
更不要破口大罵

39. Xiao Kaiyu, *Cishi cidi*, 192–93.
40. Hsia, "Obsession with China," 533–54.
41. Xiao Kaiyu, *Cishi cidi*, 190.
42. Cited in Yang Songnian, *Kua guojie shixiang*, 162–67.

請不要以為我故意把
一篇論文的題目寫成了詩
沒有人會相信嫦娥
曾經跟太空人學過太空漫步
但她一定在敦煌觀摩過
彩帶舞一倒是不爭的事實

Anticipating the reader's skeptical reaction to the title of his poem, Luo Qing's poetic persona introduces a series of evidence to justify his stance: goddess Chang'e may have never encountered the astronauts of modern times, but she must have learned her skill of flying from the fairies in the Dunhuang cave murals; Zhuangzi and Laozi do not know themselves any better than contemporary schoolkids, who have mastered the ancient sages' wisdom through cartoons and comic strips. Thus,

> Still, the greatest is Confucius, the sage of the ages, who is
> Open-minded and wise, seeing through this point
> He let people dress him up anyway they want, walking around in costumes from
>   different dynasties
> Going anywhere and doing anything, never finicky about anything

還是聖之時者孔丘
開通又明智，得看透了這一點
他任人打扮，穿著歷朝歷代的
衣冠到處活動，從不挑三揀四

What Luo Qing is poking fun at is the revelry of anachronism in which past and present, the serious and the whimsical, are all mixed with each other, all in the name of the postmodern. A symptom of temporal inconsistency, anachronism is often associated with conceptual anomaly and political disorientation. It may manifest itself as the consequences of cultural hybridization and psychological misrecognition. In the postmodernist context, however, anachronism becomes the alibi that gives rise to an epistemological carnival. It sets free temporality and thus liberates—or makes anarchic—history.

Du Fu matters here because in Chinese literary culture the poet has been enshrined as the arch-chronicler of history in poetic terms. If, as Luo Qing sarcastically suggests, anachronism serves as the essential mechanism of human civilization, one can then conclude that history is anything but a process of *engaged* human experience, either empirically or imagined, and as such Du Fu's poetry may as well be read as a hodgepodge of misreadings and rereadings of the past as the present. Luo Qing was a forerunner of postmodernist poetics in the 1980s. But, in the poem under discussion, he appears most critical of the deconstructive "free play" with history and time:

> Judge Bao can consult with fictional Sherlock Holmes,
> Empress Wuzetian can be a rip off Cleopatra of America,
> All TV audiences agree that
> Imperial Consort Yang Guifei has to look like a modern sex bomb,
> I am merely saying Du Fu was under my influence,
> Why all the fussing and frowning?

包青天可以參考虛構的福爾摩斯
武則天可以剽竊美國的埃及艷后
所有的電視觀眾都同意
楊貴妃要健美的現代豪放女來演才像
現在我只不過是説説杜甫受我影響而已
大家又可必皺眉歪嘴大驚小怪

Luo Qing harbors a grievance against the postmodern play with the literary canon, a canon represented by Du Fu in his poems, likening it to the contemporary cultural industry filled with mimicries and parodies. But the way he caricatures the postmodernist flirtation with anachronism risks exposing his own frivolity and aligning himself with the target of his critique. Luo Qing seems aware of the inherent tension of his rhetorical strategy, and he surprises his reader by taking a sober, political turn at the end of the poem.

> Should someone dare to take to the streets because of this
> Protesting and demonstrating and playing the gadfly
> The rally will be infiltrated for sure by those who
> Support separatism for a land that is long since torn apart

如果有人膽敢因此走上街頭
示威抗議胡攪蠻纏
隊伍一定會遭人插花遊行
趁機主張分裂早已四分五裂的國土

In view of the current political situation in Taiwan, Luo Qing's references to political rallies and calls for Taiwanese independence ("separatism") suddenly draw attention to the realpolitik that engulfs the island society, thus grasping for a historical relevance that is anything but postmodern anachronism. Luo Qing makes clear his political stance in the following lines:

> At that time it will further make manifest the line written by Du Fu
> "The state broken, its mountains and rivers remain"
> Is under not only my own
> But also all of our—shadow   sound

屆時將更加突顯杜甫創作的
那句"國破山河在"
不單受了我
同時也受了我們大家的，影   響

In a wry and jarring tone, the poet takes note of how Taiwan, already split from the Mainland, is subject to further fracture in this perilous political climate. His deliberate "misuse" of the opening line of Du Fu's famous "View in Spring" suddenly becomes a painful testimony as to the fate of Taiwan at the end of the modern century. Whereas Du Fu lamented the collapse of the Tang Empire, Luo Qing is saddened by the multiple political, cultural, and linguistic traces of fragmentation in Taiwan—fragmentation that resulted from the Japanese colonial occupation between 1895 and 1945, the 1949 National Divide, and calls for independence in recent years. Luo Qing insinuates his disapproval of the indigenous discourse and presents his own anachronism *as a tactic* vis-à-vis historical necessity as conceived of by many "New Taiwanese" nowadays. At the end of his poem, Luo Qing's reflection on the island's broken nationhood collapses into disjointed language. The final phrase of his poem, *yingxiang* 影響 ("influence"), is grammatically and graphically falling apart, becoming the two discrete characters of *ying* 影 and *xiang* 響, or shadow and sound. Thus, gone is the "influence" of Chinese legacies, such as that of Du Fu; one is left only with the ghostly shadows and lingering sounds of the past.

With Luo Qing's poem, we may return to the play *Six Characters in Search of the Author*, with which the chapter starts. In the play, the disappearance of the author triggers a cluster of modernist syndromes that leave the characters to create their own authenticity. Critics have pointed out that through the play Pirandello rejuvenates the traditional convention of the play within a play by asking about the legitimacy of authorial subjectivity and its "irrepresentability" in the modern context. He helps call attention to the metafictional nature of not only the theater but also the human condition in general.

My study of six contemporary Chinese poets search for Du Fu, however, leads us to a different conclusion for the case of Chinese modernism. From Feng Zhi's Goethean contemplation of humanity's fate in wartime China to Luo Qing's sarcastic observation of postmodernist values at play, what remains striking is the fact is that Du Fu and his poetry have continuously been invoked as a yardstick by which the causes and consequences of modern experience can be measured and contested.

The question of Chinese literary modernity, therefore, has to be posited in a different way. If Pirandello and his Western peers seek to describe a world full of metafictional mirror reflections, a solid world that melts into the air, modern Chinese poets seem to us to inhabit a metahistorical world. By metahistorical, however, I do not mean that they are aiming at a rhetorical construct of the past, of the kind prescribed by Hayden White and followers; rather, I mean that they enact a poetic incantation of the meaningfulness of the past and its ethical, if not political, implications in the present. Du Fu, the "author" of "poetry as history," is never missing on the platform of Chinese modernism. He remains for the poets an indispensable interlocutor, a kindred spirit. For them, to emulate and simulate Du Fu is to point to the essential problem of making Chinese poetry modern.

Works Cited

Primary Sources (Including Texts, Commentaries, and Translations)

Chu ci jijiao jishi 楚辭集校集釋. Edited by Cui Fuzhang 崔富章. Wuhan: Hubei jiaoyu chubanshe, 2003.

Chuxue ji 初學記. Compiled by Xu Jian 徐堅 et al. Beijing: Zhonghua shuju, 1962.

Feng Zhi 馮至. *Feng Zhi quanji* 馮至全集. Shijiazhuang: Hebei jiaoyu chubanshe, 1999.

Gan Bao 干寶. *Sou shen ji* 搜神記. Beijing: Zhonghua shuju, 1979.

Gu qingliang zhuan 古清涼傳. Taishō 2098, 51:1098b10–21.

Guo Zhida 郭知達, annot., *Xinkan jiaoding jizhu Du shi* 新刊校定集注杜詩. Photoreprint of 1226 edition, Shanghai: Zhonghua shuju, 1982.

Han shu 漢書. Compiled by Ban Gu 班固. Beijing: Zhonghua shuju, 1962.

Hargett, James M., trans. *Riding the River Home: A Complete and Annotated Translation of Fan Chengda's (1126–1193) Diary of a Boat Trip to Wu (Wuchuan lu)*. Hong Kong: Hong Kong Chinese University Press, 2008.

Hawkes, David. *A Little Primer of Tu Fu*. Oxford: Oxford University Press, 1967.

Huang Sheng 黃生. *Huang Sheng quanji* 黃生全集. Anhui: Anhui daxue chubanshe, 2009.

Huang Xi 黃希 and Huang He 黃鶴, annot. *Bu zhu Du shi* 補注杜詩. Yingyin Wenyuange Siku quanshu edition. Taibei: Taiwan shangwu yinshuguan, 1985.

Jin Shengtan 金聖嘆. *Jin Shengtan xuanpi Du shi* 金聖嘆選批杜詩. Taibei: Ximei chubanshe, 1981.

Knechtges, David R., trans. *Wen xuan; or, Selections of Refined Literature*. Vols. 1–3. Princeton, NJ: Princeton University Press, 1982, 1987, 1996.

Laozi yizhu 老子譯注. Annotated by Feng Dafu 馮達甫. Shanghai: Shanghai guji chubanshe, 1991.

Liang Wern Fook. "Taking the 2.4 k Run with Du Fu" 與杜甫共跑 2.4. *Lianhe zaobao* 聯合早報. July 13, 2003.

Liji zhushu 禮記注疏. In *Shisanjing zhushu* 十三經注疏, compiled by Ruan Yuan 阮元.

Liu Xiang 劉向. *Liexian zhuan* 列仙傳. Edited by Yang Pu 楊溥. Photo-reprint. Shanghai: Shangwu yinshu guan, 1936.

Liu Xie 劉勰. *Wenxin diaolong xiangzhu* 文心雕龍詳注. Annotated by Zhou Zhenfu 周振甫. Nanjing: Jiangsu jiaoyu chubanshe, 2005.

Liu Yiqing 劉義慶. *Shishuo xinyu jiaojian* 世說新語校箋. Annotated by Yang Yong 楊勇. Beijing: Zhonghua shuju, 2006.

Li Zhao 李肇. *Guoshi bu* 國史補. Shanghai: Shanghai guji chubanshe, 1979.

Lunyu zhushu 論語注疏. In *Shisanjing zhushu* 十三經注疏, compiled by Ruan Yuan 阮元.

Luo Fu 洛夫. *Yinwei feng de yuangu: Luo Fu shixuan 1955–1987* 因為風的緣故：洛夫詩選一九五五—一九八七. Taibei: Jiuge chubanshe, 1988.

Lu Qinli 逯欽立, comp. *Xian Qin Han Wei Jin nanbeichao shi* 先秦漢魏晉南北朝詩. Beijing: Zhonghua shuju, 1983.

Lu Yuanchang 盧元昌. *Du shi chan* 杜詩闡. Ji'nan: Qi Lu shushe, 1997.

Mao shi zhushu 毛詩注疏. In *Shisanjing zhushu* 十三經注疏, compiled by Ruan Yuan 阮元.

Mather, Richard B., trans. and annot. *Shih-shuo hsin-yü: A New Account of Tales of the World*. 2nd ed. Ann Arbor, MI: Center for Chinese Studies, University of Michigan, 2002.

Meng Haoran 孟浩然. *Meng Haoran shiji jianzhu* 孟浩然詩集箋注, annotated by Tong Peiji 佟培基. Shanghai: Shanghai guji chubanshe, 2000.

Mengzi zhushu 孟子注疏. In *Shisanjing zhushu* 十三經注疏, compiled by Ruan Yuan 阮元.

Owen, Stephen, trans. and ed. *The Poetry of Du Fu*. 6 vols. Boston: Walter de Gruyter, 2016.

Pu Qilong 浦起龍. *Du Du xinjie* 讀杜心解. Beijing: Zhonghua shuju, 2000.

Qiu Zhaoao 仇兆鰲. *Du shi xiangzhu* 杜詩詳注. Beijing: Zhonghua shuju, 1979.

Quan Tang shi 全唐詩. Beijing: Zhonghua shuju, 1960.

Quan Tang wen 全唐文. Beijing: Zhonghua shuju, 1996.

Sanguo zhi 三國志. Compiled by Chen Shou 陳壽. Beijing: Zhonghua shuju, 1962.

Shan Fu 單復, annot. *Du Du shi yu de* 讀杜詩愚得. Taibei: Datong shuju, 1974.

Shangshu zhushu 尚書注疏. In *Shisanjing zhushu* 十三經注疏, compiled by Ruan Yuan 阮元.

Shi Daoshi 釋道世, comp. *Fayuan zhulin jiaozhu* 法苑珠林校注, annotated by Zhou Shujia 周叔迦 and Su Jinren 蘇晉仁. Beijing: Zhonghua shuju, 2003.

Shi jing zhushu 詩經注疏. In *Shisanjing zhushu* 十三經注疏, compiled by Ruan Yuan 阮元.

Shisanjing zhushu 十三經注疏. Compiled by Ruan Yuan 阮元. Taibei: Yiwen yinshuguan, 1955.

Shitao 石濤. *Sekito To Ho shii satsu* 石濤杜甫詩意冊. Tokyo: Sansaisha, 1968.

Song ben Du Gongbu ji 宋本杜工部集. Compiled by Wang Zhu 王洙. In *Xu guyi congshu* 續古逸叢書 series. Shanghai: Shangwu yinshu guan, 1957 rpt.

Su Shi 蘇軾. *Su Shi wenji* 蘇軾文集. 6 vols. Beijing: Zhonghua shuju, 1986.

Taiping guangji 太平廣記. Compiled by Li Fang 李昉 et al. Beijing: Zhonghua shuju, 1961.

Taiping yulan 太平御覽. Compiled by Li Fang 李昉 et al. Beijing: Zhonghua shuju, 1995.

Wang Shimin 王時敏. *Wang Shimin xie Du Fu shiyi tuce* 王時敏寫杜甫詩意圖冊. Beijing: Zijingcheng chubanshe, 2007.

Wang Sishi 王嗣奭. *Du yi* 杜臆. Shanghai: Shanghai guji chubanshe, 1983.

Wang Wei 王維. *Wang Youcheng ji jianzhu* 王右丞集箋注. Annotated by Zhao Diancheng 趙殿成. Beijing: Zhonghua shuju, 1972.

Wei shu 魏書. Compiled by Wei Shou 魏收. Beijing: Zhonghua shuju, 1974.

Xiandai Zhongguo wenxue daxi: xiaoshuo erji 現代中國文學大系：小說二集. Edited by Zhao Jiabi 趙家璧, vol. 5. Shanghai: Liangyou tushu gongsi, 1935.

Xiao Difei 蕭滌非 et al., eds. *Du Fu quanji jiaozhu* 杜甫全集校注. 12 vols. Beijing: Renmin wenxue chubanshe, 2013.

Xiao jing zhushu 孝經注疏. In *Shisanjing zhushu* 十三經注疏, compiled by Ruan Yuan 阮元.

Xiao Kaiyu 蕭開愚. *Cishi cidi: Xiao Kaiyu zixuan ji* 此時此地：蕭開愚自選集. Kaifeng: He'nan daxue chubanshe, 1997.

Xiao Tong 蕭統, comp. *Wen xuan* 文選. Annotated by Li Shan 李善. Shanghai: Shanghai guji chubanshe, 1986.

Xi Chuan 西川. *Yinmi de huihe: Xi Chuan shixuan* 隱密的匯合：西川詩選. Beijing: Gaige chubanshe, 1997.

Xie Shichen 謝時臣. *Duling shiyi tuce* 杜陵詩意圖冊. In *Gugong bowuyuan cangpin daxi* 故宮博物院藏品大系, edited by Yuan Jie 袁傑, vol. 8. Beijing: Zijincheng chubanshe, 2008.

Xin Tang shu 新唐書. Beijing: Zhonghua shuju, 1975.

Yang Lun 楊倫, annot. *Du shi jingquan* 杜詩鏡銓. Shanghai: Shanghai guji chubanshe, 1980.

Yan Qilin 顏其麟, ed. *San xia shihui* 三峽詩匯. Chongqing: Xi'nan shifan daxue chubanshe, 1989.

Yan Zhitui 顏之推. *Yanshi jiaxun jijie* 顏氏家訓集解. Compiled by Wang Liqi 王利器. Shanghai: Shanghai guji chubanshe, 1980.

Yip Wailim. *Ye Weilian wushinian shixuan* 葉維廉五十年詩選. Taibei: National Taiwan University Publication Center, 2012.

Yiwen leiju 藝文類聚. Compiled by Ouyang Xun 歐陽詢 et al. Shanghai: Shanghai guji chubanshe, 2007.

Yu Xin 庾信. *Yu Zishan jizhu* 庾子山集注. Annotated by Ni Fan 倪璠. Beijing: Zhonghua shuju, 1980.

Zhang Jin 張溍. *Dushu Tang Du shiji fu wenji zhujie* 讀書堂杜詩集附文集註解. Taibei: Datong shuju, 1974.

Zhao Cigong 趙次公, annot. *Du shi Zhao Cigong xianhou jie jijiao* 杜詩趙次公先後解輯校, edited by Lin Jizhong 林繼中. Shanghai: Shanghai guji chubanshe, 1994.

Zhong Rong 鍾嶸. *Shi pin jizhu* 詩品集注. Compiled by Cao Xu 曹旭. Shanghai: Shanghai guji chubanshe 1994.

Zhouli zhushu 周禮注疏. In *Shisanjing zhushu* 十三經注疏, compiled by Ruan Yuan 阮元.

Zhouyi zhushu 周易注疏. In *Shisanjing zhushu* 十三經注疏, compiled by Ruan Yuan 阮元. *Zhuangzi jishi* 莊子集釋. Annotated by Guo Qingfan 郭慶藩. Beijing: Zhonghua shuju, 1995.

Secondary Sources

Abramson, Marc Samuel. *Ethnic Identity in Tang China*. Philadelphia: University of Pennsylvania Press, 2008.

Alpers, Paul J. "Apostrophe and the Rhetoric of Renaissance Lyric." *Representations* 122, no. 1 (Spring 2013): 1–22.

Apter, David, and Anthony Saich. *Revolutionary Discourse in Mao's Republic*. Cambridge, MA: Harvard University Press, 1994.

Bachelard, Gaston. *The Poetics of Space*. Trans. Maria Jolas. Boston: Beacon Press, 1969.

Bender, Lucas Rambo. "Du Fu: Poet Historian, Poet Sage." PhD diss., Harvard University, 2016.

Breytenbach, Breyten. "The Long March from Hearth to Heart." *Social Research* 58, no. 1 (Spring 1991): 69–83.

Cavell, Stanley. *In Quest of the Ordinary: Lines of Skepticism and Romanticism*. Chicago: University of Chicago Press, 1988.

Cavell, Stanley. *Must We Mean What We Say? A Book of Essays*. Cambridge: Cambridge University Press, 1976.

Cavell, Stanley. *This New yet Unapproachable America: Lectures after Emerson after Wittgenstein*. Albuquerque, NM: Living Batch Press, 1989.

Chen, Jue. "Making China's Greatest Poet: The Construction of Du Fu in the Poetic Culture of the Song Dynasty (960–1279)." PhD diss., Princeton University, 2016.

Chen Yinxin 陳貽焮. *Du Fu pingzhuan* 杜甫評傳. Beijing: Beijing daxue chubanshe, rpt. 2011.

Cheung, Dominique. *Feng Chih*. Boston: Twayne, 1979.

Chittick, Andrew. "Pride of Place: The Advent of Local History in Early Medieval China." PhD diss., University of Michigan, 1997.

Chou, Eva Shan. "Allusion and Periphrasis as Modes of Poetry in Tu Fu's 'Eight Laments.'" *Harvard Journal of Asiatic Studies* 45, no. 1 (June 1985): 77–128.

Chou, Eva Shan. "Beginning with Images in the Nature Poetry of Wang Wei." *Harvard Journal of Asiatic Studies* 42, no. 1 (June 1982): 117–37.

Chou, Eva Shan. *Reconsidering Tu Fu: Literary Greatness and Cultural Context*. Cambridge: Cambridge University Press, 1995.

Chu Gansheng 褚贛生. *Nubi shi* 奴婢史. Reprint, Shanghai: Shanghai wenyi chubanshe, 2009.

Culler, Jonathan. *The Pursuit of Signs: Semiotics, Literature, Deconstruction*. Ithaca, NY: Cornell University Press, 1981.

Dai Weihua 戴偉華. *Diyu wenhua yu Tang dai shige* 地域文化與唐代詩歌. Beijing: Zhonghua shuju, 2006.

Dorr, Aimée. "What Constitutes Literacy in a Culture with Diverse and Changing Means of Communication?" In *Literacy: Interdisciplinary Conversations*, edited by Deborah Keller-Cohen, 129–53. Cresskill: Hampton Press, 1994.

Emerson, Ralph Waldo. "Experience." In *The Essays of Ralph Waldo Emerson*, 243–68. Cambridge, MA: Belknap Press of Harvard University Press, 1987.

Fang Yu 方瑜. *Du Fu Kuizhou shi xilun* 杜甫夔州詩析論. Taibei: Youshi wenhua shiye gongsi, 1985.

Feng Ye 封野. *Du Fu Kuizhou shi shulun* 杜甫夔州詩述論. Nanjing: Dongnan daxue chubanshe, 2007.

Frankel, Hans. "The Contemplation of the Past in T'ang Poetry." In *Perspectives on the T'ang*, edited by Arthur F. Wright and Denis C. Twitchett, 345–65. New Haven, CT: Yale University Press, 1973.

Gao Haiyan 高海燕. "Zhongguo Han chuan Fojiao yishu zhong de sheshen sihu bensheng yanjiu shuping" 中國漢傳佛教藝術中的捨身飼虎本生研究述評. *Dunhuang xue jikan* 敦煌學輯刊 1 (2014): 170–80.

Grossman, Allen, with Mark Halliday. *The Sighted Singer: Two Works on Poetry for Readers and Writers*. Baltimore: Johns Hopkins University Press, 1992.

Hao, Ji. "Poetics of Transparency: Hermeneutics of Du Fu (712–770) during the Late Ming (1368–1644) and Early Qing (1644–1911) Periods." PhD diss., University of Minnesota, 2012.

Hao, Ji. *The Reception of Du Fu (712–770) and His Poetry in Imperial China*. Leiden: Brill, 2017.

Hartman, Geoffrey H. "Wordsworth Revisited." In *The Unremarkable Wordsworth*, 3–17. Minneapolis: University of Minnesota Press, 1987.

Henry, Eric. "Chu-ko Liang in the Eyes of His Contemporaries." *Harvard Journal of Asiatic Studies* 52, no. 2 (1992): 589–612.

Hightower, James R. "Allusion in the Poetry of T'ao Ch'ien." *Harvard Journal of Asiatic Studies* 31 (1971): 5–27.

Hori Toshikazu 堀敏一. *Chūgoku kodai no mibunsei: ryō to sen* 中国古代の身分制：良と賤. Tōkyō: Kyūko Shoin, 1987.

Hsia, C. T. "Obsession with China: The Moral Burden of Modern Chinese Literature." In *A History of Modern Chinese Fiction*, 533–54. New Haven, CT: Yale University Press, 1971.

Hua Wenxuan 華文軒, ed. *Du Fu juan* 杜甫卷. In *Gudian wenxue yanjiu ziliao huibian* 古典文學研究料彙編. Beijing: Zhonghua shuju, 1964.

Huang Canran 黃燦然. *Wode linghun: Shixuan 1994–2005* 我的靈魂：詩選 1994–2005. Hong Kong: Tiandi tushu, 2009.

Huang Yizhen 黃奕珍. "Lun 'Fenghuang tai' yu 'Wanzhang tan' 'feng' 'long' zhi xiangzheng yiyi" 論〈鳳凰臺〉與〈萬丈潭〉"鳳"、"龍"之象徵意義. In *Du Fu zi Qin ru shu shige xiping* 杜甫自秦入蜀詩歌析評, 83–128. Taibei: Liren shuju, 2005.

Hu Kexian 胡可先. "Du Fu yanjiu de xin qushi: Zhongguo Du Fu yanjiu hui dibajie nianhui ji Du Fu yanjiu guoji xueshu taolunhui xueshu zongjie" 杜甫研究的新趨勢：杜甫研究會第八屆年會暨杜甫研究國際學術討論會學術總結. *Du Fu yanjiu xuekan* 杜甫研究學刊 4 (2017): 89–93.

Hung, William. *Tu Fu: China's Greatest Poet*. New York: Russell and Russell, 1952.

Jiang Xianwei 蔣先偉. *Du Fu Kuizhou shi lungao* 杜甫夔州詩論稿. Chengdu: Ba Shu shushe, 2002.

Johnson, Barbara. "Apostrophe, Animation, Abortion." In *A World of Difference*, 184–99. Baltimore: Johns Hopkins University Press, 1988.

Johnson, Williams A., and Holt N. Parker, eds. *Ancient Literacies: The Culture of Reading in Greece and Rome*. Oxford: Oxford University Press, 2009.

Kneale, J. Douglas. "Romantic Aversions: Apostrophe Reconsidered." In *Mind in Creation: Essays on English Romantic Literature in Honour of Ross G. Woodman*, edited by J. Douglas Kneale, 91–105. Montreal: McGill-Queen's University Press, 1992.

Knechtges, David R. *The Han Rhapsody: A Study of the Fu of Yang Hsiung (53 B.C.–A.D. 18)*. Cambridge: Cambridge University Press, 1976.

Knechtges, David R. "Ruin and Remembrance in Classical Chinese Literature: The '*Fu* on the Ruined City' by Bao Zhao." In *Reading Medieval Chinese Poetry: Text, Context, and Culture*, edited by Paul W. Kroll, 55–89. Leiden: Brill, 2015.

Kroll, Paul W. "Anthologies in the Tang." In *The Oxford Handbook of Classical Chinese Literature (1000 BCE–900 CE)*, edited by Wiebke Denecke, Wai-Yee Li, and Xiaofei Tian, 303–15. Oxford: Oxford University Press, 2017.

Kroll, Paul W. "Zhang Jiuling and the Lychee." *T'ang Studies* 30 (2012): 9–22.

Lattimore, David. "Allusion and T'ang Poetry." In *Perspectives on the T'ang*, edited by Arthur F. Wright and Denis C. Twitchett, 405–49. New Haven, CT: Yale University Press, 1973.

Lewis, Mark. *The Flood Myths of Early China*. Albany: State University of New York Press, 2006.

Li, Feng, and David Prager Branner, eds. *Writing and Literacy in Early China: Studies from the Columbia Early China Seminar*. Seattle: University of Washington Press, 2011.

Li Jiping 李季平. *Tangdai nubi zhidu* 唐代奴婢制度. Shanghai: Shanghai guji chubanshe, 1986.

Li Jizu 李濟阻. "Du Fu Longyoushi zhong de diming fangwei shiyi tu" 杜甫隴右詩中的地名方位示意圖. *Du Fu yanjiu xuekan* 杜甫研究學刊 2 (2003): 44–51.

Li Pengfei 李鵬飛. *Tangdai feixieshi xiaoshuo zhi leixing yanjiu* 唐代非寫實小説之類型研究. Beijing: Beijing daxue chubanshe, 2004.

Liu, James. *The Art of Chinese Poetry*. Chicago: University of Chicago, 1962.

Loewe, Michael, ed. *Early Chinese Texts: A Bibliographical Guide*. Berkeley, CA: Society for the Study of Early China, 1993.

Lopez, Donald S., Jr. "Belief." In *Critical Terms for Religious Studies*, edited by Mark C. Taylor, 21–35. Chicago: University of Chicago Press, 1998.

Lu Yuandun 路元敦. "Lun Du Fu shi yu *Wen xuan* zhi guanxi" 論杜甫詩與《文選》之關係. Master's thesis, Xinjiang Normal University, 2007.

McCraw, David R. *Du Fu's Laments from the South*. Honolulu: University of Hawai'i Press, 1992.

McMullen, David. *State and Scholars in T'ang China*. Cambridge: Cambridge University Press, 1988.

McNair, Amy. *Donors of Longmen: Faith, Politics, and Patronage in Medieval Chinese Buddhist Sculptures*. Honolulu: University of Hawai'i Press, 2007.

McRae, John. *Seeing through Zen: Encounter, Transformation, and Genealogy in Chinese Chan Buddhism*. Berkeley: University of California Press, 2003.

Mei, Tsu-lin, and Yu-kung Kao. "Tu Fu's 'Autumn Meditations': An Exercise in Linguistic Criticism." *Harvard Journal of Asiatic Studies* 28 (1968): 44–80.

Mo Lifeng 莫礪鋒. "Du Fu dui Zhuge Liang de zansong" 杜甫對諸葛亮的贊頌 In *Gudian shixue de wenhua guanzhao* 古典詩學的文化觀照, 128–38. Beijing: Zhonghua shuju, 2005.

Mo Lifeng 莫礪鋒. *Du Fu pingzhuan* 杜甫評傳. Nanjing: Nanjing daxue chubanshe, 1993.

Naba Toshisada 那波利貞. *Tōdai shakai bunkashi kenkyū* 唐代社會文化史研究. Tokyo: Sōbunsha, 1974.

Owen, Stephen. "The Cultural Tang." In *The Cambridge History of Chinese Literature, Vol. 1: To 1375*, edited by Stephen Owen, 286–373. Cambridge: Cambridge University Press, 2010.

Owen, Stephen. "Deadwood: The Barren Tree from Yü Hsin to Han Yü." *Chinese Literature: Essays, Articles, Reviews* 1, no. 2 (1979): 157–79.

Owen, Stephen. *The End of the Chinese "Middle Ages": Essays in Mid-Tang Literary Culture*. Stanford, CA: Stanford University Press, 1996.

Owen, Stephen. *The Great Age of Chinese Poetry: The High T'ang*. New Haven, CT: Yale University Press, 1981.

Owen, Stephen. "Place: Meditation on the Past at Jinling." *Harvard Journal of Asiatic Studies* 50, no. 2 (1990): 417–57.

Owen, Stephen. *The Poetry of the Early T'ang*. New Haven, CT: Yale University Press, 1977.

Owen, Stephen. *Readings in Chinese Literary Thought*. Cambridge, MA: Harvard University Asia Center, 1992.

Owen, Stephen. *Remembrances: The Experience of the Past in Traditional Chinese Literature*. Cambridge, MA: Harvard University Press, 1986.

Owen, Stephen. "The Self's Perfect Mirror: Poetry as Autobiography." In *The Vitality of the Lyric Voice: Shih Poetry from the Late Han to the T'ang*, edited by Shuen-fu Lin and Stephen Owen, 71–102. Princeton, NJ: Princeton University Press, 1986.

Owen, Stephen. *Traditional Chinese Poetry and Poetics: Omen of the World*. Madison: University of Wisconsin Press, 1985.

Owen, Stephen. "What Did Liuzhi Hear? The 'Yan Terrace Poems' and the Culture of Romance." *T'ang Studies* 13 (1995): 81–118.

Patterson, Gregory. "Elegies for Empire: The Poetics of Memory in the Late Work of Du Fu (712–770)." PhD diss., Columbia University, 2013.

Peng Yan 彭燕. "Du Fu yanjiu yibainian" 杜甫研究一百年. *Du Fu yanjiu xuekan* 杜甫研究學刊 3 (2015): 105–25.

Petersen, Charles. "Must We Mean What We Say? On Stanley Cavell." *n+1*, February 11, 2013. https://nplusonemag.com/online-only/online-only/must-we-mean-what-we-say/.

Qin Xiaoyu 秦曉宇. *Yu ti: Dangdai Zhongwenshi xulun* 玉梯：當代中文詩敘論. Taibei: Duli pinglun, 2012.

Quintilian. *The Orator's Education*. Edited and translated by Donald Russell. 4 vols. The Loeb Classical Library, 124–27. Cambridge, MA: Harvard University Press, 2002.

Rosemont, Henry, Jr., and Roger T. Ames. *The Chinese Classic of Family Reverence: A Philosophical Translation of the* Xiaojing. Honolulu: University of Hawai'i Press, 2009.

Rouzer, Paul. "Du Fu and the Failure of Lyric." *Chinese Literature: Essays, Articles, Reviews* 33 (2011): 27–53.

Rouzer, Paul. *On Cold Mountain: A Buddhist Reading of the Hanshan Poems*. Seattle: University of Washington Press, 2015.

Schaberg, David. "Travel, Geography, and the Imperial Imagination in Fifth-Century Athens and Han China." *Comparative Literature* 51, no. 2 (1999): 152–91.

Schafer, Edward H. *The Golden Peaches of Samarkand: A Study of T'ang Exotics*. Berkeley: University of California Press, 1963.

Schafer, Edward H. "The Idea of Created Nature in T'ang Literature." *Philosophy East and West* 15, no. 2 (1965): 153–60.

Schneider, David K. *Confucian Prophet: Political Thought in Du Fu's Poetry (752–757)*. New York: Cambria Press, 2012.

Shang, Wei. "Prisoner and Creator: The Self-Image of the Poet in Han Yu and Meng Jiao." *Chinese Literature: Essays, Articles, Reviews* 16 (1994): 19–40.

Simmel, Georg. "The Ruin." In *Essays on Sociology, Religion, and Aesthetics*, edited by Kurt H. Wolff, 259–66. New York: Harper and Row, 1965.

Stevenson, Daniel, trans. "A Sacred Peak." In *Buddhist Scriptures*, edited by Donald S. Lopez Jr., 84–89. New York: Penguin, 2004.

Street, Brian V. *Literacy in Theory and Practice*. Cambridge: Cambridge University Press, 1984.

Su Yiru 蘇怡如. "Du Fu zi Qin ru Shu shi dui da Xie shanshuishi zhi jicheng yu yili" 杜甫自秦入蜀詩對大謝山水詩之繼承與逸離. *Wen yu zhe* 文與哲 2010 (16): 203–36.

Teiser, Stephen F. "Engulfing the Bounds of Order: The Myth of the Great Flood in Mencius." *Journal of Chinese Religions* 13–14 (1985/1986): 15–43.

Tian, Xiaofei. *Beacon Fire and Shooting Star: The Literary Culture of the Liang (502–557)*. Cambridge, MA: Harvard University Asia Center, 2007.

Tian, Xiaofei. "Slashing Three Kingdoms: A Case Study of Fan Production on the Chinese Web." *Modern Chinese Literature and Culture* 27, no. 1 (Spring 2015): 224–77.

Tian, Xiaofei. *Visionary Journeys: Travel Writings from Early Medieval and Nineteenth-Century China*. Cambridge, MA: Harvard University Asia Center, 2011.

Tillman, Hoyt Cleveland. "Reassessing Du Fu's Line on Zhuge Liang." *Monumenta Serica* 50 (2002): 295–313.

Van Crevel, Maghiel, "Xiao Kaiyu." Poetry International Web. <https://www.poetryinternational.org/pi/poet/975/Xiao-Kaiyu>

Varsano, Paula, ed. *The Rhetoric of Hiddenness in Traditional Chinese Culture*. Albany: State University of New York Press, 2016.

Von Glahn, Richard. *The Country of Streams and Grottoes: Expansion, Settlement, and the Civilizing of the Sichuan Frontier in Song Times*. Cambridge, MA: Harvard University Press, 1987.

Wang Hanwei 王菡薇. "Mogao ku bihua yu Dunhuang wenxian yanjiu zhi ronghe: Yi Bei Wei 254 ku bihua 'Sheshen sihu' yu xieben '*Jin guangming jing* juan di'er' weili" 莫高窟壁畫於敦煌文獻研究之融和：以北魏254窟壁畫捨身飼虎與寫本金光明經卷第二為例. *Zhongguo meishu xueyuan xuebao* 中國美術學院學報 5 (2010): 42–45.

Wang Ruigong 王瑞功. *Zhuge Liang yanjiu jicheng* 諸葛亮研究集成. Ji'nan: Qi Lu shushe, 1997.

Wang Sanqing 王三慶. *Dunhuang leishu* 敦煌類書. Gaoxiong: Liwen wenhua, 1993.

Wei Wenbin 魏文斌 and Gao Haiyan 高海燕. "Gansu guancang zaoxiang beita sheshen sihu bensheng tuxiang kao" 甘肅館藏造像碑塔捨身飼虎本生圖像考. *Zhongyuan wenwu* 中原文物 3 (2015): 63–73.

Wilkinson, Endymion. *Chinese History: A New Manual*. 4th ed. Cambridge, MA: Harvard University Asia Center, 2015.

Yajima Genryō 矢島玄亮. *Nihonkoku genzaisho mokuroku: Shūshō to kenkyū* 日本国見在書目錄：集証と研究. Tokyo: Kyūko shoin, 1984.

Yan Gengwang 嚴耕望. *Tangdai jiaotong tu kao* 唐代交通圖考. Taibei: Academia Sinica 1986.

Yang Songnian 楊松年, ed. *Kua guojie shixiang: shihua xinshi pingxi* 跨國界詩想：世華新詩評析. Taibei: Tangshang, 2003.

Ye Jiaying 葉嘉瑩. *Du Fu qiuxing bashou jishuo* 杜甫秋興八首集説. Shanghai: Shanghai guji chubanshe, 1988.

Yip, Wai-lim. *Diffusion of Distances: Dialogue between Chinese and Western Poetics*. Berkeley: University of California Press, 1993.

Zhang Hui 張暉. *Zhongguo shishi chuantong* 中國詩史傳統. Beijing: Sanlian shudian, 2012.

Zhang Nali 張娜麗. "*Dunhuang ben* Liuzi qianwen *chutan* xiyi—jian shu *Qianzi wen* zhuben wenti" 《敦煌本〈六字千文〉初探》析疑—兼述《千字文》注本問題. *Dunhuang yanjiu* 敦煌研究 69 (2001): 100–105.

Zhang Runjing 張潤靜. *Tangdai yongshi huaigu shi yanjiu* 唐代咏史懷古詩研究. Shanghai: Sanlian, 2009.

Zhang Songjian. "One Poet, Four Faces: The Revisions of Tu Fu in Modern Chinese Poetry." *Frontiers of Literary Studies in China* 5, no. 2 (June 2011): 179–203.

Zhang Wanmin 張萬民. "Bianzhe you bujian: Dang Wai-lim Yip zaoyu Stephen Owen" 辯者有不見：當葉維廉遭遇宇文所安. *Wenyi lilum yanjiu* 4 (2009): 57–63.

Zhang Xinpeng 張新朋. *Dunhuang xieben* Kaimeng yaoxun *yanjiu* 敦煌寫本《開蒙要訓》研究. Beijing: Zhongguo shehui kexue chubanshe, 2013.

Zhang Zhonggang 張忠綱 et al., eds. *Du ji xulu* 杜集敍錄. Ji'nan: Qi Lu shushe, 2008.

Zheng Acai 鄭阿財 and Zhu Fengyu 朱鳳玉, ed. *Dunhuang mengshu yanjiu* 敦煌蒙書研究. Lanzhou: Gansu jiaoyu chubanshe, 2002.

Zhou Jianjun 周建軍. *Tangdai Jing Chu bentu shige yu liuyu shige yanjiu* 唐代荊楚本土詩歌與流寓詩歌研究. Beijing: Zhongguo shehui kexue chubanshe, 2006.

Contributors

Lucas Rambo Bender is assistant professor of East Asian languages and cultures at Yale University. He is currently finishing a monograph on Du Fu.

Jack W. Chen is associate professor of Chinese literature at the University of Virginia. He is the author of *The Poetics of Sovereignty: On Emperor Taizong of the Tang Dynasty* (Harvard University Asia Center, 2010) and co-editor of *Idle Talk: Gossip and Anecdote in Traditional Chinese Literature* (University of California Press, 2013) and has written various articles on medieval historiography, donkey braying, social networks, and reading practices.

Ronald Egan is professor of sinology at Stanford University. His research focuses on Chinese literature, aesthetics, and cultural history of the Tang-Song period. His publications include books on the literary works and lives of Ouyang Xiu and Su Shi. He has also published a general study of innovations in Song dynasty aesthetic thought, entitled *The Problem of Beauty: Aesthetic Thought and Pursuits in Northern Song Dynasty China*. His most recent book is *The Burden of Female Talent: The Poet Li Qingzhao and Her History in China* (Harvard University Asia Center, 2013), also now available in a Chinese edition.

Christopher M. B. Nugent is professor of Chinese and the chair of the program in comparative literature at Williams College. His research focuses on the literary culture of the sixth through tenth centuries, with a particular focus on the material production and circulation of texts and the process of literary training. His first book, *Manifest in Words, Written on Paper: Producing and Circulating Poetry in Tang Dynasty China*, was the winner of the 2012 Joseph Levenson Book Prize, Pre-1900 Category. He is currently completing a monography entitled *The Textual Practices of Literary Training in Medieval China*.

Stephen Owen is James Conant Bryant University Professor Emeritus at Harvard University. He is the author of numerous books, the most recent of which is *Just a Song: Chinese Lyrics from the Eleventh and Early Twelfth Centuries* (Harvard University Asia Center, 2019).

Gregory Patterson is assistant professor of Chinese and comparative literature at the University of South Carolina. His research interests include medieval Chinese poetry and literary culture, cultural memory, and the history of sinology. He is currently completing a book on memory and mediation in Du Fu's poetry from the Three Gorges region.

Paul Rouzer is professor in the Department of Asian Languages and Literatures at the University of Minnesota, Twin Cities. He is most recently the author of *On Cold Mountain: A Buddhist Reading of the Hanshan Poems* (University of Washington Press) and *The Poetry of Hanshan (Cold Mountain), Shide, and Fenggan* (De Gruyter, Library of Chinese Humanities). His research interests include Buddhist aesthetics, Sinitic poetry in East Asia, and the representation of Buddhism in modern global culture.

Xiaofei Tian is professor of Chinese literature in the Department of East Asian Languages and Civilizations at Harvard University. Her most recent book is *The Halberd at Red Cliff: Jian'an and the Three Kingdoms* (2018).

David Der-wei Wang teaches modern Chinese literature and comparative literature at Harvard University. His recent works include *The Lyrical in Epic Time: Chinese Intellectuals and Artists through the 1949 Crisis* (2015) and *A New Literary History of Modern China* (2017).

Index

www.ingramcontent.com/pod-product-compliance
Lightning Source LLC
Chambersburg PA
CBHW080919100426
42812CB00007B/2324